ANCIENT BUNDELKHAND

Ancient Bundelkhand

Religious History in Socio-Economic Perspective

Kirit K. Shah

Gian Publishing House
DELHI-110007

Gian Publishing House
22/6, Shakti Nagar, Delhi-110007
Phone : 7213053

ISBN 81-212-0189-6

PRINTED IN INDIA

Published by Mrs. Gayatri Garg for Gian Publishing House, Delhi.
Printed at Jindal Printers, Delhi.

DEDICATED TO MY PARENTS

TARA-TARUN

Preface

Research in regional history is now well into vogue, yet there are regions which remains neglected. Bundelkhand is certainly one of them, though it is the heart of Indian sub-continent. My interest in it dates back to the days when I was posted in one of its towns. I delved deep into its past to prepare my doctoral dissertation and the book is based, to some extent, on the data I collected in course of my exploration at the time. The theme of my thesis was 'Religious History' but my research and reading in the decade intervening has enabled me to place before the scholarly world all that is worth remembering and recording about ancient and early-medieval Bundelkhand.

Defining Bundelkhand is a difficult task as much in terms of tracing the origin of its geographico-cultural entity as in terms of fixing its frontiers on this terra-firma. None among the available books on the region has gone beyond British view of the matter, whereas I found in ancient and early-medieval inscriptions that it had an independent identity as a political or administrative unit.

Periodization in Indian history has been a perennial problem for scholars and the original division of Hindu-Muslim-British is now normally replaced by or equated with Ancient-Medieval-Modern in perfect tune with the so-called secular attitude to the subject. Accordingly, coming to powor of Qutub-ud-din Abak at Delhi in A.D. 1206 is taken to be the terminating point of the Ancient period. However, quite for some time, the period comprising 650-1200 A.D. is invariably referred to as 'Early Medieval'. I would like to clarify that the last dated document utilised for the present work comes from Hammiravarman, a contemporary king of Sultan Ala-ud-din Khilji, when we are well into the medieval period. The book, therefore, does not describe merely 'Ancient Bundelkhand', it journeys deep into the 'Medieval' enabling the reader to cover a longer distance than he hopes to on the basis of the title.

Available historical literature on Bundelkhand can broadly be divided into two sections : books dealing directly with Bundelkhand and those dwelling on the Candellas and their times. Foremost among the former is "*Bundelakhaṇḍa Kā Saṃkṣipta Itihāsa*" by Gorelal Tiwari (Deviprasad Aitihāsik Pustakamālā—10, Kashi Nāgari Prāchāriṇī Sabhā, First Edition, V.S. 1990) which was, indeed a poineering work but basically a political narrative fixing dates and names down the thread of time. Surveying some three millennia within a space of four hundred pages and starting with prehistory coming thereon to the year of its publication, the author has offered only a sketchy description of the ancient and early medieval Bundelkhand. Even otherwise, having been published half-a-century back, the book is frankly out of date. Meriting special mention among recent publications is M.L. Nigam's "*Cultural History of Bundelkhand*" (Sandeep Prakashan, Delhi 1983). The period it covers is indicated below the title—B.C. 3rd century to A.D. 650, thereby leaving out the pre-Mauryan and Post-Harshan periods altogether. One fails to understand the grounds on which the narrative is picked up and snapped off, since the crowning period in the cultural history of Bundelkhand was certainly that of the Candellas when temples literally sprang up from the earth on every hill and halmet. Secondly, the author laboured very little on the concept of Bundelkhand. Adopting the British view, available readymade, he has included places as far apart from Garhwa, Bhita and Kausambi in the North, to Tigwa in the South, Bharhut in the East and to Sanchi, Vidisha and Udaigiri in the West in his area of study. To what extent do I differ from him in my idea of Bundelkhand will become clear from the fact that none of the places, mentioned above, figures in my description of archaeology in Bundelkhand. Thirdly, he has devoted one chapter each to history, society, economy and religion taking and treating each aspect in isolation, whereas I think none of these can be studied in isolation. The sub-title of my book sufficiently indicates that religious life has been seen in contemporary socio-economic perspective. Yet, another recent publication is "*Bundelakhaṇḍ Kā Purātattva*" from the pen of Dr. S.D. Trivedi (Jhansi Museum, Jhansi, 1984). A small book about 100 pages, it offers an account of Bundelkhand's archaeology and thus, is basically a source book for reconstructing and researching into the history of Bundelkhand. I have devoted the whole of my chapter III to describing archaeological wealth of the region covering many more places than what Dr. Trivedi has denoted.

Coming now to the second category of books, the earliest is "*History of the Chandellas of Jejākabhukti*" by Prof. N. S. Bose (Firma, K. L. Mukhopadhyaya, Calcutta, 1956). Primarily a political history, it has been thoroughly revised by subsequent monographs on the subject. Of identical nature and contents is Dr. S.K. Mitra's "*Early Rulers of Khajuraho*" (Firma, K.L. Mukhopadhyaya, Calcutta, 1958) though it can not be termed as purely political history, since he also added chapters on social and economic conditions and art-architecture. Hardly different is the work of K.C. Mishra in Hindi titled "*Candellas aur Unakā Rājatvakāla*" (Nagari Pracharini Sabha, 115, *v.d.* 2011). Last in this line, but much more deserving of mention, is Prof. R.K. Dikshit's "*The Candelas of Jejākabhukti*" (Abhinav Publications, New Delhi, 1977) which analyses and incorporates all the research done upto now on the political history of the Candellas and is unlikely to be superseded for another decade or so. The author intended to bring out a second volume on cultural achievements as well but the idea remained unfulfilled. Thus, all the works listed above, deal exclusively with the Candellas and that too, with

Apart from Saugor University Library, I worked in those of Bharatiya Vidya Bhavan, Bombay and Deccan College and P.G. Institute, Poona. I am beholden to the staff of these for the facilities and cooperation they offered. So also to the office staff of Deptt. of A.I.H.C. & Archaeology, University of Saugor.

The book assumed its final form at Chandigarh which is the home-city of one of the doyens of Indology : Prof. Jagannath Agarwal. To this octogenarian, but indefatigable scholar, I owe the excellence wherever in this book. Words would fail me to record my sense of gratitude to him. My friend and colleauge, Shri. D.K. Handa is a worthy pupil of this worthier teacher. By going through the entire type script of my book and suggesting improvements. He did a favour to me for which I lack words to thank. Mr. Ravi Prakash, a Research scholar in Sanskrit, Punjab University, helped me in interpreting some of the important passages in inscriptions. I feel obliged to him. Years ago I had taken some photographs figuring in the work. Getting a good print of them was a problem which appeard beyond solution as photographer expressed his inability owing to the condition of the negatives. How can I fail, therefore, to name Dr. R.K. Jain of Govt. College of Art, Chandigarh, who provided me with presentable copies through his colleague photographer. But for him,much of my labour would have been sheer loss. For want of adequate and appropriate illustrations, I had to approach the Archaeological Survey of India. An old friend, Shri M.D. Khark, Director, Monuments, saw to it that I get the desired photos without delay. I thank him here.

June 30, 1987
Chandigarh

K.K. SHAH

PHOTO-COURTESY

Figs. 1 to 5	Department of Ancient Indian History, Culture and Archaeology, University of Sagaur, Sagar.
Figs. 6, 9, 22, 25, 26, 27, 28, 29, 30, 33, 34	Director, Archaeological Survey of India, New Delhi.
Figs. 11-12	Curator, Lucknow Museum, Lucknow.
Figs. 7, 31, 38, 39, 40, 41, 44	Superintending Archaeologist, Temple Survey Project (North), Bhopal.
Figs. 48 to 53	The Director, Bhopal Circle (A.S.I.) Bhopal.
Figs. 54 to 58	The Directoe, State Archaeology and Museums, Bhopal.

However, we regretfully mention that Fig. No. 3 of a Nagī Icon from Lokhri Yogini Centre (Distt. Banda) cannot be published as the only available photograph was lost.

K. K. SHAH

TABLE OF TRANSLITERATION

आ = ā	ऋ = Ṛ	ट = ṭa	ढ = ḍha
ई = ī	च = c	ठ = ṭha	ण = ṇ
ऊ = ū	ङ = ṅ	ड = ḍa	श = ś
ष = ṣ	ञ = ñ	anusvara = ṁ	

LIST OF ILLUSTRATIONS

SKETCHES

Contents

1

On Defining Bundelkhand

(One might very well ask what need there is to define Bundelkhand when it is so well-known a concept. But to use an oft-quoted phrase, Of course coined in another historical context, Bundelkhand is still a 'geographical expression', its area being divided into the states of Uttar Pradesh and Madhya Pradesh. The need arises, in the first place, from the fact that there is hardly any agreement among the scholars and writers about its geographical extent and, in the second, though a lot has been written about its history and culture none, so far, has delved deep into the origin and antiquity of its name. An humble attempt, therefore, has been made below, in this direction).

Way back in 1828 was published Pogson's "*A History of the Boondelas*"[1] which was in fact a translation of an old manuscript named "*Kshutr-Purkash*" a poetic composition by a bard named Lal recording the wars, celebrity and succession of the ancient Rajas and the valour, intrepidity and heroism of the war-like 'Boondelas'. They were certainly prominent in the political and social structure of medieval Bundelkhand and the Imperial Gazetteer[2] is right in holding that the name is taken from that of the Bundela Thakurs, the most important class inhabiting it.

As late as 1908, Vincent A. Smith wrote "The use of the word Bundelkhand is vague and indefinite, the only official recognition of it, being the application of the collective term 'Bundelkhand Agency' to a group of petty native states of Panna, Charkhari, and others which are comprised within the larger group known as Central India Agency".[3]

It follows, therefore, that the name has hardly any high antiquity and cannot be taken beyond the period of British domination. We would like to find out from historical investigation what name or names, if any, the region had prior to the advent of the English and how and when the Bundelas manifested on the stage of Bundelkhand. One might wrongly conclude from these bold questions which we have set to ourselves that some new and solid evidence has come to our notice, whereas the fact is, in the present state of our knowledge, any attempt at solving them is merely to grope in the dark with only dim and uncertain light of local legends and timeless tradition. An attempt, nevertheless, is worth-making since we have to work in the history of the region and an objective analysis of all the available evidence and opinions on the subject might help us to reach, if not the solution, at least, a way to it. Very rarely, indeed, one can reach finality in the realms of ancient history of India.

Earliest among the appellations with which the area was christened is Cedi and interesting to note, this name has been dated to the Ṛgvedic period[4] when the Aryan knowledge of Indian geography was largely confined to the Land of the Five Rivers. B.C. Law located it lying near the Jamuna contiguous to the kingdom of the Kurus roughly corresponding to modern Bundelkhand.[5] Echoing almost identical opinion V.V. Mirashi thought that Cedi was originally the name of the country along the southern bank of the Jamuna from the Chambal on the north-west to the Karvi on the south-east.[6] What is further noteworthy in his observations is his view that in later times Cedi came to signify the modern province of Baghelkhand. We have here a clear case of geographical names travelling literally territorially down the corridor of Time and confusing the posterity in the realms of historical research.

Needing further note is the fact that almost all the references to this name come from literature, none being yielded by the epigraphic records of the region. But when they do mention, it is with reference to Kalacuri kings and their dominions who had long shifted to Tripuri and were governing the area mostly south of the Narmada. The Candella chiefs who ruled practically over the whole of Bundelkhand mention Cedideśa as their southern neighbour.[7] As a matter of fact, Vāmarāja, an august ancestor of the Kalacuris, is known to have ruled with Kālañjara as his capital and that explains the appellation Caidyas for Kalacuri kings.

When exactly the word Cedi went into disuse we have no means to ascertain from, but under the Imperial Guptas the area had no official appellation and was being referred to simply by its river frontiers—the Kalindi in the north and the Narmada in the south. Eran stone pillar inscription of emperor Budhagupta omits the name of this Gupta province and yet makes specific mention of Mahārāja Suraśmicandra, the contemporary governor charged with protecting the people.[8]

The Parivrājakas were contemporary rulers of the latter Imperial Guptas. Fleet equated Dabhālā or Dehālā of Parivrājaka records with modern Bundelkhand.[9] The equation is obviously arbitrary since we possess absolutely no evidence that Mahārāja Hastin ruled the whole region between the Jamuna and the Narmada. Parts of it, however, may have been included in the Parivrājaka dominions. As for the name Dabhālā, no other document, literary or inscriptional, testifies to its having ever been applied to Bundelkhand.

The hold of Harshavardhana over Bundelkhand, whether direct or indirect, we may accept as fairly certain[10] and Bāṇa, his biographer, has left for us a good and graphic account of our area in his works. Of course, his description cannot be fully taken for Bundelkhand as he uses the general term Vindhyāṭavi. Yet the fact that Harsha, along with Rajyaśri and Divākaramitra, starting from the latter's hermitage reached in a few marches, his camp stationed along the Ganges[11] is a hint, broad enough, to take that the episode relating to the rescue of Rajyaśri occurred somewhere in the area of our study. Yet in our search of contemporary name for Bundelkhand Bāṇa fails us with all his graphic and grandiloquent description whereas Hsuan-Tsang, devoting hardly more than a para to the region, supplies us with one. Chih-Chi-To or Chi-Ki-To of the Chinese pilgrim has been taken by Cunningham[12] to stand for Bundelkhand. Much ink, ever since this equation was first made, has been spilt in supporting as well as rejecting it. Smith supported it on the ground that the term is phonetically equivalent to Jijhoti,[13] an epithet by which the Brāhmaṇas and Banias of Bundelkhand still distinguish themselves, whereas H.C. Ray[14] and N.S. Bose[15] rejected the view basing their opposition on the derivation of Jijhoti from Jejākabhukti—a name given to Bundelkhand by the Candella king Jejjā or Jayaśakti who ruled long after the departure of Hsuan-Tsang from India. Latest in the line of those opposing the identification of Cunningham was R.K. Dikshit who felt that the description of the Chinese pilgrim is so indefinite that little can be made out of it in determining the identity of the province or its capital. He further believed that the distances given by the traveller do not suit the proposed identification[16] and, that is why, Smith had to reconcile the apparent discrepancy by making further assumption that Eran, and not Khajuraho, was the capital of Jijhoti. He did not want, therefore, to budge even an inch in the matter from the unequivocal statement of the Mahoba stone inscription to the effect that there was a king Jejā by name, after whom Jejākbhukti was named just as this Pṛthvī after Pṛthu.[17]

We have no right, perhaps, to question his absolute faith in the authority of an early record but we simply wonder what made him think that the capital city of the Chinese description must correspond to Khajuraho when even its earliest available monument and epigraph do not date it beyond ninth century of the Christian era. Eran, on the other hand, does amply demonstrate with its pottery, coins, inscriptions and religious ruins having been an important city of the region from the dawn of history down to sixth century A.D. and its decline so soon after the exit of Toramāṇa and Goparāja seems as much unlikely as the eminence and elevation of Khajuraho to being the capital city so early. Hence the assumption of Smith is fairly reasonable and his consequent identification of Chih-Chi-To with Bundelkhand cannot be rejected simply because it is unsupported by an inscriptional record. We need hardly point out that a good many claims contained in the kingly *praśastis* of early medieval India turn out hollow when verified and cross-checked from other sources. As for the veracity or vagueness of Chinese description, we may be guided by the views of an eminent scholar who delved very deep into the contemporary Chinese records and found them to be 'trustworthy', though at places affected by his fervour for Buddhism.[18] Hsuan-Tsang has left us minute details of the places he visited but modern historian in his anxiety to avoid credulity is prone to disavow the data handed down by him. Thus the view of Dikshit that the description of Hsuan-Tsang is vague and indefinite and the distances given by him do not suit the identification, has no validity and the whole question may be examined afresh in proper perspective, and on a broader basis.

Let us first take up the name Jejākabhukti. That the region was so hailed during the Candella times admits of no doubt. Apart from the clear testimony of the Mahoba record, noted above, we also come across references to it in those of the contemporary dynasties. Madanpur inscriptions of King Pṛthvīrāja Cāhamāna refer to Candella dominions with this very appellation[19]. In Bangla Memorial Stone inscriptions we have Jejāhuti[20] whereas Narwar inscription of Yajvapāla king Gopāla refers to the region as Jejābhukti.[21] But the point, missed by all historians in this regard, is that the fact of area being named by king Jejā is referred to not in his own record (none being available upto now) or any of his immediate successors but in a document of king Kīrtivarman, thirteenth king in line and separated by more than 200 years and about 10 generations. What is further significant, no king after Kīrtivarman refers to this historic act in official record. Of course, King Jejā is held as an important ancestor even by the remotest of his successors but his naming of Bundelkhand does not figure anywhere except the Mahoba record of Kīrtivarman. Clearly the fact was never a part of the genealogical portion to be inserted in official inscription or could it be that the mention was only to capitalize on a fact already existing ? We possess wealth of evidence lending credence to either of the above possibilities and indications there are that both together lead us to the reality of the situation.

First of all we have to note that the proper noun Jejā was not a special invention or monopoly of the Candellas. The name was well in vogue much before the arrival of Candellas on the stage of history. As early as A. D. 532-33 we have a Mahārāja Dejja, a Rāṣṭrakūṭa ruler, figuring in Gokak Plates.[22] If the reference is objected to on grounds of remoteness in time and space, then we may cite Mahārāja Jejja, also of Rāṣṭrakūṭa lineage, ruling in Bundelkhand itself hardly a couple of generations before Jejā of the Mahoba inscription.[23] That the name was not a special appellation used by the ruling classes is shown by Siyadoni stone inscription where we meet with sūtradhāra Jejapa in 29th line.[24] Even the ladies of the time carried a variant of it, for the First Inscription from Vaillabhaṭṭa Svāmin Temple at Gwalior gives us Jajjā as the name of the mother of Alla—the hero of that *Praśasti*.[25] The connection of the word Jajja or Jejja with the Sanskrit word *Yajña* is clear enough and we would come to this point in a little while. For the present, suffice it to note that if Jejjā of Candella line could name the area as his *bhukti*, so also could Jejja of the Pathāri pillar record, with the difference that we have a solitary mention for the former and none in case of the latter, though he was earlier in time. If early Candella chiefs held a portion of Bundelkhand as fief from the Pratihāras, contained in the component part of the name as bhukti, so also perhaps, could the Rāṣtrakuṭa ruler holding it from the parent Rāṣṭrakūṭa line. In any case, the possibility can not be lightly dismissed that the term, either in its refined form Jejākabhukti or rude application Jijhoti, must have been current long before the coming of the Candella chief and he simply seized upon the fact already existing.

Another and equally interesting aspect of the matter is that the boundaries of Jejākabhukti are believed to be marked still by the distribution of Jujhotiā Brāhmaṇas, Banias and Ahirs who are supposed to derive their designation from the territorial name.[26] If the use of the term is coeval with the king Jejā or slightly subsequent to his naming of the area as is the belief of R.K. Dikshit, one would certainly like to know what was their designation prior to this event. Brāhmaṇas definitely dwelt in the area much earlier than the Candellas and we wonder if they did not use any term to distinguish themselves from their counterparts elsewhere in the sub-continent. A consistent silence is maintained by our sources on the point and at the same time, they establish no connection between the refined term Jejākabhukti and rude one Jujhotiā, which we have merely to postulate. Could it be that the term has origin other than that mentioned above ?

Let us look at the problem from a different angle. We have noted earlier that the word Jajja or Jejja is derived, in all probability, from the Sanskrit word *Yajña* meaning sacrifice, which was the main feature of Vedic religion. Knowledge and study of the *Yajurveda* is basic to the performance of sacrifice and, of all the four *Vedas*, it is by far the most important for the purpose. Barring an exception here or there we find that majority of the Brāhmaṇas in Bundelkhand figuring in inscriptional records were students of the *Yajurveda*. One of them happened to be even the head of the *Maitrāyaṇi* school.[27] Eran stone pillar inscription of Budhagupta records that Indraviṣṇu, a scholar ancestor of local *viṣayapati*, is mentioned as such and hailed as Brāhmaṇa sage studying his *Veda*. Out of 309 donees in the Semra plates of Parmardideva, 183 were followers of *Yajurveda* caraṇa.[28] Leaving aside epigraphs even if we turn to literature we meet with Divākaramitra, a boy-friend of Maukhari emperor Grahavarman,a follower of *Maitrāyaṇi Shākhā* embracing Buddhism later on and taking to Vindhyan wilds.[29] Now the connection of Brāhmaṇas being *Yajurvedin* in refined Sanskrit and Jujhotiā in common parlance cannot be absolutely ruled out. In fact Nalinākṣha Dutt has actually derived the word Jajhoti from Yajurhotā which is an observance of the Yajurveda.[29]a And the Brāhmaṇas, wherever they lived, enjoyed the highest place in social hierarchy, so Banias and Ahirs adopting their qualifying epithet seems perfectly logical. Of course, the data cited and discussed above, does not establish our point beyond doubt it, at least, demonstrates that there is nothing inherently improbable in equating Chih-Chi-To of the Chinese with modern Bundelkhand or its part.

As a matter of fact one word indicating the whole of the region and being consistently used in all the sources was never the case. In Candella times, even when prince Jejā had already named the region, we find one of his near successors being referred to as Citrakūṭa-bhūpāla by a contemporary neighbouring ruler.[30] In Muslim chronicles it is never called Jejākabhukti and they mostly name it after its capital Khajuraho.[31] The rākar (red or yellow) soil between Jhansi and Lalitpur was the origin of yet another name — *Pītaśail Viṣaya* for this part of the province.[32] The fact of Vindhyas characterising the region resulted in yet another name *Vindhyadeśa*.[33] Of all such names finding solitary mention by far the most interesting seems to be *Yuddha deśa*[34] with clear reference to its river frontiers. It is rather difficult to make out its possible origin but we may surmise that it issued out of the situation in which the Rāṣṭrakūṭa invaders fought their adversaries in the plains of Bundelkhand. Even when the battles came off elsewhere the route, generally taken by the Rāṣṭrakūṭas, ran through Bundelkhand. Dhruva defeated Vatsarāja somewhere near Jhansi.[35] So also did Govinda III his adversary Nāgabhaṭa II. Indra III followed the Bhopal-Jhansi-Kalpi route. The march of Kṛṣṇa III into Bundelkhand is also recorded. Thus in the tripartite struggle, Bundelkhand was verily war-prone and war-worn, the fact being beautifully reflected in the name Yuddhadeśa.

It is strange that a good many terms we have seen and cited by which the territory was designated, yet nowhere we find ourselves any near the word Bundel or an epithet allied to it. We have seen that Bundela Thakurs, though in minority, being the dominant class in the area, the British coined or adopted the term Bundelkhand to designate the land disregarding the majority consisting of Jujhotiās. It is worthy of mention that the earliest appearance of the Bundelas cannot be taken beyond 14th century A.D. and whatever little knowledge we have of the founder of their class is based on legends and stories figuring in bardic accounts of Bundela courts, hardly the material for sober history. One such work under the title *Kshutr Purkash* has already been referred to which was prepared under the patronage of Rājā Chuttur Saul. The book gives a mythical origin to the Bundela clan and connects them with Lord Rāma of Ayodhya and marks them out as Kṣatriyas of Solar line. Needless it is to mention that the account betrays an attempt by the bard to impart a respectable social position to the Bundelas in Hindu hierarchy. It is indeed a fact that nowhere in ancient records or literature we have any reference to the clan. According to Smith the Bundelas, although counted as Rājputs, admittedly are of mixed blood and probably descended from an intermarriage between a Gaharwār Rājput chief and a Khangār girl.[36] He places the appearance of the first Bundela chieftain between the years A.D. 1335-40. In bardic account, the founder is named Punchum and shown in the act of offering his life to the Goddess Vindhyavāsinī Bhavānī when she suddenly appeared and the drop of blood already fallen miraculously assumed the form of a child suckled by the divine mother. The class so issuing out of a *būnd* (drop) was fittingly named 'Bundela'. Smith gives the name of the founder as Arjunpāl who was similarly encouraged by the Goddess with a promise that he should found Bundela Rāj.[37] Be that as it may, this much is evident that Bundelas emerged from some autochthonous group owing largely to their martial qualities in the transitional period between the decline of the Candellas and manifestation of the Muslims. The court account of their origin from a *būnd* is obviously a bardic fabrication to explain the clan-name which perhaps issued out of some other source not satisfactorily identified so far.

Gorelal Tiwari, who was the first scholar to write a short history of Bundelkhand believed that the name originated from Vindhyelkhand.[38] Of course, the Vindhyas form the sole mountain range of the region. Yet his suggestion is not acceptable since the term 'Vindhyelkhanda' was hardly ever current in common parlance or kingly records.

B.P. Tripathi based his views on philological laws and attempted to trace the root of the word 'Bundela' from the ancient tribe of the Pulindas who inhabited the region. Such are the laws of philology according to him that Bundelkhand, which was originally named after Pulindas, came to be known as 'Bolind' in course of time and ultimately gave birth to the present word 'Bundela'. He also refers to a script called Polindi or Bolindi which was current in ancient times,[39] though it is not clear whether it was used only in central India and whether any record written in it has so far been discovered. We have nothing to comment on the philological aspect of the question but the fact of the Pulindas having dwelt in Bundelkhand stands amply attested by epigraphic records and Sanskrit literature. Earliest among the inscriptions in which they figure are Aśokan Edicts though their exact geographical location cannot be made out.[40] Their concentration in certain areas of central India in substantial numbers is evident from the Nawagrāma grant of Mahārāja Hastin.[41] In fact the expression *Pulinda-Rāṣṭra* occurring in this Parivrājaka inscription, leaves us in no doubt that even after centuries of Aryanisation, pockets of Pulindas wielding political power continued to exist side by side with Brahmanical settlements, though under an Aryan overlord, as late as A.D. 517. The word *rāṣṭra* clearly stands for an administrative unit of the Parivrājaka kingdom but the prefix *Pulindarāja* speaks of a dominion of the chief of the Pulindas. Many more such Pulinda dominions must have existed, though not mentioned in available records. Of course, continuous contact through the ages clearly led to conversion for we have, slightly later, a priest from these non-Aryan dwellers named Pulindabhaṭṭa, getting a grant of two villages —Vyāghrapallika and Kachārapallika from Mahārāja Sarvanātha of the Ucchakalpa line.[42] It appears that some sort of social stratification and classification had set in and the tribe was no longer homogeneous as in the past.

That some of the Pulindas went on with their wild existence is proved by a late thirteenth century record. Ajayagadh Rock Inscription of the time of Bhojavarman tells us that Ananda, the local governor, reduced to submission the wild tribes of Bhillas, Sabaras and Pulindas.[43] Aboriginal tribes of central India, with whom these are to be identified, have been a constant headache for the administration from the early Aryans to the modern British. Ordinarily they must have owed certain allegiance to the monarch when strong, yet lived for the most part free of control and indulged in their hereditary propensities for fighting and plunder, for we come across a couple of other local chiefs also in our records claiming to have suppressed them.[44]

Turning now to literature we find that the Pulindas are first mentioned in the *Aitareya Brāhmaṇa* along with the Śabaras, with whom they have always been associated and sometimes confounded.[45]

Brahmāṇḍa[46] *and Matsya Purāṇas*[47] place the country of the Pulindas in the Vindhya region. So also does Kālidāsa, the noted poet and dramatist.[48] The District Gazetteer of Sagar mentions Pulinda-deśa as name for the western part of Bundelkhand[49] though we have no idea of the source on which the statement is based.

It is neither necessary nor possible to quote all the literary references to the Pulindas. It is sufficiently clear from the evidence cited above that Pulindas prominently figure in the history, society and politics of Bundelkhand down to the decline of the Candella power. Strange enough, they are not heard thereafter. The metamorphosis of the word Pulinda into Bundela by the operation of philological changes, we are not in position to accept, for the historical stages of the change cannot be properly marked out but the non-appearance of Bundelas earlier than fourteenth century A.D. and disappearance of Pulindas later than the thirteenth is significant. This is not to say that all the Pulindas after a brief interregnum reappear—as Bundelas. May be most of them continued with their old identity but the possibility of a section, perhaps martial in character, acquiring new name, more or less akin to the old, cannot be entirely ruled out. The process of Hinduisation was an ongoing one and foreigners as well as aborigines found their place in the Hindu hierarchy in consonance with their character, profession etc. The non-Aryan origin might also explain why the Bundelas do not occupy an eminent position among the Rājputs to which community they claim to belong. In course of time when they acquired political prominence in the whole of Bundelkhand, the legend concerning their birth from a '*būnd*' and a mythical connection with the sun-descended Kṣatriyas was too willingly invented by the courtly chroniclers. By the time the British came on the stage of Bundelkhand's history, the Bundelas were well-entrenched in the local society and polity, so the territory was designated after their clan-name.

The problem of defining Bundelkhand geographically is thornier than the one we tried to solve above. The popular imagination and opinion on the subject is largely influenced by the well-known verses of Bundeli bards which have wide currency in the public, educated as well as illiterate.[50] One of them refers to the river-frontiers by which the area is bounded on all four sides viz. the Jamuna, the Narmada, the Chambal and the Tons, whereas the other describes it figuratively basing the idea on a pastoral motif immensely interesting and imaginatively beautiful as are these couplets, they seem to have been born out of popular appreciation and enthusiasm attending the temporary ascendency of the Bundela clan and, for this very reason, are hardly the material to guide us in the matter of fixing the boundaries of Bundelkhand. They deserve to be disregarded.

In our search for a historical basis we are handicapped by the fact that until the advent of the Candellas, Bundelkhand did not acquire a distinct political identity.

Even on the socio-cultural plane it shared a lot in common with adjoining areas and hardly anything marked it off as a distinct unit.

Language can very well be the yardstick to measure the geographical extent and was accepted as a basis to redraw the State boundaries of Indian Union in 1956. Bundeli is a variant of Hindi and is the common and conversational tongue used by the people of the area we have to study. Thanks, indeed, to B.D. Mishra who has drawn a map of the area containing Bundeli speaking people mapping out a far larger area for Bundelkhand than it possessed even in the palmy days of Candella or Bundela ascendency.[51] Subjecting all the previous surveys and theories on the topic to critical examination, he has assigned to it nineteen districts of Madhya Pradesh (some of them partly included) and four districts of Uttar Pradesh. Praiseworthy though his labour is, we cannot accept his map since linguistic basis alone, in complete disregard of historical and geographical considerations, is unfair for selecting and setting bondaries to an area when we are to work into its hoary past and more so when that language developed much later than the period covered by our study.

Far more reasonable and acceptable, therefore, appears to be the view of K.L. Agrawal who includes four districts of Uttar Pradesh (now increased to five by the creation of Lalitpur district) and six districts or Madhya-Predesh.[52] Listed below are their names :

1. Banda
2. Hamirpur
3. Jalaun
4. Jhansi
5. Lalitpur (of Uttar Pradesh) and
6. Datia
7. Tikamgarh
8. Panna
9. Chhatarpur
10. Sagar and
11. Damoh (of Madhya Pradesh)

These districts constitute a distinct unit which is south of the Jamuna and north of the Narmada and which was wholly or partly the Cedi Janapada in pre-Christian times. Later on, this very area was formed into an administrative unit by the Gupta emperors with Kalindi and Narmada as its river frontiers as already noted above. Still later, the frontiers of Candella Kingdom encompassed these districts.[53] On the linguistic plane we have seen that these districts have a distinct language of their own. Geographically they are a compact unit. It stands to reason, therefore, that the area covered by the eleven districts, mentioned above, may be taken to be constituting Bundelkhand. Thus we can have a well-defined area for the purposes of our study possessing a long historical basis and bounds. But from this it should not be construed that areas outside it, but touching its boundaries or in the immediate vicinity, will be left out of our view altogether. The area mapped out above is just for the sake of convenience to study the archaeological material and inscriptional evidence in it. Bundelkhand, being in the heart of Indian sub-continent ever remained exposed to influences from all the four sides, and so, particularly in the domain of religion we cannot isolate it strictly to the boundaries drawn above. The *Mahāstūpas* of Sānchi and Bharhut are not far from the boundaries we have fixed and yet we possess no Buddhist remains in our area assignable to their times. That does not mean Buddhism was non-existent in Bundelkhand at that time. We have to be flexible in our approach.

REFERENCES

1. B.R. Publishing Corporation, (Report) Delhi, 1974.
2. Vol. IX (New Edition), Today and Tomorrow's Printers and Publishers, New Delhi. p. 68.
3. The History and Coinage of the Chandel (Chandella) Dynasty of Bundelkhand (Jejakabhukti) from 831-1203 A.D., I.A., Vol. XXXVII, 1908, p. 130.
4. Nigam, M.L.: *Cultural History of Bundelkhand*, Sundeep Prakashan, Delhi, 1983, Preface, p. VII.
5. *Historical Geography of Ancient India*, Ess Ess Publication, Delhi, 1967, pp. 312-13.
6. E.I., XXVII, p. 168.
7. Pande, R.B.: *Historical and Literary Inscriptions*, Chowkhamba Sanskrit Studies, Vol. XXIII, Varanasi, 1962, p. 195.
8. *Ibid.* p. 106.

   कालिन्दी नर्म्मंद योर्मध्यं पालयति लोकपाल गुणै ।
   ज्जंगति महाराज श्रियमनुभवति सुरश्मिचन्द्रे च ।।
9. C.I.I., Vol. III, Indological Book House, Varanasi, 1963, No. 25, p. 113-14.
10. Devahuti, D, *Harsha—A Political Study*, Oxford, 1970, p. 95.
11. Cowell, E.B. (tr.) : *The Harṣa-carita of Bāṇa*, Royal Asiatic Society, London, 1897, p. 258.
12. A.S.R., Vol. XXI, p. 58.
13. I.A., XXXVII, 1908, pp. 130-31.
14. D.H.N.I., Vol, II, p. 670.
15. *History of the Candellas*, K.L. Mukhopadhyaya, Calcutta, 1956, p. 14.
16. *The Candellas of Jejākabhukti*, Abhinav Publications, New Delhi, 1977, p. 13.
17. E.I., I., No. 27, V. 10

   जेजाख्ययाथ नृपति: स बभूव जेजाभुक्ति: :
   पृथोरिव यत: पृथिवीयमासीत् ।।
18. Devahuti, D., *op. cit.*, p. 4.

19. A.S.R., XXI, pt. II, p. 174.
20. E.I., XXXI, p. 323.
21. Ibid., XXXIII, No. 4, L. 10.
22. Ibid, XXI, p. 289.
23. Pathari pillar inscription of king Parabala, E.I., IX, No. 34, p. 248, Vs. 5-7.
24. Pande, R.B., op. cit., p. 173.
25. E.I., I., No. 20, p. 156, V.9.
26. Dikshit, R.K., op. cit., p. 173.
27. C.I.I., Vol, III (Revised), No. 39, L. 4-6.
28. E.I., IV, No. 20, p. 153ff.
29. Cowell, E.B., op. cit., Ch. VIII, p. 233.
29a. Dutt, Nalinaksha *Buddhist Sects in India*, Indological Book House, Varanasi, 1977. p. 303: The name Jujhoti is known to *Skanda Purāṇa* also, vide B.P., p. 2
30. Dikshit, R.K., op. cit., p. 37.
31. Ibid., pp. 14 and 89.
32. Ibid., p. 10, Note 3.
33. Ibid., p. 72.
34. Ibid., p. 12, Note. 2.
    रेवायमुनयोर्मध्ये युद्धदेश इतीर्यते ।
35. This and all other facts following it which illustrate the name *Yuddhadeśa* have been taken from A.I.K., p. 5.
36. The History and Coinage, op, cit., p. 130; Trivedi, S.D. is also of the view that the area came to be christened as Bundelkhand in fourteenth century A.D. though he has assigned evidence in support of the date (B.P., p.1).
37. J.A.S.B. (New Series), Vol. 50, pt. III, 1881, p. 31.
38. बुन्देलखण्ड का संक्षिप्त इतिहास, प्रयाग, 1933, पृ॰1.
39. बुन्देलखण्ड की प्राचीनता, वाराणसी, 1965, पृ॰ 7-9.
40. Pande, R.B., op. cit., p. 17, L. 10 and note 2 also.
41. E.I., XXI, No. 20.
42. Fleet, No. 31.
43. E.I., I., No, 38 (II), VS. pp. 21-22.
44. Jhansi Inscription of Sallakṣaṇasimha, E.I., I., No. 25, L.7.
45. E.I., XXI, p. 106.
46. **श्री व्यासमहर्षिप्रोक्तं ब्रह्मांड पुराणम्** (संस्कर्त्ता-आचार्य जगदीश शास्त्री, मोतीलाल बनारसा दास, (Reprint) दिल्ली, 1983, पृ॰ 23.
    "पुलिन्दा विन्ध्यमौलिया वैदर्भा दण्डकै: सह" 2.16.58.
47. श्री राम प्रताप त्रिपाठी शास्त्री, **मत्स्य महापुराण**, हिन्दी साहित्य सम्मेलन, प्रयाग, संवत 2003, पृ॰265.
48. पण्डित श्री रामचन्द्र मिश्र: **रघुवंशम्**, सुलभ संस्कृत ग्रन्थमालायास्तृतीयं पुष्पम्, श्री कामेश्वर सिंह दरभंगा संस्कृतविश्वविद्यालय, दरभंगा, 1979.
    "व्यलङ्घयद् विन्ध्यमुपायनानि पश्यत पुलिन्दैरुपपादितानि. 16.32.
49. P. 65.

50. त्रिपाठी, भा. प्र. : वही, पृ० 23 & 34

(अ) इत जमुना उत नर्बदा, इत चम्बल उत टोंस।
छत्रसाल सो लरन की रही न काहू हौंस॥

(ब) भैंस बंधी है ओरछे, पड़ा होशंगाबाद।
लगवैया हैं सागरे, चपिया रेवा पार॥

51. मिश्र, भ. दी. : बुन्देली की सीमाएँ, मध्य भारती, जिल्द 14-16, पृo 139.

52. अग्रवाल, क.ला. : विन्ध्य क्षेत्र का ऐतिहासिक भूगोल (शोध प्रबन्ध) सागर विश्वविद्यालय, 1972, पृo 75.

53. E. I., I., No. 19 (II), V. 45.
आकालन्जरमाचमालव नदी तीर स्थिते भास्वत:
कालिन्दी सरितस्टादित इतोप्या चेदिदेशावधे:।
आतस्मादपि विस्मयैक निलयाद गोपाभिद्या नाद गिरे-
र्य: शास्ति क्षितिमायतोर्जित भुज-व्यापार लीलार्जिताम्॥

2

Polity in Socio-Economic Perspective

(Geography of a region is always a key in many respects, to its economic condition, social formations and political evolution. This is not to say that the geography of Bundelkhand imparted any uniqueness to its economy, society and polity. The natural frontiers of Bundelkhand are not impassabe and so it has a lot in common with adjoining areas. As a matter of fact, being the heart region of India it ever remained exposed to influences of various kinds from all the directions and absorbed a great deal which may not be directly attributed to its geography. Nevertheless, fundamental features of any aspect of a people's life cannot be correctly and adequately analysed without studying the geographical background against which the society shapes up. The survival of aborigines has much to do with the dense forests and mountaineous fastnesses. Likewise the non-appearance of a local centre of power, till very late, has also to be explained in terms of its geographical character. In case of economy, the impact is much more manifest. Thus the society, economy and polity develop along the lines set by the geography and all together affect the religious life, beliefs and practices of a community. Below is given in brief an account of the geo-political and socio-economic background alongwith a detailed epigraphic survey which would help us develop a better understanding of the process, rate and nature of interaction and acculturation than possible otherwise.

Lying within the folds of Vindhyan range, Bundelkhand is a marked geographical unit. The base of the hills rests on gneiss while the hills themselves are made of sandstone. A good-many temples of the region are built of this sandstone and this is how the role of geography in the study of religion becomes manifest.

The Vindhyas loom large in the legends and literature relating to the region. The widely current episode of their having impeded the course of the sun is mentioned in a number of inscriptions. The *Kādambarī* contains a beautiful reference to it.[1] The Sabara general of the area appeared as though he were the very child of Vindhya mountain. His wide expansive chest reminded the writer of a Vindhyan rock. Śakti is worshipped in her special form as Vindhyavāsinī and figures prominently in the story of the founder of the Bundela clan.[2] A temple was constructed and consecrated to Lord Śiva with the name Vindhyeśvara.[3] Little wonder Vindhyelkhaṇḍa and Vindhyadeśa are believed to be earlier names of the area.[4]

From the hills numerous streams flow north or north-east towards the Jamuna of which the most important are the Betwa, Dhasan, Birma, Ken, Baghain, Paisuni and Southern Tons. Barring a few exceptions majority of the rivers go dry even before the summer sets in. Needing a particular note here is the fact that till the beginning of the present century hardly four percent of the cultivated area was irrigated.[5]

The alluvial plain contains a large proportion of disintegrated trap which gives it dark colour. The fact is forcefully brought home in the description of Bāṇa who compares the black soil of Bundelkhand fields with black iron and refers to its production being primarily through spade culture.[6]

The vernacular equivalent of the black soil is *mār* and is especially adapted for growing wheat. Another variety with lighter colour and differing qualities is known as *Kābar*. What hardship the peasant had suffered in ploughing it through the ages becomes evident in the native proverb which says *Kābar* is too wet to plough one morning and too dry to plough the next. From Jhansi to Lalitpur we have a soil called *rākar*, the prevailing colour of which is yellow. Black soil is retentive of moisture but requires irrigation in unfavourable seasons and in dry weather opens out in large cracks.

About one-third of the autumn crop is Jowar and one-seventh cotton. The chief spring crop is gram varying between 50 to 80 percent. Irrigation from the wells is difficult owing to the low spring level and the storage tanks made by closing the valleys do not command large areas. The solitary canal of the British days drawn from the Betwa chiefly served Jalaun district.

Bundelkhand is peculiarly liable to suffer from deficient rainfall. Others among the natural calamities are prevalence of rust after a wet or cloudy winter and the growth of a weed or grass called *kāns* which spreads rapidly and involves a lot of labour for rooting out. In 1867 the crops failed and in 1868-69, there was famine attended with great loss of cattle. Again in 1872 loss of cattle stalked the land in the wake of murrain.

Another cycle of bad years commenced from the early nineties. 1892 and 1893 brought blight and rust whereas 1894 followed with floods resulting from excessive rains. Drought came in 1895 and 1896, which was, to say the least, disastrous.

The population of Bundelkhand decreased by 10½ percent between 1891-1901. Debt assumed serious proportions in all parts of the tract.

Systematic and well-documented collection of the climatic and geographic data commenced with the British and to their meticulous records we owe the whole of this detailed survey done above.[7] The geo-climatic events and conditions highlighted by them must not be radically different from remote past we are working in and so, there cannot be serious objection to our visualising the politico-economic picture of those days which is necessarily affected by them, since our own sources are silent and scanty on the subject. To illustrate our point, the unmetalled roads of Bundelkhand are even now impassable during rains owing to the tenacious mud formed on them. The situation must have been the same in Candella or pre-Candella times posing a problem of communication to every administration down to the British and always militating against the building of a durable empire even by the ablest of monarchs.

We have seen that Vindhyan mountains are the main feature in the topography of Bundelkhand. Added to this we may note dense forests in the west-south and south-eastern parts. This fact alone is enough to explain the presence of aborigines in the area in such large numbers from prehistory to the present times. The mountainous fastnesses provided them numerous shelters away from the approach of Sanskritisation to continue with their 'arrested' civilization. Though a great many among them gradually were absorbed within Brahmanical fold finding an occupational niche in the caste-structure, the fact that some of the local chiefs and officers in our records are mentioned as bringing them back to discipline clearly highlights that these non-Aryans remained a constant factor in the polity of Bundelkhand.

Lastly the very geographical position of Bundelkhand[8] is such that all through it acted rather as a gateway between the North and the South than the nucleus of an imperial system. It became and remained a sort of corridor for invading armies trading caravans and religious missionaries wanting political expansion, commercial penetration and religious propagation respectively, in their march to trans-Vindhyan territories. To put the position in proper terminology, the region continued to be 'peripheral' hardly ever reaching 'core' status. Even when the Candellas, verily the sons of the soil, tried to build up a local centre of power, their success in transforming this age-old identity was only partial.

A number of routes ran through the region. It is not without significance that lies there in the heart of the region, a palaeolithic site regarded as a meeting ground of Sohan and Madras industries. From very early times Kausambi was connected with Vidisha and, further on, to Ujjayini, the road most probably going through the valleys of the Betwa. It is believed that the present railway line passing by Vidisha and touching Jhansi and Kalpi on way to Kanpur hints at the old route.[9] The very name Vidisha is interpreted to mean a place from where many roads go to different directions.[10] The holy spots of Sanchi and Bharhut became places of pilgrimage from the Mauryan period and people from far and near frequented them for centuries to come but the fact of their being located on important routes must be seen in the background leading later to their elevation. The location of Gujarra Edict of the Mauryan emperor also indicates a route passing by it. Many more references to caravan merchants going through Bundelkhand can be collected. In fact we have in Yakṣa Maṇibhadra a special deity presiding over the fortunes of the caravan merchants in the region in the early centuries of the Christian era. This special character of the deity should be seen in the context of apprehension and insecurity involved in plying on these routes. As early as the Jātaka period we have instances of robbers working havoc on the wayfarer.[11] Bāṇa too was well-aware of plundering habits of the people living in the vicinity of these roads. He depicts the villagers of the region wearing ragged clothes for fear of thieves.[12] Obviously much of this thieving and plundering activity should be attributed to the presence of forest tribes. Coming back to our main point, it is noteworthy that the real root of Cāhamāna-Candella conflict in the time of Paramardideva lay in quarrel over Sirsa, a strategic point between Mahoba and Delhi where converged a number of roads.[13] In medieval times the direct road from Karra to Bhilsa passed through Mahoba.[14]

Viewing the matter from a different angle we come across urban centres springing up and flourishing along these routes, bringing a bit of prosperity to the area otherwise poor in productivity and growth. Some of these stood on river banks. Eran achieved eminence from the dawn of civilization and Sotthivati did so during the Buddhist period.[15] Vidisha, Kausambi and Tripuri may also be mentioned among early urban settlements though located outside the area we have demarcated. The Candella period witnessed efflorescence of a great many towns and cities. Tradition avers that, in its palmy days, Mahoba included fifty two towns or bazars.[16] The explanation appears to be that Mahoba happened to be the chief town in a *baoni* or paragana of fifty two towns and villages. It would be unfair to discount the tradition absolutely for we do have a number of references to prosperous towns in epigraphic records of the period. Where these fail us, we possess a wealth of archaeological remains attesting the fact. Khajuraho needs no description. From Siron (Lalitpur dist.) we have just one record but it speaks volumes leaving not a shadow of a doubt about the humming trade activity transacted in the town.[17] An Ajayagadh record testifies to the existence of thirty six towns, obviously in Bundelkhand.[18]

We may now pass on to prepare the political background to our theme. The historians usually confine themselves to writing a political history debating the dates and dynasties figuring in scanty available records (there being just one for the pre-Gupta period in our area) and fixing as well as revising chronological arrangements. In our opinion the exercise would not serve any purpose, at least, in our context. In the first place, hardly half a dozen records we possess handed down by the pre-Candella period and no connected account, therefore, is possible. The so-called histories of Bundelkhand which have appeared till now, do little more than whistling in the dark as far as ancient period is concerned. It would be no use walking a road that has numerous and big gaps without even bridges to continue our march. In the second place, whichever cult came into prominence owing basically to the personal predilection of the king, other cults did not suffer correspondingly, since Brāhmaṇical tradition which ruled supreme in the realms of religion prescribed more or less same beliefs, practices and rituals for all the major as well as minor cults. If iconographical features of the enshrined deity are left out of consideration, then there is not much to distinguish a Śiva temple from the one dedicated to Viṣṇu. At Khajuraho one may go a step further. The Pārśvanātha temple raised in heterodox faith of the Jainas is remarkably similar in shape and details to those of othodox tradition. As a matter of fact, we have examples of dynasties in which the rulers, even when they happened to be father and son, did not worship the same deity. In Pratihāra royal family this eclectic spirit is proved by the fact that four generations beginning from Devarāja were devotees respectively of Viṣṇu, Śiva, Bhagavatī and Sūrya.[19]

Hence it would be in the fitness of things to discard the beaten track of listing the rulers from stray references, and prepare the background in terms of emergence and evolution of structure of politics. The classes and castes that monopolised and enjoyed political power must have affected a lot the religious life and the precious little definite, that we possess by way of records and coins, could be put to the best use.

The earliest inhabitants of the area were no doubt ancestors of a few of the aborigines still clinging to it in a corner wild or hill-top high. Illustrating the law of uneven development on our subcontinent, the aborigines of Bundelkhand are a few of the fragments of prehistoric world still scattered over India, remnants to our own day of the Stone Age. The Imperial Gazetteer enumerates Kols, Khangars and Saharias among them, putting their number at 2,693,000 in 1891 and 2,456,000 in 1901, accounting only for the then British Bundelkhand.[20] A recent study mentions Agarias, Bhumyas, Baigas, Ghasias, Gonds, Kols, Korwas, Oraons, Paraliyas and Sahariyas dwelling in U.P. districts of Bundelkhand.[21] On M.P. side, by far the most numerous are Gonds. So much so that in medieval times the tract came to be christened as Gondwana. Bhils and Baigas are other tribal communities on M.P. side. We have to be flexible in our attempt to establish their identity in hoary past and if anthropological and ethnographical studies done on them are not acceptable in totality for our purpose, such of the traits as tally with their description in ancient literature cannot be altogether ignored. They were in Bundelkhand much before the Aryan advance, have lived throughout to our own times and so their role in and contribution to the society, polity, economy and religion of the higher civilization has to be underlined even if we have no written account available from them. They verily constitute, so to say, the living past of India to a great extent. Wafted now by the wind of time to the main—stream of Indian life and civilization they retain the fond memories of their former existence and just one small piece of evidence is enough to drive home our point. More than a century ago, the noted historian Vincent Smith collected and published 'Popular songs of the Hamirpur

District'. Figuring among them is Kol's song that has much more to convey to the students of history than the stereotype land-grants of the lords of the land. Its translation is quoted below in full :

> "Behold the ways of the dwellers in the wood. In hills and caves they dwell, never neither for night nor day build kols a wall. In men who abide in towns and villages never will they put trust. The camp of travellers they always plunder, regarding not the law of God nor of man. In dreams even, corn they never see, wood fruits they eat—so their life passes. Among the Kols the chief is he whom all men united cannot subdue."[22]

The pictures presented does not belong to any particular age or year and yet its value as a document highlighting prominent features of the life of non-Aryan and non-literate dwellers of Bundelkhand cannot be underestimated. We will see slightly later that a lot of what we know about tribals from anthropological studies can be properly verified and authenticated with the help of Sanskrit works written by ancient authors. No history of Bundelkhand therefore, has any claim to completeness unless it treats the unwritten account of these tribals as part of all that happened in times past and is worth preserving for posterity.

That Palaeolithic Man inhabited the region of Bundelkhand is now a fact established beyond doubt. Regarding tool industries of this period H.D. Sankalia says, "The most interesting and instructive area is Lalitpur. Here within a radius of a mile from the railway station several workshops were discovered." About Biana Nālā nearby he concluded that it was "found by early man to be a suitable site for habitation. The tools disclose transition from the early Stone Age."[23] The rivers Sonar Kopra and Bearma in Damoh district "yielded industries of all the three periods. Apart from the stone tools, the early man has left a rich legacy of rock-paintings, the earliest among them being taken to 4000 B.C. K.D. Bajpai who made a discovery in Banda district holds the view that the paintings revealed a civilization older than that of the Indus Valley, but with a highly developed aesthetic sense.[24] V.S. Vakankar and S.K. Pandey have done commendable work in unearthing this valuable source of history in the region.[25] Sagar, Chhatarpur and Datia districts have a great many painted rock-shelters.

Rich though our legacy is, we can not make out from this material what sort of organised community living the early men had, if there actually was any. Bidding farewell to their yin-state, a part of the prehistoric people ushered in the yan-state of settled civilizing somewhere around 2000 B.C. because, therefrom, we get solid evidence of Chalcolithic culture available at the only systematically and scientifically excavated site viz. Eran in Sagar district. Arnold Toynbee traces the genesis of civilization in the response of man to the challenge of Nature.[26] Difficult it is to say, in our present state of knowledge, whether the original settlers of Bundelkhand left their stagnant existence and switched ever to the dynamic in consequence of any such challenge. In any case, theirs proved to be the 'arrested civilization' to use another Toynbeean expression, for they are still primitive tribes and in the words of Edward Balfour, "These people have separate names—Pahāris, Kols, Gonds, Bhilas, Colis or Colaris."[27] K.D. Bajpai gives their ancient equivalents—Niṣādas, Śabaras, Pulindas.[28] References to these last in literature and inscriptions we have already noticed in the earlier chapter. The Śabaras indicate in general any of the primitive tribes and have been favoured with a good coverage in the *Harṣa-carita* and the *Kādambarī* of Bāṇa. A remarkable pen-picture he gives us which is well worthquoting—

"How full of folly is their life and censured by the good are their deeds! For they believe it to be a religious rite to make offerings of human flesh. Their food consists of wine, flesh and such things, which are condemned by the good. Their physical exercise is hunting. Their *Śāstra* is the howling of jackals. Their advisers of good and bad are the owls. Their talent consists in knowing (the ways of) birds. Their acquaintances are dogs. Their kingdom is over tenantless wilds. A drinking bout is their chief festive occasion. Their friends are their bows, which serve them in perpetrating cruel deeds. Their helpers are their arrows, with their tips besmeared with poison, and looking like snakes (whose fangs are full of poison). Their music is such as works havoc among the simple deer. Their wives are other people's women made captive. Their association is with the ferocious-natured tigers. Their worship of the deities is (made) with the blood of wild beasts. Their offerings (to deities) are (made) with flesh. Their sustenance is by pilfering......In whatever forest they may happen to be residing, the same forest they entirely tear up by the roots."[29] Admitting certain amount of exaggeration and some coating of imagination, born largely out of the Brāhmaṇical antipathy of Bāṇa for their uncouth and non-Brāhmaṇical mode of living, we may still tally a good many features of the Śabara tribe with those noticed in British observations. Chitkaur Devi, the Gond goddess, is given sacrifice of a pig and a chicken, by cutting the throats of animals and letting their blood drop on the central part of the threshing floor.[30] Lieutenant Predergast came across a tribe of Gonds who were cannibals and ate their own relations only.[31] A sept among the Dhanwar is named *Manakhia* which means man-eater and it is possible that its members formerly offered human sacrifices.[32] The Bhuiyas did so every third year at their shrines till the country came under the British Rule.[33] The Bhatras worship the god of hunting who is known as Mātideo and resides in a separate tree in each village.[34] Marriage by capture is very widely prevalent among savage races and where the custom has given place to more peaceable methods of procuring a wife, survivals commonly occur. Among a section of the Gonds the regular capture of the girl is still sometimes carried out though the business is usually arranged by the couple before hand. A minor variant of the practice may be seen in the procedure where the bride is required to hide somewhere and has to be found or carried off by the bridegroom or his brother.[35] As for the rooting out of trees, we may cite the legend concerning the origin of the Baigas in which they claim to have received divine sanction to make their living by felling trees and have never taken to any other calling.[36] In the *Harṣa carita*, Bāṇa makes reference to spade-culture being practised in Vindhyan villages[37] and it is pertinent to note in this regard that a section of the Gonds still carries on cultivation without a plough, their only agricultural implement being a kind of hoe or spade.[38] Thus even after a gap of more than a millennium the description holds largely good finding numerous echoes in British observations and we may legitimately resort to either of these sources to discuss the nature of interaction between Aryan intruders and non-Aryan natives leading to a distinct process of acculturation in course of time.

Among the aborigines, Bhils are the only tribe to have been noticed by their current name. Whereas Jhansi stone inscription of Sallakṣanasiṃha mentions that they were kept in order by some local chiefs,[39] the Ajayagadh rock inscription records them alongwith Śabaras and Pulindas having been reduced to submission by the local governor.[40] Suffice it to say with the help of the data, discussed above, that when Homo Palaeolithicus of Bundelkhand embarked on his exertions towards transformation into Homo mechanicus and further into Homo sapiens, Bhils, Pulindas and Śabaras were inhabiting the region.

Having established the identity of these pre-Aryan dwellers beyond doubt, we may switch back to our subject of polity. We cannot generalise in this regard. Some of the tribes continue even now at their food-gathering stage whereas others took to settled life at least by second millennium B.C. and became authors of Chalcolithic culture at Eran. Some could not progress beyond hunting stage as is evident from the account of Bāṇa. Others elected felling of trees, clearing and burning of forests and practising shifting cultivation to make a living. Accordingly some are even now at the stage of tribal unity and polity. Others evolved some sort of political organization. Our data does not permit us to say more on the point and the big question-mark confronting us is the authorship of Eran Chalcolithic culture.

M.L. Nigam has discussed the possibility of Harappans coming to Kausambi as fugitives and founding a settlement.[41] He bases his view on the presence of early defences, closely resembling the Harappan citadel. In case of Eran, too, he believes in the Harappan influence reaching through Kathiawar and western India. But here he bases his opinion on the evidence of pottery.[42] He seems to be alone in holding these views. Mere citadel can not be taken to hint at the possible Harappan connection. Hence, the validity of above views may well be doubted until some confirmatory evidence comes to light.

Technology has a central role in civilization and Iron has a central role in technology. A keen controversy is raging round the question of dating the appearance of iron at Eran. It is maintained that the iron-finds almost all over India dated by carbon-14 method and as corrected by dendochronology show that iron technology began in India not later than middle of the second millennium B.C. and that it originated independently instead of being borrowed from West Asia or anywhere else.[43] In Eran sequence the emergence of iron is placed in Period II (B.C. 1300-700) which is the earliest recorded date for iron in India.[44] The opponents of the theory hold the view that as yet there is hardly any basis for the assumption of pre-1000 B.C. beginning of the Iron Age in Madhya Pradesh. The evidence, available so far points to a date nearer the '7th century B.C.' for the earliest occurrence of iron in this region.[45]

Be that as it may, for us the fact deserving of note is evidence of Eran having been a fortified settlement not only by a defence wall but a moat as well.[46] It is enough to attest some form of polity into which the people were organised. If there was a monarch, we have no evidence to the effect. An oligarchy cannot be altogether ruled out, though this, too, is at best a conjecture.

Early Aryan advance or instrusion into the area has to be ascertained from Sanskrit literature. Brāhmaṇisation of Bundelkhand appears to have been initiated by the *ṛṣis* who ventured into the Vindhyan wilds. Local tradition asserts that the area contained the *āsramas* of such eminent *ṛṣis* as Vālmīki, Vedavyāsa, Atri and Agastya.[47] It is interesting to note that hillocks standing in the vicinity of Gujarra, where we get the only available Mauryan record of our area, are locally called *Siddhon kī toriyā*—which mean hillocks of the perfected ones.[48]

Especially important in this regard seems to be the prescription of *viśvajīta* sacrifice according to which temporary residence with the Niṣādas was obligatory.[49] The *Kādambarī* also confirms the fact of the Vindhyas having been resorted to by the holy sages.[50]

We have already noted that Cedi was the earliest name of Bundelkhand. The word is supposed to have originated from the name of king—Cidi who was the grandson of king Vidarbha. In the *Rgveda* the king of Cedi figures as making a gift of ten kings, obviously as slaves to a priest who officiated at one of his sacrifices.[51] Another Ṛgvedic monarch Kasu brought many kings under his sway. Perhaps some of the so-called kings were in reality non-Aryan chieftains. Thus it appears alongwith peaceful penetration by the saintly sages, armed advance went hand in hand.

A picture of the process we can have from the lesser epic as well. The historicity of the *Rāmāyaṇa* is being established by the archaeologists. The location of Laṅkā is an issue debate on which has assumed national dimensions. Much new evidence has been collected on the subject and there are good grounds to believe that Rāvaṇa and his tribe lived somewhere in Central India. There are holy bathing places (*tīrthas*) named after Indrajīta and Rāvaṇa which are not known to exist elsewhere in India.[52] In no other part, perhaps, we have the people calling themselves *Rávaṇa—Vaṃśis*.[53] Bāṇa has made comparison of Vindhyāṭavi with the capital city of Rāvaṇa.[54] The name Rāvaṇa frequently figures in Candella records and we have no idea if, it so occurs in inscriptions elsewhere in the country. In Semra Copper Plates alone it is recorded thrice.[55] Siyadoni stone inscriptions mentions it once.[56] On geographical side Kiṣkindhā is placed to the north of the Vindhyas.[57] Citrakūṭa, of course, is located in Bundelkhand. Marriage by purchase as well as force was as much in vogue in Rāvaṇa's tribe[58] as it is among the aborigines, noticed above. Language and customs of the Vānaras have a lot in common with the Śavaras who are found in Sagar district.[59] We also have Savara mountains in central India. Most striking among the resemblances is wearing of animal masks by Ravaṇa's followers[60] as well as aborigines of central India. In rock-paintings also we come across a large number of such representations. The facts, cited above, cannot be lightly brushed aside and even if they do not establish the point conclusively, their appeal to us for reading into the *Rāmāyaṇa* the interaction and armed encounter between the two civilizations cannot be missed. In any case, the ventures of Lord Rāma, prior as well as subsequent to his exile in the Vindhyan range, must be seen in terms of an ongoing process of Sanskriti-Sation initiated by the sacrificing Brāhmaṇas.

Archaeological evidence, on the other hand, points to a date fairly late for the penetration of Aryans in the area. The absence of P.G. ware on the one hand and the presence of microliths associated with red-painted sherds on the other, followed by iron and N.B.P. at Eran are taken to mean longer and uninterrupted occupation by the original settlers.[61] It appears initial Aryan efforts at political subjugation remained confined upto Kauśāmbi and areas in its vicinity. A long list of kings can be prepared from early Sanskrit literature to show their connections with Cedi dynasty or *janapada* but placing them in time and preparing proper genealogy or chronology with even a faint idea of their (exact) dominions is a task at which none has succeeded so far. For instance Śiśupāla of the Greater Epic is believed to have ruled from his capital Chanderi in Guna district[62] (touching the boundary of the area we have fixed) but there is no evidence to substantiate the belief. Yudhiṣṭhira is supposed to have installed his son in the sovereignty of the Cedis.[63] Here again, we are neither sure of the date nor the exact frontiers in which his subjects lived. As a matter of fact, till we come to the Mauryans no name or date we can take as certain, and the polity that emerges in this dim light appears to be equally divided between the Aryans and the non-Aryans. Such of the areas as came under Aryan occupation or influence witnessed the subordination of earlier dwellers to the Kṣatriya invaders, whereas vast jungle tracts and hilly fastnesses continued under tribal polity with a chief and his comrades-in-arms. The position of those Neolithic people, who had already taken to cultivating fields and domesticating cattle, producing food and building houses, as at Eran, seems to be middle one. They must have made stiff resistance before being absorbed. In this context only we can comprehend how even by the Later Vedic Age only a few of the aborigines had been assigned caste status in Brāhmaṇical books. Needing particular note among these caste names are Āndhra, Kirāta, Niṣāda, Pulinda and Śabara.[64] Slightly later we have Bhils and Kols in the list of *antyajas* classed with all those who were beef-eaters.[65] One thing stands out clear from what we have noted above. Centuries were to roll by for the process of Sanskritisation to complete and so we would be wrong in generalising on any matter.

Kauśāmbi seems to have been the key point opening the gates to Bundelkhand. The structural remains, found here in excavations, bear out the rites of '*Śyenaçiti*' and *Puruṣamedha* having been performed here and are in close conformity with early Vedic literature.[66] Nicaksu, the Māhābharatan descendant of Parikṣit, came and occupied the site sometime earlier than 6000 B.C. Kauśāmbi, most probably, therefore, became the base for onward Aryan advance.

The first Mauryan made complete conquest of Bundelkhand. None of the non-Aryan tribes could withstand the onslaught of the imperial army. That they did not mend their ways after subjugation, one can easily make out from the warning his grandson had to issue for all the forest dwellers. Without mincing matters he addressed them in his XIII Rock Edict, "The Beloved of the Gods believes that one who does wrong should be forgiven as far as it is possible to forgive him. And the Beloved of the Gods conciliates the forest tribes of his empire, but he warns them that he has power in his remorse and he asks them to repent, lest they be killed. For the Beloved of the Gods wishes that all beings should be unharmed, self-controlled, calm in mind, and gentle."[67] Perhaps political conquest was not as difficult as the cultural and the tribes must have resented the new mode of life imposed from the above. British studies make it clear that some of the tribes till the current century disliked switching over to plough cultivation abandoning the shifting one. Tilling of the land was considered inferior occupation by the Baigas, who never willingly took to it.[68] Hence the smouldering resentment among these malcontents may have broken out in open at times against which Aśoka had to issue the warning. An additional factor in this regard seems to be the thieving and plundering habits of these people also noted earlier.[69] We have seen important trade routes passed through Bundelkhand and concern of Aśoka for their safety and maintenance is clear from his records. Good communications had a central role in the centralised administration of the Mauryans and when they were to pass through tribal territories, Aśoka would naturally want the tribes to be law-abiding and peaceable. Another factor angering Aśoka seems to have been shifting cultivation practised by some of the tribes and the desire to exploit the forest wealth prompted him to prohibit the wanton burning of forests in V Pillar Edict.[70]

With the Mauryans came Brāhmaṇical system and supremacy to Bundelkhand. The political power in local affairs rested with the Brāhmaṇas since in contemporary thought it was believed that the factors bringing unqualified success to the king were the support of the Brāhmaṇas, the good advice of the ministerial council and action in accordance with the *Sāstras*.[71] No mention is necessary that *Śāstras* through the ages have been a close Brāhmaṇical preserve and the ministerial council mostly had members from their class only. We have no contemporary records to show that officials largely came from among them but the non-Aryans hardly stood any chance.

Power and wealth go together. The fact boldly stands out since the very purpose of Gujarra inscription and that of Ahraura seems to assure the poor that they can as well effect their association with gods by adhering to Aśokan *Dhamma*.[72]

Apart from usual official hierarchy working elsewhere as well, two officers need special note in our context. Among the superintendents, one specially concerned with forest produce must have been posted here as also an *aṃtamahāmatta* to look after the less civilized tribes.[73]

Perhaps the Brāhmaṇas did not enjoy the monopoly in the structure of power. They had to share in some respects with the trading class. Profuse punch—marked coins have been unearthed in excavations at Eran dating from about C. 3rd century B.C. to the end of 3rd century A.D. An earthen jar yielded 3,268 coins mostly of copper and a few with silver coating.[74] The evidence cannot but be interpreted in terms of brisk trade and dynamic economy which also help in rearing a local centre of power.

This is exactly what seems to have happened soon after the unrelaxing control of the Mauryan emperor was withdrawn. A little more than a century ago, Cunningham picked up from Eran a coin of King Dharmapāla assignable to late 3rd century B.C.[75] A circular lead-piece was also discovered at Eran in course of excavations on which we have the name Indragupta in characters of Mauryan Brāhmī.[76] We know absolutely nothing about the two kings except their names, mentioned above, but the fact of their being independent rulers is quite obvious and the possibility of mercantile support in this regard cannot be entirely ruled out. After all, building of an army and concomitant royal paraphernalia could not come about without hard cash and the traders would be too willing to help in return for a place of priority in the local centre of political power. If the Gupta ending in the name of second king is an indication, a member of their own class climbed to power.

Whichever *varṇa* the rulers came from, their alliance with trading class seems to have been shortlived. We do not expect any genealogy or chronology of the kings coming to light, the period being too early for such a recording and the excavations at the place being already exhaustive. In fact, the relationship between Dharmapāla and Indragupta is not easy to establish. In any case, the monarchy met an early end and a commercial oligarchy was inaugurated. A baked clay-sealing bearing the legend Erikiṇa is taken to indicate republican form of government with Eran as capital.[77] Of about the same time are some die-struck coins containing the name Erakaṇa in Brāhmi characters. The semi-circle symbol on them is regarded as representing the shape of the old town and river symbol is believed to stand for the Bina river on which the town was located.[78] The government of Erikiṇa, whether monarchical or oligarchical was obviously a local one and its command did not go much beyond some villages in the vicinity. It was easy, therefore, for the ambitious rulers of the adjoining areas to extend their sway and absorb the young of government. A clay sealing coming to light in course of excavations bears the name of Siṃhasena, son of Śaka king Īśvaramitra.[79] Another house that cast its covetous eyes on the prosperous trading town was that of the Nāgas. Numismatic evidence adequately attests to the Nāga and Saka hold and for the period immediately preceding that of the Guptas, we have an epigraphic record as well. The Eran stone pillar inscription[80] of Śaka king Srīdharavarman makes him out a contemporary of Samudragupta to whom probably he submitted and was confirmed in his possession.

Himself a foreigner, he seems to have displaced another foreign adventurer Mahārāja Avarisgha who is known to us from his sole surviving evidence—a crystal intaglio.[81]

The end of Srīdharavarman is merely to be conjectured. He was surely the last in the line, if there was any, and fell fighting for his chief. Of Samudragupta we have only one stone inscription other than his Prayāg *Praśasti* and that comes from Eran.[82] For the rest of Bundelkhand in the absence of an inscription, we could as well depend on his bold claim of having made all the kings of the forest regions to become his servants. (*paricārakikṛta-sarvv-āṭávika rājasya*).[83] The statement is sweeping enough to include those of the aboriginal chieftains that lived in the area of our study lording over their respective tribes. After concluding his campaign the emperor made the whole area between the Kalindi and the Narmada into a province placing its administration under a separate governor.

Rāmagupta may have been the first occupying that position. The historicity of this ruler is now fairly well established and what makes us think of him as the earliest Gupta governor is the fact that almost the whole of numismatic and epigraphic evidence supporting his historicity has been found at Eran and its adjoining region.[84]

We have briefly mentioned earlier that the Mauryans made and maintained their empire with Brāhmaṇical support. So also did the Guptas now. In fact, heading, as they were, the political manifestation of Brāhmaṇical revival, their interest in championing Brāhmaṇical social system and values was stronger and clearer. Under them the system found a firm footing in the area and Brāhmaṇisation of Bundelkhand began in right earnest. However, the process was not completed even when the British came chiefly because the geography offered enough shelter to the retreating non-Aryans from the advance of the Brāhmaṇas, who now acquired the monopoly of all political power.

The origin of the imperial family is not known for certain though the possibility of its being Brāhmaṇa is as convincing as being Kṣatriya or Vaiśya. Samudragupta proudly proclaims himself as 'the enclosing structure of Dharma'[85] which obviously stands for *Varṇáśrama* order and Brāhmaṇical rites. His self-equation with the Brāhmaṇical gods Kubera, Varuṇa, Indra and Yama leaves not even the shadow of a doubt about the role of Brāhmaṇas in his administration since he was to govern according to the Śāstras of which they were the sole custodians. In his Eran inscription itself his comparison with ideal Aryan emperors Pṛthu and Rāghava is significant in this regard.[86] His great-grand son Skandagupta was so sincere in maintaining the social order that while he ruled 'no man whatsoever from among his subjects deviated from duty' which obviously was fixed by his station in life.[87] By far the most convincing proof regarding Brāhmaṇas sitting at the top of the structure of power is Eran stone pillar inscription of Buddhagupta, a portion of which is well worth quoting.[88]

"By the Mahārāja Mātṛviṣṇu who is excessively devoted to Bhagavān, who by the will of Destiny, was married by sovereignty, as if by a maiden choosing herself (her own husband); whose fame extends upto the borders of the four oceans; whose wealth is unimpaired high mindedness; (and) who has been victorious in battle against many enemies:

Who is the son of the son's son of Indraviṣṇu, who was devoted to his religious rites; who performed sacrifices; who studied his Veda; who was a Brāhmaṇa sage: (and) who was the head of the *Maitrāyaṇiya* school of *Yajurveda* :—who is son's son of Varuṇaviṣṇu, who imitated the virtuous qualities of (his) father :—(and) who is the son of Hariviṣṇu, who took after his father (and) was the cause of the advancement of his race;......" Commemorating the erection of a flag-staff in honour of the divine (god) Janārdana, the record ends on a significant note, "May it be well to all the people, headed by the cows and the Brāhmaṇas."

We could very well mistake the description of Mātṛviṣṇu given in the first part of the passage, for that of Samudragupta or Chandragupta II or Skandagupta, such, indeed, being the epithets with which he styles himself. Yet he was merely a local *Viṣayapati* posted at Eran. His predecessors were orthodox Brāhmaṇas by birth and profession but he changed the ladle for the sword and felt proud of glory in battle more than in headship of the *Maitrāyaṇīya* school. The Brāhmaṇic hold on administrative hierarchy may be seen in the fact that even the barbaric invader Huṇa King Toramāṇa did not dare select anyone else for the post other than his younger brother Dhanyaviṣṇu, also mentioned in the record cited above. The supremacy of the Brāhmaṇas is proclaimed in the last sentence.

But this supremacy they enjoyed only in society. In the structure of politics the warrior class had the highest place. That precisely seems to be the reason compelling Mātṛviṣṇu to change his ancestral calling. This social mobility in terms of changing hereditary occupation was not only downward from the first to second *varṇa* but also upward from the third to second. In Tumain inscription of Kumāragupta I, we come across five merchant brothers—Srīdeva, Harideva' Dhanyadeva, Bhadradeva and Saṅghdeva—becoming the abodes of Kṣatriya valour in Tumbavana[89] and the fact that they deemed it necessary to make the mention of this change or achievement should be enough to convince us that *Kṣātra dharma* had special appeal in contemporary polity.

It is interesting to note that some of the non-Aryan warrior chiefs also found accommodation in the structure of politics although in subordinate position. Note in this regard, has already been taken of the Nawāgrāma Grant of Mahārāja Hastin in which a *rāṣṭra* unit of his administration is named as Pulindarāja.[90] It seems the whole fief of the chief had been formed into a rāṣṭra paying a fixed tribute to the Brāhmaṇic (Parivrājaka) overlord. In passing may be noted the khoh copper plate of the Mahārāja Śarvanātha (year 214) which speaks of Pulindabhaṭa having been favoured by the grant of villages Vyāghrapallika and Kachārapallika. It is easy to make out that the donee was a non-Aryan priest devoted to the worship of Goddess Piṣṭapurikā in whose favour now he made over the villages to Kumārasvāmin.[91] As a matter of fact, both the records throw a flood of Light on the process of interaction and acculturation in which some of the non-Aryans were absorbed in the Brāhmaṇical social system—at times reaching even the priestly and warrior status.

Under the Imperial Guptas, the Brāhmaṇas acted as *Viṣayapati* at Eran. It was very near to being the sovereign which one of them truly became under the Vardhana emperor.[92] Hsuan-Tsang is clear on the point though the identity of this king we cannot establish. The whole of the Early-Medieval period may be divided into two almost equal phases with the Gurjara-Pratihāras governing the first and the Candellas governing the second, but both the ruling houses are believed to be Brāhmaṇic in origin.[93] The Candella records trace the origin of the royal clan to an eponymous sage Candrātreya. At least one record, the Semra Copper Plate inscription of king Paramardideva, contains reference to some Brāhmaṇa donees with Candrātreya gotra and one mentioned as *Pratihārānyava.*[94] But this Aryo-Vedic and Brāhmaṇic origin based on royal records of the dynasties concerned is not acceptable to a section of historians which regards all the Rajput clans as having issued partly from Hinduized Scythian foreigners and partly from autochthonous aboriginal tribes of the land. Vincent Smith believed that the Pratihāras were converted from the former and the Candellas came from the latter.[95] He was not prepared to place any faith in epigraphic records which connected the kingly families to solar and lunar Kṣatriyas of mythical past. To him such accounts appeared to be specially manufactured by the Brāhmaṇic beneficiaries for their princely patrons. It is difficult to decide either way as popular tradition to which Smith turned cannot be altogether ignored.

The case of the Candellas can be taken up as theirs is the only line that governed Bundelkhand continuously for more than four centuries and could, with some certainty, be held as of local origin. In fact, under their rule Bundelkhand came into her own and reached a stage of unity, progress and prosperity not attained earlier or ever since. Smith may well be right in locating the roots of this royal family in the region itself and that might explain the phenomenon of Bundelkhand coming into her own.

Popular tradition holds that Paramardi lost his kingdom in consequence of disobeying the four conditions laid on the founder of his race. Three of these commandments were negative—not to drink wine, not to put Brāhmaṇas to death, not to form improper marriage connections—and one was positive—to preserve the name of Varmma.[96] The tradition may not be acceptable in totality, yet working in an area and period where authentic historical records are few and far between, one should not miss the hints thrown by it.

In the prohibition pertaining to wine one can see the Brāhmaṇical antipathy beautifully reflected in the Bāṇa's description of the Śabara savages of central India.[97] It is not unlikely that the aboriginal founder chief of the Candella clan was asked to pledge his line to total abstention or on being raised to rulership and obtaining recognition from the Brāhmaṇical ideologues, he voluntarily conformed to the code of conduct for kings.

In the second condition also one can read the prevailing exemption claimed by the Brāhmaṇas from capital punishment under the law.[98] From the Gupta period onwards the immunity and privileges of the Brāhmaṇas are specifically mentioned and here the founder was merely to pledge his family to honour them. Such was the devotion of royal family to Brāhmaṇical law that one of the kings is known to have been afraid to offend against it.[99]

With regard to third condition also we could say that the founder was required to pledge his family to *Varṇa* rules relating to marriage as laid down in the *Smṛti* works.[100] A couple of examples we could quote on the point from the royal records. Harṣa, the sixth king, is mentioned to have married with suitable rites a suitable lady of equal caste (*Savarṇā*) named Kañcukā from the Cāhamāna tribe.[101] One fails to understand what need there was to use the specific epithet *Savarṇā*. Interestingly, this queen figures prominently in the records of even remote descendants.[102] Puppā, the queen of the next king Yośovarman, is also referred to as hailing from a noble family (*mahá Vaṃse samut-panná*).[103] But for the third condition figuring in the popular tradition, we would not have attached any importance to the epithets noted above. The Candellas seem to be self-conscious on this point of marrying into equal caste which lends some credence to the tradition.

The fourth condition appears to aim at elevating the Candellas to Kṣatriya status. Use of 'Varman' as suffix to personal names had also its basis in *Varṇa* rules in *Smṛti* law. In traditional account everyone of the first twenty Candella kings has 'Varman' forming part of his name till we come to Paramāla[104] but as these names do not tally with those figuring in family records we may leave this fact out of consideration. It is true that all the names found in their land-grants do not have 'varman' as their component parts, yet out of 17 kings ruling before Paramardi, nine have the varman-ending. So also four of his successors, which is equally significant. The founder of Candella line according to inscriptions was Nannuka, but historians believe that Candravarman was his *biruda*.[105]

Be that as it may, we feel that popular tradition on this point of origin cannot be dismissed off—hand and could well be taken into account in the context of aboriginal background of the Candellas.

Another fact worth-noting in this connection is that Candellas are conspicuously missing in the standard list of thirtysix royal Rājput clans.[106] Of course, the name Chandaka is sought to be identified with their family but the effort is unconvincing. When other contemporary dynasties—such as the Paramāras, Cāhamānas and Pratihāras—figure so clearly, there is no reason why the Candellas suffered a change.

Asopa has worked hard on the origin of Rajputs and has made out a sound case to prove that Candellas were Brāhmaṇas.[107] According to him the word Candrella is a territorial appellation composed as it is of Candra+illa. (Proper name + noun meaning territory). The suffix Ātreya could be used by anyone belonging to Atri gotra. He concludes, therefore, all Candellas need not be Candrātreyas but the Candrātreyas were Candrella by habitation. Now the main consideration by which he seems to be guided is the *gotra* of the Candellas. What we fail to understand is why the Brāhmaṇa donees with Candrātreya gotra figure only in Candella land-grants. Similarly the mythical sage Candrātrerya and the story surrounding his birth are known only to Candella records. If at all Candrātreya was a recognised and current *gotra*, the possibility cannot be ruled out that the Candellas acquired it from the purohitas officiating at their sacrifices. As regards the derivation of word Candellas, we would like to mention that Asopa has failed to notice its use as proper name for man as well as woman. A queen of king Madanavarman was Candeladevi[108] whereas another queen Kalyāṇadevī was grand-daughter of a noble Cādala, who belonged to the race of Dadhīci and was object of reverence for Kṣatriyas.[109] Thus Asopa's origin theory as well as derivation of the dynastic name are not altogether unexceptionable.

Equally so are the theory and evidence of the critics who take the Candellas to have risen to eminence in Brāhmaṇical society from the ranks of aboriginal settlers of central India. Such an absorption is not absolutely unlikely bearing in mind the available evidence of an ongoing process of Sanskritisation, yet after examining their theory as well as arguments in support thereof we are nowhere near a convincing explanation regarding the origin of the Candellas. The protagonists of the theory rely chiefly on tradition which preserves the memory of many villages having been inhabited by Gonds, Kols, Bhārs, and Chamārs in times gone by. The Gaharwars were an aristocratic section of the Bhārs. They were great tank-builders. In Hamirpur district alone they are credited with having built no less than eleven embankments noted below.[110]

1. Baraipura
2. Bhandrā
3. Bhatewar
4. Bijainagar
5. Bilkhi
6. Kari Pahari
7. Paswara
8. Pawa
9. Nareri
10. Nanyaura
11. Selamuaf.

Interestingly enough, the only other power associated with the building of tanks in the history of Bundelkhand is that of Candellas and, at least, in country around Mahoba the number of tanks ascribed to them is equal to what is attributed to the Gaharwār rule who are believed to have preceded the Candellas. Smith noted that a Gaharwar tank can be recognised from the absence of cut stone whereas Candella embankments are generally formed of dressed granite blocks.[111] Further, most of Candella tanks were associated with temples whereas a Gaharwār lake never was.

Vincent Smith, the chief protagonist of the autochthonous origin, cited many more facts gleaned from such coincidences. To him the indications were fairly distinct that the Candella clan originated in the midst of the Gonds with whom other similar tribes were intermixed. The Candella Zamindars of Khajuraho claimed to be autochthonous tracing their origin to Mānyagarh where was located the traditional shrine of their tutelary deity Mānya Deo. The royal Candellas worshipped the deity at Mahoba also. The image appeared to Smith quite akin to the Gond deities. The third and only other shrine of the deity survives at village Barel in Hamirpur District occupied formerly by the Bhārs. The poet Chand associated Mānyagarh with a Gond chieftain. Lastly for him the marriage of Candella princess Durgāvatī to a Gond chief of Garhamandla is no less significant.[112]

The fundamental weakness of Smith's theory is that it is based entirely on tradition and coincidence getting no support from historical records. If the Candella Zamindars of Khajuraho believe themselves to be autochthonous it may simply mean they have lived there since times immemorial. The likeness of Mānya Deo to Gond deities could again be a coincidence which should not necessarily be taken to indicate a Gond origin of the Candellas. All the deities of Brāhmaṇism did not have iconic form, a few certainly had aniconic. The hold of a Gond chief at Mānyagarh and of Bhars at Barel has to be viewed in proper historical perspective for which we have hardly any material. What surprises us most is the last argument of Smith in which the marriage of medieval Candella princess Durgāvatī to a Gond king convinced him of their Gond origin whereas he conveniently forgot that Nandā Devi, another Candella princess, had been married to the Kalacuri King Kokalla I much earlier.[113]

However, there is nothing inherently improbable in Candellas having originated from one of the primitive peoples inhabiting the area and the fact that myths explaining the phenomena of their sudden shooting into prominence were invented in bardic tradition as well as royal records lends colour to this possibility. Brāhmaṇic widow Hemavatī and the holy saint Candravarman cannot be dismissed altogether as devoid of significance. Even if they are taken as imaginary and invented ancestors, their tale does reflect an uneasiness on the part of the Brāhmaṇic beneficiaries to offer an explanation regarding the noble origin of their princely patrons. Fleet's observations in regard to invented genealogies are well worth quoting, though made with reference to south Indian royal families. Without mincing matters, he is on record as having remarked, "there are plain indications that, just about the period—the last quarter of the ninth century A.D.—all the reigning families of southern India were beginning to look up their pedigrees and devise more or less fabulous genealogies."[113a] The words could as well and as much be applicable to a central Indian royal house which stepped on the stage of history about the same time. There seems to be some substance in the suspicion of Kielhorn that the gotra-name Candrātreya......owes its origin to the desire of the bearer to have a more Sanskritic name.[114] If this suspicion of Kielhorn is seen in conjunction with the fact that donees bearing this gotra are found only in Candella land-charters, the possibility of Candellas having come from aboriginal stock stands stronger if not authenticated.

We have noted above that tradition knows of a Gaharwār rule having preceded that of the Candellas but we are yet to come across a historical record to verify the fact. History knows of the Pratihāras or Parihāras having acquired a hold over a part of the province and being succeeded by the Candellas around A.D. 831 at Mahoba. The antiquity of the Parihāras has been taken to the time of Ptolemy[115] though the identification made is hardly convincing. Much ink has already been spilt in an effort to establish when and how the Pratihāras were overthrown in Bundelkhand and whether the Candellas started their career as feudatories to them or independent of them. Our entering into the controversy would hardly serve any purpose.

What has been missed by other scholars is the fact that the Pratihāras were never completely overthrown. All through the Candella period Pratihāra chiefs continued ruling their respective fiefs undisturbed even under the new power. Bhārat Kalā Bhavana Plate of Mahārājādhirāja Harirāja dated about A.D. 982 speaks of a Pratihāra line ruling in Jhansi-Guna region.[116] We come across another Pratihāra chief Mahārājaputra Vāghadeva ruling in Damoh district as late as first quarter of the fourteenth century.[117] A Parihāra chief, Māhila figures in the *Pṛthvīrāja Ráso* and the *Lay of Ālhá* conspiring continually against the Candellas and trying to bring about their downfall.[118] May be he was burning to take revenge for the earlier overthrow of an ancestor of his own family by the Candellas. Hence what seems to have happened exactly is that the Candellas supplanted the imperial Pratihāras as overlords in Bundelkhand and the local rulers—Pratihāras or others—were left undisturbed in their possession. It may be added that the imperial Pratihāras extended their rule in Bundelkhand in the wake of tripartite struggle and a few of their battles with the Rāṣṭrakūṭas came off somewhere in the region.

However the change from the Pratihāra rule to that of the Candellas is not as important for us as is the structure of politics emerging and shaping up under them. This is the so-called feudal period of Indian polity. The features distinguishing feudal structure find faint beginnings under the Pratihāras and get fully sharpened under the Candellas. But feudalism in the real sense never approaches the scene.

R.S. Sharma believes that the political essence of feudalism lay in the organisation of the whole administrative structure on the basis of land whereas its economic essence lay in the institution of serfdom in which the peasants were attached to the soil held by the landed intermediaries placed between the king and the actual tillers, who had to pay rent in kind and labour to them.[119] He has applied the concept to Indian agrarian scene of the Early Medieval Period mainly on the basis of land-charters and has been able to read in them a few of the feudal tendencies characterising the contemporary social and political structure. We could very well examine his thesis in relation to Bundelkhand. Among the documents available the earliest and most important is Barah Copper Plate of Bhojadeva, through which the Pratihāra monarch made over the *agrahára* of Valāka located in Udumbara *Viṣaya* of the Kālanjara *Maṇḍala* in the Kānyakubja *bhukti* to the Brāhmaṇas born of the Bhaṭṭa-Kāchar-Svāmin family with all its income barring such as had already been granted to gods and Brāhmaṇas.[120] It is quite clear from the grant that only the income from the village was allotted. In no way the peasants were attached to the soil or reduced to serfdom. None of the administrative rights is surrendered. The endowment was purely religious (being for the increase of the merit of monarch's parents) and permanent (to last till the Moon, the Sun and the Earth exist).

Bhārat Kalā Bhavan Plate of Harirāja is another charter available to us. It was issued not by a ruler of the imperial Pratihāra line but a local one. Adhirāja Harirājadeva, son of *bhūpádhipa* Nīlakantha was staying at Siyadoni on the occasion of a solar eclipse.[121] In accordance with Śāstric injunction, he took bath in the waters of Vetravatī and granted two *hala* measures of land in the village of Tauḍa-grāma attached to Lalitpurvāla together with a site for no less than ten houses in the village of Tithasevanigrāma to a Brāhmaṇa Deda. Again it is clear that the donee was either to cultivate the land himself or get it cultivated. No alienation of authority, administrative or other is involved as he was merely to enjoy the income from a mere piece of land granted. The relation of the King with the people in the village is hardly affected or altered.

Other time of Bhoja we have two more documents[122] known as Vaillabhaṭṭasvāmin Temple inscriptions from Gwalior. They record donations to two temples built by Alla, the son of Vaillabhata. Worthy of note here is the fact that the donations were made neither by the king nor any of his officers but by the citizens of the town. By the first donation, the whole town gave to the temple of Navadurgā a piece of land belonging to the village Chudapallikā which was its own property for creating a flower garden. By the second endowment the town gave the field cultivated by Dallaka in the village of Jayapurāka and another cultivated by Memāka. The two fields were obviously town property and the cultivators appear to be tenants. Now they become tenants of the temple to which the fields were assigned. It is difficult to treat them as serfs or peasants attached to the soil. The remaining two donations have nothing to do with land since they concern a monthly supply of lamp-oil to be made by the guild of oil-millers and a monthly supply of flower-garlands to be made by the guild of the gardners who dwelt on the top of srī Gopagiri.

Siyadoni stone Inscription is perhaps the longest among Pratihāra records, it being a copy of twenty seven separate donations.[123] Interestingly, only one of these pertains to the gift of land. Here again, as at Gwalior, the whole town gifted a field to the temple of Sri-Nārāyaṇa Bhaṭṭāraka, Set up by the merchant Cāṇḍuka. Nothing more is said about the gift hence the question of its contributing to feudal relationship in any way does not arise. However, the second part of the inscription refers to a prince making over a town-Rayākka-to some Brāhmaṇas. Probably here also the case was that of income being assigned rather than the ownership or administration. The document is silent on the point.

Among the lesser Pratihāra potentates of a much later period, we have Malayavarman, out merely on a hunting excursion, and yet, miraculously capturing the celebrated fort of Gwalior. His Kurethā copper Plate is dated 1221 A.D., Verse 16 of which mentions him granting a village called Kudavāthe in favour of the Brāhmaṇas brothers Vatsa and Haripāla.[124] The grant specifically includes grazing ground, salt pits, mango and madhūka trees and things under the ground as well as above it with the exception of lands already assigned to the gods and Brāhamaṇas. The phraseology used seems to convey the conferment of sovereignty over the scholar brothers as far as the village was concerned. But the actual assignment was merely monetary as becomes clear from the command of the king to the *Mahattama—janapadāna* (village-elders) asking to pay the Bhaga Bhoga and other dues to the donees. The king also desired that no member of the royal family should cause obstruction to the enjoyment of the grant by the donees. Nowhere in the grant the king seems to have surrendered his sovereign rights over the people of the village. It is interesting to note that the king made the assignment of income from the village only after the consent of his minister and the priest.

The companion Copper Plate from Kureṭhā is a grant by Narararman belonging to the same Pratihara line of which Malayavarma was an earlier member.[125] Dated in A.D. 1248 the document records the grant of village Gudhhagrāma to Vatsa who is here qualified by the designation *nāyaka* indicating some sort of official or feudalory status that he now enjoyed. What is further noteworthy, the record speaks of neither the boundaries nor the taxes nor other customary details as found in the first inscription. Probably here, too, the assignment was only financial in nature though the donee being an officer, some enjoyment of administrative powers on his part cannot be altogether ruled out. Here, again, it is interesting to find that the king obtained consent for the grant from not only the *mahāmantri* and the *purohita* but from the *Mahādevī*, the *jyeṣṭha-kumāra*, the *pratihāra*, and the *akṣapaṭalika* as well. The specific mention of these relatives and functionaries reminds of the *ratnins* of the hoary past who similarly exercised some control in contemporary polity, though the parallel is in no way exact one.

Oddly enough, neither of the grants contains the phrases indicating eternal duration of the assignment. It is not to last till the Sun, the Moon and the Earth exist. Perhaps the fact is implied. But the second grant being secular might have been for life-time. R.S. Sharma is of the view that the practice of religious grants was more widespread in the kingdoms of the feudatories of the Pratiharas than in the regions which they directly governed.[126] This brings us now to the Candellas who are believed by some scholars to have been Pratihāra feudatories for a few generations from the founder of the line onwards.

Earliest among the land-charters of the Candellas is the Nanyaura Copper Plate of King of Dhaṅga-deva.[127] On auspicious day of the year A.D. 998 issued from Kāśikā, the plate records the grant of village yulli to one Bhaṭṭa Yaśodhara. The village was given with its water and dry land, with its low and high land, with its mango and madhūka-trees, with its fertile and saline soil upto its four well-known boundaries." This long legal phraseology doubtlessly indicates the transfer of the village as such and not its income only. But it is difficult to conclude that the village thence on became a fief of the donee because the king nowhere transfers the administrative and judicial rights. At least it is not clear from the record. Secondly the command that he clearly conveys to the people through the grant merely enjoins upon them, "Give the share of the produce, the money rent and so forth and (having done so) live happily." He does not ask them to be obedient to the beneficiary. Hence what was sought to be assigned was the income from all sources. The donee could appropriate to himself all such land of the village as was unowned, unassigned and uncultivated. But the charter in no way made him feudal lord since people of the village were not his tenants, for less serfs attached to the soil. Here it may be pointed out that Prof. Kielhorn has missed the real meaning of the words "Bhoga-hiranya". He thought them money-rent whereas they stand for kinds of taxes. Thus the peasants of the village continued tilling as before with hardly any change in their status.

Next Copper Plate available to us comes from king Devavarman, dated in the year A.D. 1050, by which the village Kaṭhahau was made over to a Brāhmaṇa Abhimanyu on the occasion of Queen-mother Bhuvanadevī's anniversary.[128] In addition to the phrases qualifying the gift village of the earlier record seen in the preceding para here we have "with its hills and water courses, with its mines of iron and salt, with the treasure in its forests, well-defined as to its four abuttals upto its proper boundaries, the grass and pasturelands" but "exclusive of what has before this been given to the gods and to Brāhmaṇas." That this last negative clause was not a pure formality becomes clear when we come to Semra Plates of Paramardideva where the donor king had to specify numerous exceptions which governed the areas granted. The donee, therefore, was not the exclusive owner of the gift village in all the cases. Again, the positive phrases qualifying the village merely indicate the intention of the donor not to leave any source of income uncovered, rather than to allot administrative or judicial powers over the inhabitants of the village, who are required only to pay the customary dues and taxes to the donee. The Brāhmaṇa beneficiary is further authorised "to enjoy or permit to enjoy, or give to another, sell, plough or cause to be ploughed the land in unbroken succession of his sons and son's sons so long as the moon and the sun, the earth and the sea endure". The whole description doubtless is aimed at transferring absolute rights to the donee in unequivocal terms but these again are property rights and by no means enough to render him a sovereign.

The Charkhari Copper Plate settles the point with utmost certainly and coming from the same king it is all the more significant.[129] It purports to record the grant of village Bhūtapallikā to Paṇḍita Kikkana by King Devavarmadeva. It plainly assigns the revenue to the donee scholar and omits altogether the long legal clauses noted above. The whole of the formal address to the people of the village has been compressed just in one sentence asking them to bring the taxes and dues to the donee thence on. Normally specific mention was made of the nature of donee's property rights—that of pledging, selling or otherwise using suiting his convenience.

Even that also is missing here. Thus the Plates in no way contribute to the feudal features of contemporary society.

In case of any doubt still lingering on the point, we have Augasi Plate of Madanavarman with which he granted only ten ploughs of land at village Vamhardā to a Brāhmaṇa Rabhalaśarman yet all the long legal clauses and phrases associated with the grant of a whole village figure in it.[130] Possibly the actual allotment was that of revenue-income and not of the piece of land. The point is further clarified from another inscription of the same king discussed below. Whatever sense we might take, the beneficiary was nowhere near to being a sovereign.

Bhārat Kalā Bhavan Plates of Madanavarman are much more interesting than any of the records referred to above. The grant order is addressed to the people of Valhaudā-grāma in Mahisiṇeha *Viṣaya*.[131] The donee is Paṇḍita Someśarman who received 2¼ *padas* out of 8 *padas* of cultivated land in the said village. The second beneficiary is Dikṣita Nārāyaṇaśarman. Earlier he had been allotted Aṣṭavālagrāma in exchange for lands in his possession scattered over various villages such as Pipalahā, Vasauhā, Gaulā, Dādari and Denavada. By the present Plate the king allowed him a second exchange allotting him four *padas* of land in lieu of Aṣṭavālagrāma and other lands located at villages named Pipalahā, Valahaudā and Davahā which had been granted to him by Nāduka, a priest attached to queen Lakhmādevi and Someka.

The third beneficiary figuring in the record is Sahajuśarman who received 1¾ *padas* of land at Valhaudāgrāma in exchange for his lands at Pipalahā-grāma and Mahuali-grāma that had been granted to him by Mahārājñī Vālhaṇadevī and Rājñī Candeladevī. It goes without saying that gift from the queens had been made with specific permission of the King.

The contents of the Copper Plate clearly reveal that it is not even a religious grant in the right sense since two of the beneficiaries are merely accorded permission to consolidate their landed property spread over various villages in different districts. The text of the document, nevertheless, contains familiar phrases and clauses qualifying the endowment. The royal command directing the villagers to bring the state dues to the donees thenceon indicates that the exchange was not of one piece of land for several pieces in the named villages but one consolidated share of revenue income in lieu of several such shares. The technical term of measurement fixing the quantum of endowment of exchange, therefore, stands for an estimated standard share of revenue. If on the other hand, the term is taken to mean piece of land, the long legal qualifying clauses are rendered redundant and it would appear that the royal record office kept readymade some charters with set conditions and fixed formulas in legal language constituting the text into which this endowment-cum-exchange order was fitted. Whichever way we interpret this much seems certain that the record was unlikely to make any of the donees into even a petty feudal lord.

Of the next king Paramardideva, we have two charters from the Bhārat Kalā Bhavan, Vārānasi.[131] A By the first one dated in 1182 A.D. he made over the revenue of Vavaudā-grāma to one Paṇḍita Padmadharaśarman with the usual condition known from the records noticed above. The second document issued in the year A.D. 1191 A.D. from the Maṇikarṇikā-ghāt at Vārānasi records the grant of 10 *lavas* of land at Italā-grāma. The donee, again, is none other than Padmadharaśarman. Together the two inscriptions clarify that the monarch intended to allot the revenue rather than sovereign rights. Otherwise the grant of a village in one case and a measure of land in another couched in the same set phraseology is difficult to explain.

The Pachar Plate of Paramardideva dated in the year A.D. 1175 records the grant of 10 *halas* of land at Lauvagrāma to one Paṇḍita Keśavaśarman.[132] The inhabitants are asked to bring the State dues to the donee. Interestingly, the gift clauses contain provisions authorising him either to cultivate or get cultivated, gift, mortgage or sell the donated land. If any extra-meaning is to be attached to these clauses and that, too, a literal one, the charter may be taken to convey a 10 *hala* piece of land in addition to the revenue income of the village. But this is not only being arbitrary and inconsistent on our part, but also unwarranted in the light of evidence seen above, as also in view of similar charters omitting any such provision. One more Bhārat Kalā Bhavan Plate we possess, that of king Harirāja, granting two-*hala* measure of land at Taudā-grāma[133] but no such provisions accompany the gift. However, it can not be denied altogether that the practice in some cases may have been to grant piece of land and in others the income.

That we are correct in so interpreting our evidence becomes clear from Mahoba Plates of Paramardideva in which the gifted land measuring 60 *vadhas* and cultivable by five ploughs has been mentioned with proper demarcation of natural boundaries with particular reference to neighbouring property-holders.[134] The assignment does not in any way need the qualifying clauses in legal language. Obviously the grant was made on one of the ready-made charters available with the royal revenue record office containing the customary text of such documents. No other explanation can be convincingly offered for the variations seen above. In any case, the donee of this document also had hardly any chance to develop into a feudal chief.

Longest of all the legal documents is Semra Copper Plates[135] of Paramardideva by which the granted revenue of eleven villages—Khaṭaudā—dvādaśaka, Tāṇṭā-dvādaśaka, Hāṭa-aṣṭādaśaka, Seṣayigrāma, Pilikhiṇapañcela, Itāva-pañcela, Isarahāra-pañcela, Uldana, Kakarādaha, Nasahahatthidaha, Paṭhā-to 309 donees studying different Vedic *caraṇas Sākhās*. The share of each donee is indicated after his name. The record does not leave even the shadow of a doubt that the revenue income is intended to be assigned. What is further significant the charter makes unequivocal mention of no less than eight exceptions governing the grant and indicating thereby that the donees did not enjoy exclusive and absolute hold over the donated villages.

The Charkhari charter of Paramardideva[136] was issued in favour of four beneficiaries granting village Sagaudā to them making specific mention of the share they were to hold in its revenue income. An interesting fact emerging from the charter is the exception made of the five *halas* of land already gifted to Lord Buddha showing once more that such grants were intended merely to provide maintenance to the donee than to make him local lord of the manor.

Passing now to the next king Trailokyavarman, we find the situation substantially the same. His Tehri charter was issued in the year 1208 A.D. assigning the revenue of village Mandaurā to one *Nāyaka Kuleśarman.*[137] Hardly any change we notice in the technical terminology save for the fact that the familiar phrase conveying the religious object of the grant is curiously missing in this inscription. The title of the donee as well as those of his father and grand-father also seem significant in this regard. They speak more of a position in the administrative or political hierarchy than that of scohlarly world.

The fact is frankly admitted in Garra Copper Plates of the same King.[138] The donee of the twin-plates is one and the same Rāuta Sāmanta on whom the villages Kadohā and Lohāsihāni were bestowed (in two different districts) by way of maintenance for death (*mṛtyuka-vṛttau*) unquestionably that of donee's father on the field of battle. The charter is singular among Candella inscriptions in being for secular purpose and first of that king. As the language employed is practically that of other records, already considered, the effect is simply of transferring the revenue to the beneficiary who acquires none of the administrative rights under it. Particular note need be taken that the villages bestowed were located in two different districts.

The third available copper-Plate of the time of Trailokyavarman also lacks the religious element. It is plainly a *vitta-bandho* or deed of mortgage.[139] Dated in Kalacuri year 963, the Rewa Copper Plates record the pledging of the village Alira by the Śaiva teacher Śāntaśiva to Rāṇaka Dhareka who is given all the rights of collecting taxes. This fact further lends strength to our view that religious land-grants in effect meant assignment of the revenue-income so far as this part of the country is concerned.

The only available charter of King Viravarman is also secular in object issued in the year A.D. 1254. It records the grant of village Tumṭuma to Rauta Abhi belonging to Candreśvara family in recognition of the valour displayed by the beneficiary in the battle of Sondhi against Dabhyuhapa-varman.[140] What passes our comprehension is the fact that even after this undisguised motive, the charter refers to increase of religious merit of the donor and his parents as the object of the grant. Once more, it could be readymade customary text being used without effecting required changes in the phraseology.

The last of the Candella grants is that of the last king Hammira arman issued in the year A.D. 1289 allotting the revenue of Kikadagrāma to two Brāhmaṇa brothers.[141] No change we notice either in the conditions fixing the position of the beneficiary or in the language.

The long and exhaustive survey, done above, of the Pratihāra and Candella land-charters amply makes it clear that the land-grants by no means contributed to the feudalisation of political structure. The beneficiaries were entitled only to the financial income from the lands or villages granted to them. They must have shot into prominence owing to the privilege so conferred but civil and judicial administration is nowhere delegated to them. The possibility of their exercising some implied authority in local matters may not be entirely ruled out but the inscriptions do not permit us even to postulate that grantee's status somehow approximated to that of the feudal lord.

We must also examine the view that existence of numerous fortresses was also a factor largely contributing to the feudal organisation under the Candellas. It is contended that a fortified place besides being used for storing collected taxes in kind, maintaining garrisons of soldiers and offering shelter to the surrounding population in times of calamity, natural or man-made was above all, the final instrument through which the prince or chief could perpetuate his power over the peasantry.[142] The Candellas are credited with having possessed twenty one fortresses, seven of which are well-known even now—Kharjuravāhaka, Vāridurga, Jayapura (Ajaygadh), Kīrttigiri durga (Deogarh) Gopagiri (Gwalior), Kālañjara and Sondhi (Seondha). The tradition ascribes to them eight forts including three already named viz,—Bārigarh, Kālañjara and Ajaygadh. The remaining five are Mānyāgarh, Marphā, Mandhā, Garhā and Mahiyar.[143] Strangely enough, Mahoba figuring so prominently in tradition and undoubtedly a seat of Candella power is not included in either of the lists. Sultan Mahmud of Ghazni is known to have confirmed Vidyādhara in the possession of fifteen forts.[144] Gaṇda, his predecessor was just one short of the number.[145]

But it is difficult to say with certainty which of the forts were built by the Candellas themselves. Neither the tradition nor material evidence avers anything in this regard. The date of Kālañjara goes back to much earlier times than the advent of the Candellas on the stage of history. The epigraphic evidence available from the forts of Deogarh and Gwalior dates them to pre-Candella times. Among the surviving monumental remains of Khajuraho traces of a fort, having there been in bygone times can hardly be made out. Far from being a military depot, Deogarh acquired prominence from very early times as holiest among the holy spots of Jainism and all the surviving Jain sculptures and temples are located on the hill in the fort. Setting aside tradition for a while, we must also note that only two among the forts named above, find mention in Candella records. They are Kālañjara and Ajayagadh.

The officers-in-charge of at least two forts—Gwalior and Ajaygadh—do figure in our records but by no stretch of imagination can they be held as vassal chiefs. The epigraphic description we have of them leaves not even the shadow of a doubt that they owed as well as acknowledged their position to the pleasure of the king.[146] The officer-in-charge of Gopagiri fort was assisted in his work by a board on which members of mercantile class also sat alongwith officers.[147] Meriting mention, again, is the fact that a city like Siyadoni, industrially advanced and commercially throbbing and beyond doubt a seat of one local lord, should not be fortified at all. Far from being a feudal tyrant, coercing or pressing the neighbouring peasantry, the officer-in-charge or local noble of the fort was supposed to discharge his duties in consultation with a Board consisting of official and non-official members, the latter drawn to represent economic interests.[148] Thus the Candellas may have attached undue importance to the forts on strategic defence considerations and a few they may have raised on their own resources, they can not be charged with having used them as "final instruments to perpetuate power on the peasantry." At least, the available evidence, discussed above, does not warrant such a supposition.

On the other hand, if India came into her own under the Imperial Guptas, so also did Bundelkhand under the Candellas. The period of progress and prosperity which commenced with yaśovarman was unprecedented in her annals. The large legacy of sculptural and architectural wealth spread over length and breadth of the region, of which a detailed survey has been done in the next chapter, speaks volumes for the dynamism that characterised the economy under the candellas.

We do not have the statistical data in terms of industrial output and commercial transactions to measure the level prosperity under the Candellas. An idea, nevertheless, can be obtained on the basis of military strength that they were able to build and field in times of war. Even Mahmud, the unbeaten invader of early-medieval India was unnerved casting a look at the Candella army and "repented of his coming and placing the forehead of supplication on the ground of submission and humility prayed for victory and conquest from the giver of all mercies"[149] King Vidyādhara is known to have commanded an army consisting of 56,000 horses, 184,000 foot and 746 elephants.[150] Verse 10 of the Mau-candella inscription says that in the assembly of Sallakṣaṇavarmadeva there was not perceived any difference whatever between the Kings doing homage to him and his other dependants from the similarity of their garments glittering with quantities of gold and jewels.[151] If the facts and figures given above are studied in conjunction with majestic and magnificent temples of Khajuraho and no less majestic and magnificent temples of less-known sites, our task of measuring the progress and prosperity of this period in comparison with that of any of the preceding ones becomes much easier.

Whence came this boom and bonanza ? The government must have done a lot by way of encouraging agricultural output, promoting trade and industry but our records hardly reveal anything in this regard. Yet the biggest boon that the Candellas conferred on Bundelkhand is evident in their inscriptions and traditions. Being sons of the soil, they could feel the pulse and sought out the right key to the progress of the region. The geography of the area has already been described highlighting the total dependence of its agriculture on rain-fall and lack of irrigation hampering the farmer to increase the yield. The Candellas set upon the tremendous task of building innumerable embankments and excavating tanks to tackle the water problem. Inscriptions are as vocal on the point as is tradition and together they establish our point. Verse 38 of the Khajuraho stone inscription makes mention of a large tank caused to have been dug by king Yaśovarman.[152] Line 10 of the Khajuraho stone inscription of Kokalla refers to Atiyaśobala of Grahapati family who built tanks full of water in which lotuses shone with the loveliness of the spreading rays of the bright-lustered moon.[153] In Jhansi stone inscription of Sallakṣaṇasiṃha also we are informed of a tank having been dug and a grove planted.[154] Mau-Candella inscription mentions more tanks than one built by the ministers figuring in it. Verse 47 refers to Gandādhara getting a tank excavated near village Deddu charming with its masonry of many broad stones. Verse 48, though broken one, makes clear reference to another tank which had water pale like the moon. Verse 49 commemorates the digging of yet another tank of good water in the proximity of the village Kendi (?).[155] As a matter of fact, the memory of some Candella Kings has been preserved simply by the large lakes excavated by them and, therefore, named after them. Kiratsāgar and Madanasāgar lakes near Mahoba have carried the names Kīrtivarman and Madanavarman down the corridor of time.[156] Kiratsāgar is about 2 kms. square and the area of Madansāgar is 4½ kms. square. To the east of Mahoba is Kalyāṇasāgar and further east is Vijaysāgar which is 6½ kms. square and is said to have been built by King Vijayapāla Candella. Mahoba was verily a city of lakes. Semra Copper Plates of Paramardideva refer to Ajayasāgar tank.[157] Such was the magnitude of water problem for drinking purposes that even the queens did not lag behind in attending to it and came forward to finance the building of wells. In Ajaygadh Rock inscription of Vīravarman queen Kalyāṇadevī is recorded to have caused excavation of a tank resembling ocean and built a well called *nirjara* (never failing) just out of compassion and 'to sustain life'.[158] The very expressions accompanying the purpose are enough to bring home to us the importance attached to the act. That water was at times a crucial factor in deciding the fortunes of combatants in war is very clearly highlighted by the circumstances in which the Muslims could capture Kālañjara. The King was disposed to surrender at one stage but not the minister Aj Deo who went on with resistance, till compelled to capitulate in consequence of a severe drought having dried up all the water reservoirs inside the fort which had been supporting 50,000 men for months past.[159] So acute must have been the problem of drinking water that the excavation of a well or *Vāpi* acquired religious dimension earning the highest merit to the person financing it. We are yet to come across an epigraphic record in Bundelkhand where a *baoli* or step-well forms a fit enough theme for composing a *praśasti*. Verses 24-25 of the Baraudi record are well-worth quoting ;

> Well-made like friendship fair ;
> Brilliant like a poem clear ;
> Unbroken like an expert arguer ;
> Pleasing to the eye like a women
> All-giving like the wealth of religious merit capable to offer all fruits ;
> Consuming heat like the light of the moon ;
> Walls whereof are like a high hill sans breach ;
> May this *baoli* continue to relieve the heat of all beings by its clean waters
> So long as Girīśa holds Girijā And Gaṅgā Sanctifies the three worlds.[160]

No less glowing are the tributes paid in the Narwar inscription in which Gaṅgadeva, seeing the decrease in religious merit ordered the excavation of a *Vāpi* to make good the loss.[161] The waters of the well, being cleaned stand for real representation of religious merit and in fact, are considered superior to all other forms of religious merit and are compared with the high-souled, high-minded and noble-hearted. The *praśasti* here closes with the prayer that the well may continue to serve for the good of the great-souled so long as Brahmā sits on the lotus issuing out of Hari's navel. We have seen elsewhere how the geography of Bundelkhand is governed by scanty rains and absence of irrigational facilities in consequence of which famine is frequent. The Candellas made an all out effort to overcome the deficiency and seem to have succeeded a good deal. The entire area is interspersed with numerous tanks and temples which tradition ascribes to 'Chandeli Rāj.'[162] Much of the majesty and magnificence of the Khajuraho and other temples would have been missing, had the surplus revenue been not generated by tackling the problem of agriculture with tank irrigation. We have already seen above while studying the land-charters that a big slice of land-revenue was assigned to the Brāhmaṇic beneficiaries as well as some secular functionaries. Possibly some of the copper plates are yet to come to light or have perished falling victim to the tyranny of time. The innumerable temples that dotted the region definitely had some landed income for their maintenance which is reported in our records in some cases and has to be inferred in others. We have also noted that in addition to Kings, other members of royal family—queens in particular—also made endowments. Bearing in mind all this, one wonders how the Candellas could not only build and field an army equal to the invading 'Hamvira' but also raise world renowned temples as a gift to the posterity. It was nothing short of miracle that they did and the only convincing explanation we can offer is their herculean effort at harnessing and generating water resources of the region.

The structure of politics under them continued to be what it was in the preceding periods with one variation. A new class—that of the Kāyasthas—emerged which shared political power with the scholar, soldier and trading classes. This is not to say that they were born of the Śudras. The Kāyasthas might have issued out of one or all of the four *Varṇas* but they do not identify themselves with any of them in our records and at times claim superiority to all of them tracing a noble lineage to some divine being.[163] Long back they had crystallized into a caste, concerned mainly with writing out charters and record-keeping but under the Candellas they rose to very highly responsible positions rivalling with the Brāhmaṇa and trading castes. We have in Ajaygadh Rock inscription of Subhaṭa, a scion of vāstavya Kāyastha family, a pure *praśasti*, as good as that of any King containing a long genealogy and proclaiming that he was not only *Koṣādhikārādhipati* of King Bhojavarman but a *saciva* as well, placed at the head of all his weighty affairs. The record further reports that the family of Subhaṭa had been associated with the ruling dynasty since the days of King Gaṇḍa.[164] Another official of the Kāyastha caste to achieve such eminence is Nana.[165] Such was the pride and joy of being a Kāyastha that betraying Brāhmaṇic pretensions they believed mere presence of theirs was holy enough to purity, no less than thirty-six towns of central India.[166]

As of yore, the Brāhmaṇas continued to occupy the highest positions in political structure. Hereditary principle held good in matters of appointment and we have plenty of examples. Parallel to the line of princes we have line of officials in several cases. Lakshmīdhara, Yaśāhpala, Srīdhara, Gokula, Bhoja, Mahipāla, Gaṃgādhara and Jagaddhara belonging to Gauḍa family served Kīrtivarman, Sallakṣaṇavarman, Jayavarman, Pṛthvīvarman, Madanavarman, Paramadideva, Trailokyavarman and Vīravarman respectively.[167]

The Brāhmaṇa ministers vied with their royal masters in claiming as well as causing composed *praśastis* in praise of their excellence and eminence. Indeed, if one were to take their records literally, all the glory and greatness of the Candellas would appear to be the making of their ministers. In Mau-Candella inscription of the time of Madanavarman, we have a dynasty of ministers parallel to that of their princely masters. Prabhāsa, the chief minister of Dhaṅga and Gaṇḍa, is mentioned as expert in the science of politics. Śivanāga like Dhiṣaṇa made the government of next King Vidyādhara one to which all the rulers of the earth were rendered for ever tributory. Mahipāla is mentioned as standard of comparison among good ministers. Ananta, the next minister, was the very heart of king Kīrtivarman in secret confidential matters. Vatsa was Chief Minister of Pṛthvīvarman and made the government of that king prosper in all its constituent parts. For Madanavarman he reduced all princes to the state of dependency by applying six expedients, each in due season, making thus the king's sovereignty characterised by a single umbrella.[168] One could justifiably dismiss or doubt the authenticity of these claims coming, as they do, from a record of ministerial family itself but we do have events from Candella history with no room for doubt when a Brāhmaṇa minister with his valour and vigour came to the rescue of the royal family in the worst of crises. Gopāla, a Brāhmaṇa chieftain did this noble service to Kīrtivarman when the Kalacuris had virtually occupied a part of Candella Kingdom.[169] He has been held by the historians a saviour in that hour of great calamity. Gopāla was lucky to have been crowned with success in his noble attempts. Not so lucky was Aj Deo. Disregarding even the king, who was disposed to surrender to the alien invader, he went on with the war. He was beaten not by the enemy but by the problem of water inside the fort.[170] He could be identified with Senapati Ajayapāla mentioned twice in Semra Copper Plates of the king, he so courageously served.[171] Incidentally our records show that besides the ministry, Brāhmaṇas manned the military services for, apart from Ajayapāla, we also have *senāpatis* Kolhka[172] and Madanapāla[173] figuring as scholar donees in royal charters. The second part of Siyadoni stone inscription also refers to a Brāhmaṇa noble laying down his life in battle.[174]

A better yard-stick to measure the magnitude of Brāhmaṇic influence on contemporary polity and administration is supplied by the titles qualifying their names in land-grants. These titles they share in common with members of other castes and by nature they are anything but scholarly. In Semra record side by side with *dvivedins* and *trivedins* we meet with *thākkuras, rājaputras* and *Senāpatis*.[175] A classic example we can quote from the Tehri Copper Plate of Trailokyavarman where the donee is Kuleśarman having the title of *náyaka* whereas his father and grand-father are mentioned with *Rauta* and *Ráṇaka* titles respectively.[176] He was a student of *Vājasaneya Śākhā* and had five *pravaras*.

Socially the Brāhmanas enjoyed the highest honour and even Kśatriyas seem to have longed for that prestige. Devadhara, the hero of Baraudi *Praśasti* introduces a Kṣatriya family of which he came but refers proudly to its resemblance to a Brāhmaṇa family.[177] However, there certainly were heroes who took pride in being Kṣatriya. In Deogarh Rock inscription we have Svāmibhaṭa proclaiming his connection with Kṣatriyas of solar race.[178] In Ajaygadh Upper Gate Jamb inscription also the hero is careful to mention his Kṣatriya caste. The post-Harṣa Period in the history of Northern India is the period of the Rājputs. If their origin is to be traced from *rājaputras*, as some scholars seem to have done, they did not come invariably from Kṣatriya family background. Evidence cited above shows Kṣatriyas were not necessarily Rājputs and the Candellas in none of their records trace a Kṣatriya lineage.

The third group playing significant role in polity consisted of commercial class. In capital accumulation they were second only to king. Like him they had the resources to finance the raising of lofty and large temples. Siyadoni inscription has immortalised the temple of Nārāyaṇa-bhaṭṭāraka set up by salt-merchant Cāṇḍuka. Of the total twenty-seven donations recorded in the document more than half are assigned to this very temple. Such was the influence of the salt-magnate.[179] Hardly any artisan class of the city missed the opportunity to earn the religious merit. Apart from Cāṇḍuka and his son Nāgāka, we have Vāsudeva, Sīluka, Bhail, Pappā and Mahāditya, all dealing in salt and assigning endowments. But the influence of these salt-merchants was largely confined to urban areas where they dwelt and did their business. There was another class referred to as *śreṣṭhins* and hailing from families, mostly mentioned as Grihapati. The members of this class were equally wealthy and erected big and beautiful temples dedicated to Jaina *tīrthankaras* of whom were they devotees. From a Khajuraho Jain temple inscription we learn that Pahilla, an illustrious man of this class, was held in high esteem by king Dhaṅgadeva. An idea of his capital resources can be easily formed from the fact that through this single record he made an endowment of no less than seven gardens to the temple.[180]

Interestingly, at times, even a member of grihpati family, traditionally given to trade and money-lending, took to a military career and did creditably well. Line 10 of the Khajuraho inscription of Kokkalla refers to Atiyaśobāla of Grihapati family throwing down enemy forces (in confusion).[181]

With rapid advance in agriculture, the primitive dwellers must have been further pushed to mountainous and forest fastnesses. This displacement apart, they must have resented spreading Brāhmanisation and any such contact in their eyes might have been contemination of their own civilization. The indignation often burst into rebellion to which we have references in contemporary records.

Jhansi stone inscription of Sallakṣaṇa simha mentions the suppression of the Bhillas.[182] A similar suppression seems to have been made by the governor of Ajaygadh where the Bhillas rose in combination with Śabaras and Pulindas.[183] Thus the problem of the primitives in the polity of Bundelkhand was a constant factor down the ages and reconciliation was nowhere near.

We have already surveyed the position of three upper classes in the structure of politics. Our sources are silent about the fourth. Not that they were altogether ignored. On one occasion, at least, even the meanest among them received a medicum of recognition from the lord of the land. Going by our records we can say that the ruler remembered them while granting land. Some of the Candella charters were addressed not only to the Brāhmaṇas and other respectable members of the rural society like Kutuṃbins Kāyasthas and *mahattaras* but to dütas, vaidyas down to medas and Cāṇḍālas as well.[184] That Cāṇḍālas were regarded hardly as human being is also evident from the copper plates where a standard among the curses meant for the confiscator of granted land is one to be born a Cāṇḍāla.[185] No better example can be quoted demonstrating the double standards of the ruling classes which regarded these otherwise unfortunate outcastes as integral parts of society when the question was one of realising taxes and requestioning services. As for the physician class we have the solitary example in which a member of their community switched over to soldiering and made his mark.[186]

Our broad survey of the structure of politics of the early medieval and preceding periods shows that the Brāhmaṇa class had near-complete monopoly of all forms of political power. Be if army, executive or administration of justice, they manned and monopolised all organs of State Being scholar-custodians of the *Śāstras* as well as interpreters, they laid down the norms to which the other classes were supposed to conform. The trading class was cheifly centred in the cities and, wealthy as it was, mattered much in urban administration. The merchants were very well placed to rise as rivals of Brāhmans in acquiring hold on State power but it never happened for two reasons. In the first place majority of the mercantile class came from the fold of Jaina faith which never had any mass following whereas the Brāhmaṇa was indispensable in every village for officiating at a number of *Saṃskāras*. In the second place the merchants kept confined to their traditional occupation never diversifying and taking to other professions whereas the Brāhmaṇs fitted themselves into whatever field offered them opportunity to enjoy power. With command on economic resources, hold on political power and influence on the masses, it was easy for them to rule in realms of religion as well.

REFERENCES

1. Kale, M.R.: A literal English translation of *Bāṇa's Kādambarī*, Vaman Yashvant & Co. Bombay, 1924, p. 26.
2. Pogson, W.R.: *History of the Boondelas*, p. 6.
3. Unchahra Fragmentary Inscription of the year V.S. 1294 E.I, XXXIII, No 22.
4. The possibility of the word Bundel having originated from Vindhvel has already been examined in the earlier chapter.
5. I.G.I. IX p. 72.
6. Cowell, E.B.: *The Harṣacarita of Bāṇa*, p. 226.
7. I.G.I., IX p. 73-74.
8. Nigam, M.L. : *Cultural History of Bundelkhand*, p. 7.
9. Ibid., p. 80.
10. Khare, M.D. : Chalcolithic Besnagar in *Indian Archaeology New Perspectives* (Ed. R.K. Sharma), Agam Kala Prakashan, Delhi, 1982, p. 220.
11. Law, B.C.: *Tribes in Ancient India*. Bhandarkar Oriental Series, No. 4 (First Edition) Poona, 1943, p. 51.
12. Cowell, E.B. : *op. cit.*, p. 227.
13. Bose, N.S. : *History of the Candellas*, K.L. Mukhopadhyaya, Calcutta, 1956, p. 190.
14. Smith, V.A. 'Contributions to the History of Bundelkhand—The Post—Chandel Period' J.A.S.B. (New Series). Vol. 50, Pt. III, 1881, p. 43.
15. Nigam, M.L. *op. cit.*, Preface, pp.VI and VIII.
16. J.A.S.B. Vol. 48, Pt. I, No. IV, 1879, p. 289.
17. Pande, R.B., *Historical and Literary Inscriptions*, Ch. VI, No. 42.
18. Rock Inscription of the time of Bhojavarman, E.I., I., No. XXXVIII, pt. II, V. 2.
षट्त्रिंशतिकरणकर्म्मनिवासपूता आसन्पूर: परमसौख्यगुणातिरिक्ता :
19. Barah Copper Plate of Bhojadeva, EI., XIX, No. 2, LI, 1-5.
20. p. 72.
21. Hasan, Amir: *Meet the U.P. Tribes*, The Academic Press, Gurgaon, 1982 p. 11.
22. J.A.S.B., 1876, pt. 1, No. III, p. 287.
23. Sankalia, H.D. : *Pre-history and Proto-history of India and Pakistan* Deccan college (New Edition), Poona, 1974, p. 107.
24. M.P. Chronicle, (Daily Newspaper), Bhopal, May 14, 1975, p. 5.
25. I.A.A.R., 1960-61, p. 62.
26. *A Study of History* (Abridgement of volumes I-VI by D.C. Somer-well), Reprint London, 1977, p. 111.
27. J.A.S.B., vol. XIII, pt. I, 1844, p. 1.
28. 'Madhya Pradesh Sculpture through the Ages'—*Marg*, Vol. XXVI, No. 3, p. 27 (Bombay, June-1973).
29. Kale, M.R. ; *op. cit.*, p. 42.
30. Russell R.V. and Hiralal : *Tribes and Castes of the Central Provinces of India*, Vol. III, Cosmo Publications, Delhi, 1975, p. 107.
31. Ibid. p. 114.
32. Ibid. Vol VI, p. 491.
33. Ibid. p. 310.
34. Ibid. p. 275.

35. Ibid. Vol. I, p. 147.
36. Ibid.Vol. II, p. 79.
37. Cowell, E.B. : *op. cit.*, p. 226.
38. Russell, R.V. and Hiralal ; *op. cit.*, Vol. III, p. 139.
39. E.I., I., No. 26, p. 215.
40. Ibid. p. 334.
41. Nigam, M.L. : *op. cit.*, Preface, p. VI.
42. Ibid. p. 17.
43. Sharma, R.K. (Ed,) : *Indian Archaeology—New Perspectives*, Agam Kala Prakashan, Delhi, 1982, p. 157.
44. Ibid. p. 214
45. Ibid. p. 263.
46. Ibid. p. 214.
47. Dikshit, R.K. : *The Candellas of Jejākabhukti*, p. 11.
48. E.I., XXXI, p. 205.
49. Law, B.C. : *Tribes in Ancient India*, p. 98.
50. Kale, M.R. : *op. cit.*, p. 25.
51. Law, B.C. : *Historical Geography of Ancient India*, p. 313.
52. I.H.Q., Vol. IV, No. 2, p. 344.
53. Ibid., Vol. IV, No. 4, p. 701.
54. Kale, M.R. : *op. cit.*, p. 44.
55. E.I. IV, p, 173.
56. Pande, R.B. : *op. cit.*, p. 168.
57. I.H.Q., Vol. IV, No. 4, p. 699.
58. I.H.Q., Vol. V, No. 2, p. 293.
59. Ibid., p. 281 and Vol. IV, No. 2, p. 344.
60. Ibid. p. 289.
61. Nigam, M.L. ; *op. cit.*, p. 13.
62. Tiwari Gorelal : *Bundelkhāṇda Ka Saṅkṣipta itihāsa*. p. 4.
63. Law, B. C. :*Historical Geography of Ancient India*, p. 313
64. Kane, P.V. : *History of Dharmaśāstra*, Vol. II, pt. I Bhandarkar Oriental Research Institute Poona, 1941, p. 44
65. Ibid. p. 71,
66. Nigam, M. L. : *op. cit.*, p. 12
67. Thapar, Romila: *Aśoka and the Decline of the Mauryas*, Oxford University Press, (Second Impression), Bombay, 1977, p. 256
(Firma KLM) Calcutta, 1967, pp. 51-62
68. Russell R.V. and Hiralal., *op. cit.*, p. 98.
69. *Supra*, p. 31.
70. Thapar, R. : *op. cit.*, p. 264.
71. Ibid. p. 96,
72. E.I., XXXI, No. 27. L. 9 : XXXVI, No. 30, L. 11.
73. Thapar, R. : *op. cit.*, p. 116 and 121.
74. Bajpai, K.D. : *Indian Numismatic studies*, Abhinava Prakashan, New Delhi, 1976, p. 7.

75. Ibid, p. 6.
76. Ibid. p. 7.
77. M.P. District Gazetteer, (Sagar District) 1967, p. 46.
78. Bajpai, K.D. : *op. cit.*, p. 6
79. Ibid. p. 11
80. C.I.I., IV, pt. II, No. 119
81. Sircar D.C. : *Studies in the Society and Administration of Ancient and Medieval India* (Firma KLM) Calcutta, 1967, pp. 51-62
82. pande, R.B. ; *op. cit.*, Ch. IV, No. 2
83. Ibid. No. 1, L. 21
84. Bajpai, K. D. : *op. cit.*, pp. 121-122
85. Pande R.B. : *op. cit.*, Ch. IV, No. 1, L. 15
86. Ibid. No. 2
87. C.I.I., III (Revised), 1981, No. 28, V. 6
88. Ibid, No. 39, L, 47
89. Ibid, No. 20, p. 279
90. *Supra.* p. 13
91. Fleet. No. 31, L. 8
92. Devahuti, D. : *Harsha - A Political Study*, p. 95
93. Asopa, J.N. *Origin of the Rajputs*, Bharatiya Publishing House (First Edition), Delhi 1976, p. 68 and 213,
94. E.I., IV, No. 20, L1. 37,53,66 (twice) and 61.
95. Smith, V.A.:*The Early History cf India*, Oxford (Fourth Edition), 1957, pp.424 and 429
96. I.G.I., IX, p. 70
97. Supra. p. 33
98. Basham, A. L.: *The Wonder that was India*, Rupa & Co., (Paperback-second Impression), Calcutta, 1967, p. 121
99. Dikshit, R. K.: *op. cit.* , p. 35
100. H.C.I.P., Vol. III, pp. 560-61
101. Pande, R.B. : *op. cit.*, p. 192
102. Dikshit, R K.: *op. cit.*, p. 37
103. Mitra. S.K.: *The Early Rulers of Khajuraho*, Firma K.L. Mukhopadhyay, Calcutta, 1958, p. 175
104. Dikshit, R.K. : *op. cit.*, p. 15
105. Ibid, p. 25. Note-1
106. Viodya, C.V.: *History of Medieval Hindu India*, Vol. II, The Oriental Book Supplying Agency, 1924, p.25
107. Asopa, J.N.: *op. cit.*, p. 212
108. Bhārat Kalā Bhavan plate of Madanavarman - E.I., XXXII, p. 120
109. Dikshit, R.K.: *op. cit.*, p.171
110. J.A.S.B. (New series), Vol. 50. pt. I, No. 1, 1881, pp. 1-2
111. Ibid.
112. History and coinage of the Chandel Dynasty-in I.A., XXXVII, May-1908, p. 107.
113. J.A.S.B. (New series), Vol. 50, pt. 1, No. 1, 1881, p.9.

113.A E.I., III, p. 171

114. I.A., XVIII,p. 237
115. J.A.S.B. (New series), Vol. 50, pt.1., No. 1 1881, p. 4
116. E.I., XXXI, No. 41
117. Dikshit, R.K., *op. cit.*, p. 178
118. Bose, N.S,: *op. cit.*, p. 192

119. Sharma, R.S. : *Indian Feudalism*, Macmillan (Second Edition), Delhi, 1980, p. 1
120. E.I., XIX,No.2,p.15 ff.
121. E.I., XXXI.No.41, p.310 ff.
122. E.I.,I, No.20, p.154 ff.
123. E.I., I, No. 21
124. E.I, XXX, No. 36, pt.A
125. Ibid. pt.B
126. Sharma, R.S.; *op.cit*., p.66
127. I.A., XVI, p. 201 ff.
128. Ibid. p. 204 ff.
129. E.I., XX,No.14 pt.A
130. I.A.,XVI, p.207 ff.
131. R.I.,XXXII, No.14
131A. Ibid.
132. E.I., X, No.11
133. E.I., XXXI, No.41
134. E.I., XVI, No.2
135. E.I., IV, No.2
136. E.I., XX, No. 14, pt.B
137. E.I., XXXI, No. 11
138. E.I., XVI, No. 20
139. E.I., XXV' No. 1
140. E.I. XX,No. 14, pt.C
141. Ibid. pt. D
142. Sharma, R.S.: *op. cit*., pp.240-41
143. Bose, N.S.: *op. cit*. p.11;
144. Dikshit, R.K.:*op.cit*.,p.95
145. I.G.I.IX,p.69
146. E.I., XXX, No.17
147. E.I., I, No.20, Second Inscription, L.20
148. Pande, R.B.: *op.cit*., p.171 and 173
149. Dikshit, R.K.; *op. cit*., p. 93
150. Ibid. p. 92
151. E. I , I, p. 198. This epigraphic description does have corroboration in Jinamandama *Kumarapala prabandha* in which the picture of mahaba and its prosperity under Madanavarman is overdrawn. Vide : R.S., Introduction, pp. VII-VIII Note-3
152. Ibid. p. 138
153. Ibid. p. 149
154. Ibid. p. 215
155. Ibid. pp. 206-7
156. I. A.,XXXVIII. p. 134
157. E. I., IV, No.20, p.155
158. E. I., I. p. 330

155. Ibid. pp. 206-7
156. E.I. A., XXXV, p. 134
157. E.I., IV, No. 20, p. 155
158. E.I., I, p. 330
159. Dikshit. R.K. : op. cit., p. 148
160. E.I., XXXIII, No. 4
161. Ibid.
162. Dikshit, R.K. : op. cit p. 11
163. E,I., XXVII, No. 19, VS. 11-12
164. E.I., I, No. 38, Vs. 30-31
165. E.I., XXVIII, No. 19
166. E.I., I, No. 38, V. 2
167. Diashit, R.K, : op. cit. p. 208
168. E.I., I, p. 196 ff.
169. Dikshit, R.K. : op. cit. pp. 112-14
170. J.A.S.B. (New series). Vol. 50, pt. II, p. 28
171. E.I., IV, No. 20, LI. 19 and 67
172. Ibid.
173. Dikshit, R.K. : op. cit., p. 197
174. E.I., I, No. 21
175. E.I., IV, No. 20, p. 155
176. E.I., XXX: No. 11
177. E.I., XXXX No. 4
178. E.I., XVII, No. 15
179. E.I., X, No. 21
180. E.I., I, p. 136
181. Ibid. p. 149
182. Ibid. p. 315
183. Ibid. p. 337
184. E.I., XXXX, No. 14; E.I., II, No. 14-B
185. E.I., II, No. 14-A
186. E.I., I, XXIII No. 4

3

Religious Geography from Archaeological Remains

(Hardly any historical records have been handed down by ancient Indians. A historian, therefore, is badly handicapped in reconstructing their life and times out of a fragmentary inscription here and a solitary coin there. Frankly speaking, all his voluminous attempts, at times, amount only to puzzling out the problems that he has himself to identify. What is true of India is bound to be so of Bundelkhand. It offers very little by way of written records. Apart from a solitary Aśokan edict and couple of Guptan commemoratives, we draw a complete blank till we come to the Pratihāras and Candellas. But our position is none the better even with early-medieval inscriptions. Chiefly land-charters, their contents are the same in all cases with variations only of dates and names of persons and places. We are constrained, therefore, to consult and depend on non-epigraphic sources. Fortunately for us, much of the archaeological evidence surviving to our day is religious in character bearing a good deal on the theme of this book. Below is given an account of antiquities with a view to acquainting the reader with their nature and location in time and space of Bundelkhand.)

I TOPOGRAPHY

The boundaries of Bundelkhand for the purposes of the present book have already been defined. Turning now to the topography of the region, names such as the Vindhyas, the Betwā, the Dhasān, the Bīnā, the Kena and the Yamunā come casually to our mind, forming, as they do, the warp and woof of the region under study.

The Vindhyas constitute the chief mountain range of the region having been held as one among the seven *Kula-Parvatas* of ancient times.[1] The treasure of Indian mythology has preserved a beautiful myth personifying the mountain and narrating its attempt to obstruct the path of Sūrya, Ṛṣi Agastya wanted to cross to the South and so at his asking the attempt was postponed till his return. The Ṛṣi is yet to cross back. Symbolically the myth represents the stage of Aryan penetration south of the Vindhyas. It finds frequent mention in ancient literature[2] as well as inscriptions[3]. Ptolemy's 'oeuindon' is taken for the Vindhyas.[4]

The Yamunā is certainly the *Kalindakanyā* of Kālidasa,[5] Kālindī of Eran Stone Pillar inscription of Budhagupta[6] and *Kalindatanayā* of Khajuraho Stone inscription[7]. The Betwā is the Vetravati of old times and mentioned as river Mālava in Khajuraho Stone inscription. River Daśārṇa of ancient literature is identified with modern Dhasān forming boundary between Jhansi and Hamirpur districts. Modern Kena falling into the Yamunā is Karṇavatī of former times.

The region is rich in romantic remains of the past and lot is yet to be redeemed from the ravages of Time and rogues of the antique world. Very few provinces of India can boast of such large legacy in the form of painted rock-shelters, temples and sculptures. One is bound to lose the count trying to list them. A portion of this iconic and architectural material has now been transferred to various museums and its thorough study is essential to recreating the religious life of the region in the period of our study.

Described below, therefore, are almost all the notable archaeological sites of Bundelkhand with an idea about their geographical location and a brief account of the antiquities that still greet us at the place. Some such sites came to light in course of explorations undertaken for the purposes of the present work. Hence they are yet to acquire place in the archaeological map of Bundelkhand.

II BANDA DISTRICT

A. *Bilharia*

Possessing a beautiful location in the midst of a valley and situated at a distance of 45 kms. from Banda town, the village contains the remains of a small stone temple standing on the top of a rocky hill locally known as Bilharia maṭha. Consisting only of a sanctum and a portico, the temple appears to have been dedicated to Viṣṇu as his figure can be noticed in the *lalāṭabiṃba* of the sanctum doorway. Profusely ornamented, as were its outer facades, the carvings contained, according to Cunningham, figures of Gajalakṣmī, Haragaurī, Ardhanārīśdvara and Sarasvati.[8]

B. *Chitrakuta*

Important evidence is available attesting to its early habitation. Accompanied by Sitā and Lakṣamaṇa, Lord Rāma, the ideal man of Indian tradition, came and rested at this 'many-hued peak,' during the period of his exile. Situated on the left bank of the Paisuni river, at a distance of about 70 kms. south-east of Banda, it had the honour to become the abode of the sage-poet Vālmīki who sang its praises in the following words:

> Auspicious hill; where all day long,
> The lapwing's cry, the Koil's song,
> Make all, who listen, gay—
> Where all is fresh and fair to see,
> Where elephants and deer roam free...[9]

The Godāvarī of the Lesser Epic has been placed a few kms. to the south of Chitrakuta[10]. Barring a few sculptures of early medieval times scattered in the vicinity of the village, we have nothing to our purpose. A little away is Dashrathaghāt preserving among its carvings figures of Seṣaśāyī Viṣṇu, Mahiṣamardinī and Sūrya.

C. *Gonda*

About 1½ kms. away from the high road leading from Karwai to Banda, the village was noted by Cunningham for two temples.[11] Of them the larger he identified as dedicated to Viṣṇu and the smaller to Lakṣmī, basing his reading on the figures occupying the *lalāṭabimbas* of the respective shrines.

D. *Kālañjara*

Mentioned as Rudrakoti in *Kūrma-Purāṇa*[12] and taken to be an abode of Śiva, its very name is believed to have been derived from Śiva's activity as Kāla or Time causing everything in the world to decay (Jarā). Located at a distance of 55 kms. from Banda town in latitude 25.1°N. and longitude 80.29°E, it is held as one of the *Tapasyāsthānas* going back to the Vedic period according to Wilson who dated the founding of the fortress to the beginning of the Christian era.[13] The Kalacuri occupation of Kālañjara is placed in the mid-third century A.D. and the event is regarded important enough to be commemorated by the foundation of an era.

Beyond doubt is the sacred character of the spot. It figures in the list of nine holy places of northern India. A bath in the tank inside the fort earned religious merit equivalent to the gift of 1000 cows. In tradition the waters of Burhia Tal are supposed to have cured king Kirtivarman of his leprosy.[14] The event, if true, must have further enchanced public faith in the holy character of Kālañjara. The idea is echoed by the author of Mahobākhaṇḍ as well.[15] By the close of Candella period a regular festival in connection with pilgrimage to Kālañjara had been instituted finding frequent mention in the dramas of Vatsarāja.[15]a

Among the antiquities surviving at the spot notable is the Nīlakaṇṭha temple of Lord Śiva. An octagonal cave in shape with a Candella *maṇḍapa* in front, the temple contains representations of twin river-godesses and the divine pair Hara-gaurī, which have been dated to the Gupta epoch. Worthy of note, further, are rock-cut representations of Śiva, Pārvatī, Gaṇesa, and Nandī near a reservoir now known as Hanumāna-Kuṇḍ and a colossal Kālabhairava, Śeṣaśāyi Viṣṇu and Varāha near lake Gaṅgāsāgara. The total number of icons may well be a thousand.

Of greater importance and deeper significance, however, is epigraphic evidence recovered here or referring to it, though found elsewhere. The earliest of inscriptions comes down from the Gupta period.[16] The place must have acquired political importance by then, if not earlier, since the date concerning its Kalacuri occupation is yet to be confirmed. The Pratihāras do not feel proud of its possession whereas the Candellas do. In Baraha Copper Plate of Bhoja.[17] Kālañjara is merely a *maṇḍala* headquarter but Khajuraho Stone inscription regards its conquest as singular success of Yaśovarman.[18] This fact stands further confirmed by the title Kālañjarādhipati assumed by the Candella Kings from Dhaṅga onwards. We are not sure if Kālañjara was ever the capital of the Candellas, since the royal records and local tradition mention Khajuraho and Mahoba respectively, but the fact of its having been a military capital is too obvious to need confirmation. The Muslim invasions of Bundelkhand mainly aimed at capturing Kālañjara. The commandership of Kālañjara was a rare reward in recognition of signal services and the revenue of one village was fixed as the salary of that functionary, who enjoyed the title of Viśiṣa.[19] Kālañjara owed this military importance to its elevated mountainous position commanding a very wide area which is beautifully reflected in the myth, already mentioned, and looms large in inscriptions as well. To quote the Khajuraho record :

"He (Yaśovarman) easily conquered the Kālañjara mountain the dwelling place of Śiva which is so high that it impedes the progress of the Sun at mid-day.[20]"

Whatever be the worth of the story, current in contemporary bardic circles and offering an account of the origin of the Candellas, Kālañjara figures prominently in it and Hemavatī, their Brāhmaṇic ancestress is believed to have shifted here from Kāshi.[21]

E. *Lokhri*

Situated at the northern foot of the Vindhya hills at a distance of 9 kms. to the north-west of Dabora station, the village contains a number of sculptures depicting Varāha, Nṛsiṁha, Gaṇeśa, and Bhairava among others. An important discovery of utmost interest to us was made about a decade ago by K.D. Bajpai who chanced upon a yoginī centre near here assignable to eighth century A.D.[22] In all, twenty-nine yoginī icons have been found meriting mention among them being representations of Aindrī Vaināyakī, Yamī, (Fig. 1), Śasi, Kaṅkālī (Fig. 2), Nāgī (Fig.3), Meṣamukhī (Fig. 4), Nārasiṃhī and Kaumārī (Fig. 5). Of Kārttikeya and Lakuīśa also we have lithic representations.

F. *Marphā*

Situated on a high projecting hill about 20 kms. to the north-east of Kālañjara, the fort bears a deserted look and is overgrown with jungle. As already noted, Marpha is among the eight forts assigned by tradition to the Candellas but hardly anything of their times has survived here. The inscriptions available belong to Late-Medieval period.[23]

G. *Rasin*

Lying about 40 kms. away from Banda on high road to Kālañjara the village is dotted with ruined shrines indicating that the place must have been a populous city in times past. Located in latitude 25.11°N. and longitude 80.44°E, the village has a wealth of antiquities belonging mostly to the Candella period. Needing note for us is Ratananātha temple, buried in a thick forest and standing on a hill overlooking verdant woods. It is locally known as Caṇḍa-Maheśvari temple. Another shrine dedicated to Gaṇeśa stands hard by the village with a twenty-four armed colossal image of the elephant-headed god. In stray sculptures, lying about the village, we have icons of Cāmuṇḍā, Hanumāna, Nṛsiṁha, Nandī and Durgā.

Interesting it is to find that another village, also known as Rasin about 7 kms. away from Banda, is an ancient site as is evident in the antiquities scattered over there. Among sculptures two representing Gaṇeśa and Durgā are worth-noting.

Our survey of Banda district is by no means complete and some more sites could be named and described in addition to those, covered above, but they hardly add to what we already know. We could pass on noting only their names—Pailāni, Laudi and Gairāhā.

Of late, a new source has emerged for the study of history. Rock-paintings came to light long back but their value in reconstructing the picture of early society and civilization is only recently being recognized. The problem of their dating is being scientifically tackled enhancing their worth as a source of history. Banda district is one of the richest in our area as regards painted rock-shelters. These nature-made dwellings of man are as far-flung in location as the frontiers of the district but as good a work of art as are sculptural and architectural remains. Notable among the villages, in the vicinity of which these shelters are situated, are Sorhat, Kariākuṅd, Bargarh, Markandi, Mazharan and Chitrakuta. At Sorhat a cart without wheels is painted being drawn by a single ox. The occupant has an umbrella shading him.

III CHHATARPUR DISTRICT

A. *Khajuraho*

Located in latitude 24.51°N and longitude 79.56°E the antiquity of this temple-town has been taken back to Ptolemy whose 'Kuraporina' Cunningham was inclined to identify with Khajuraho[24] but the available evidence does not support the suggestion. However, recent research in archaeology has established that this forested region was the abode of Stone-Age man and the tribal people until the Candellas built their temples.[25] The point is very significant as it shows the place was especially selected by the Candellas to raise their religious monuments and a good deal of interaction between the tribals and the Aryans must have followed.

In epigraphic records, recovered from the place, the Sanskritized equivalent—Kharjurvāhaka—of the current name figures. Taken literally it stands for a place having a grove of date-palms. Cunningham did notice a few when he discovered the site, though now not a single date-palm is to be seen here. Viewed from this angle, the name could arise anywhere and we should not be surprised to chance upon a couple of less known Khajurahos in the area of our study.[26]

Khajuraho is verily a temple-town and out of an unknown number some twenty-five have survived the iconoclastic enthusiasm of early-medieval invaders and cyclic tempests of Time. We have seen that a curious myth is recorded by contemporary bardic tradition seeking to explain the origin of the Candellas. It touches upon the phenomenon of Khajuraho temples as well putting their total at eighty-five built by the founder ruler Candravarman to expiate for the sins of his mother Hemavati. A little later in the same work the bard has credited divine architect Viśvakarmā with the raising of these magnificent monuments.[27] It goes without saying that this traditional account has hardly any grain of history and is based only on bardic imagination.

Too well-known are these temples to need any elaborate description here. Ever since their discovery voluminous and meticulous coverage from every conceivable angle they have received and the scholarly world is yet to arrive at unanimous meaning of the erotic sculpture appearing on their walls, throwing a challenge to generation after generation of intellectuals and art-historians. A point worth-noting in this regard is non-recognition of Khajuraho as a place of pilgrimage. It is a little surprising that a town possessing nearly thirty temples of substantial size and shining sculpture did not have a *tīrtha* status. The early-medieval and medieval works compiling a list of contemporary *tīrtha*s completely ignore Khajuraho.

A bird's eye-view of the extant temples will not be out of place here. Earliest among these is a shrine of the Śāktas consecrated to sixty-four yoginīs. Next in chronology come those of Brahmā and Lalguan Mahādeva, of which the former was originally dedicated to Viṣṇu. All these were built wholly or partly of granite.

The Matangeśvara is regarded first among the sand-stone temples. It is a Śaiva shrine. The Varāha temple is merely a *maṇḍapa* standing on four pillars.

First among the finer sand-stone temples is the Lakṣamaṇa (Fig. 6) belonging to the Vaiṣṇava sect. A *Sāndhāra Prāsāda* of the *pancāyatana* variety, is rightly assigned to the regin of Yaśovarman Candella on grounds of epigraphic evidence.[28]

Not much distant in date is the Pārsvanātha temple built at the time of king Dhaṅgadeva. Save for the Jina image in the sanctum and Jina figures seated in the doorlintel, the temple is hardly distinguishable from the Brāhmaṇical shrines standing at the site, showing thereby that the artists and architects employed in the making of temples were the same irrespective of the faith for which they were to work.

The Viśvanātha is a *Sāndhāra* temple of Śaiva affiliation and *pañcāytana* in nature. It is datable to the year A.D. 1002 on the basis of an inscription now studded into the *maṇḍapa* wall.[29]

The Jagadambī and Citragupta are *nirandhāra prāsādas* assignable to the first quarter of the eleventh century. The former of these was originally dedicated to Viṣṇu.

The largest and loftiest as well as the most magnificent and marvellous is the Kandariyā Mahādeva. Verily a gem of architecture and a treasure of incalculable sculptural wealth, it has been dated to the second quarter of the eleventh century A.D.

To the third quarter of the same century belongs the Vāmana temple and slightly later in date is a Jaina shrine dedicated to Lord Ādinātha of which only the sanctum and vestibule survive now. The Jāvāri, is a small well-proportioned *nirandhāra prāsāda* consecrated to Viṣṇu. It is placed in the period 1075-1100 A.D.

Standing at a distance of 2½ kms. from the main group is yet another Viṣṇu temple now known as Caturbhuja temple. Possessing a beautiful and well-carved imge of the god and resembling the Jāvāri in many of its architectural features, the temple is placed round about 1100 A.D. Last of the line is Duladeo, a Śaiva shrine with a *Saptaratha* plan and placed in the second quarter of the twelfth century A.D.

The Ghaṇṭai temple, so called owing to the chain and bell motifs carved in bold relief on its tall, elegant pillars, is the fragmentary shell of a structure belonging to the Jaina faith (Fig. 7). Only an *ardhamaṇḍapa* and a *mahāmaṇḍapa* stand in situ resting on four pillars. It is assigned to the end of the tenth century A.D.

The dating of the temples[30] done above, shows that building of temples commenced at Khajurāho with the Candellas coming to power and went on for a couple of centuries largely under royal patronage and is no way an overnight miracle wrought by some supernatural architect like Viśvakaramā. From the Khajuraho records we learn that all the Jaina shrines and a few Brāhmaṇical ones owe their existence to the munificence of non-princely patrons. Kokkala, figuring in inscription No. V, the maker of Vaidyanātha temple, does not come of a kingly family.[31] What further surprises us is the fact that his record waxes eloquent over the splendour and charm of Padmāvatī town, maintaining a mysterious silence about Khajuraho where the temple financed by him was to be located.

Another fact emerging from the survey is that a liberal and tolerant atmosphere characterised the religious life at Khajuraho with orthodox and heterodox cults flourishing side by side. Of course, even otherwise, Indian history records very few instances of religious intolerance but what sets Khajuraho apart is that it was held in equally high esteem by all the three major religious systems of the time and the kings not only permitted this coexistence, but encouraged it as well.

The living together and coming closer contributed to another significant development in the history of Brāhmaṇism. The idea of worshipping all the five principal deities together gained ground shaping out in the form of Smārta cult in which the chief principle was to offer simultaneous worship to Viṣṇu, Śiva, Sūrya, Śakti and Gaṇeśa. Culmination of the cult can be seen in the *pañcāyatana* shrines that contain four subsidiary temples in corners of their *jagati* intended for four principal deities other than the one to whom the main shrine was dedicated. However, Cunningham found that such shrines attached to the Lakṣamaṇa temple were all dedicated to Viṣṇu[32] which was the chief god of the chief temple as well. Possibley the maker wanted to glorify Viṣṇu to the exclusion of others adopting the idiom of Smārta ideologues.

Syncretism in Brāhmaṇic iconography is much older than monuments of Khajuraho. Here it found further elaboration and diversification. Voluminous coverage from a variety of angles has already been given to ancient art and iconography of Khajuraho which contain a rich representation of Brāhmaṇical myths associated with Kṛṣṇa, Viṣṇu and Śiva.

In addition to architectural and art relics, inscriptions also constitute a part of the Khajuraho elgacy. They throw a welcome light on the religious life and beliefs of early-medievel Bundelkhand. A few have already been referred to in foregoing chapters and the remaining we could conveniently refer and utilise at appropriate place elsewhere in the book in order to avoid repetition.

Of Buddhism very little trace has suvived in this temple-town, though Cunningham found that the Chinese pilgrim noted a number of monasteries flourishing here. The pioneer archaeologist was inclined to identify the ruined mounds in northern group of the temples as the likely sites of Buddhist monuments[33] but as we have earlier seen, it is difficult to apply the description exactly to Khajuraho. Barring a solitary Buddha figure now housed in the local museum practically nothing survives of Buddhism.

B. *Mānyagarh*

Lying on the left bank of the river Ken about 25 kms. south-east of Chhatarpur and commanding a clear view of Rajgarh, this Candella fort has been named after the tutelary deity of the Candella dynasty. The temple of the tribal god Mānyadeva is now buried in a thick forest and is difficult of access, Strange indeed, the Candellas chose Khajuraho in preference to this place to raise their religious monuments.

C. *Mau Suhania*

Characterised by a beautiful sheet of water and surrounded on all sides by pretty hillocks, the village lies about 15 kms. west of Chhatarpur. Tradition avers that it had the honour of being a minor seat of Pratihāra government,[34] a fact attested to by the presence of many granite temples in Pratihāra provincial style still surviving here.

Near Bhīmakuṇḍa stands one of the temple-groups. Consisting only of a square sanctum—cella and a pyramidal *śikhara* of horizontal tiers and inordinate style with a crowing *āmalaka*, each of these temples reminds us of the tiny cells of Causaṭha—yogini temple at Khajuraho. The *jaṅghā* and the doorway of these temples are devoid of any decorative designs. The icons having gone, it is difficult to decide upon their dedication (Fig. 8) They can be assigned to the ninth century A.D. The so called Nāgabābā temple situated beside the path leading to the state museum, Dhubela remarkably represents the group. Possessing primitive features and plain character, the temple is in good state of preservation (Sketch No. 1).

Slightly developed in plan, style and elevation is another temple, also located near Bhimkuṇḍa. With a *pañcaratha* plan as well as elevation, it possesses a curvilinear *Śikhara* and a crowing *āmalaka*. The portico that stood in front earlier is now missing leaving a few traces of its having been there.

Among other sites with monuments of Pratihāra make, but in most miserable condition, names of Kainry and Chamrua we could mention. A Jaina temple of slightly later date with Lord Śāntinātha as presiding deity exists at Urdmau about 35 kms. away from Chhatarpur.

IV DAMOH DISTRICT

A. *Bāsā Tārkhedā*

The site is unnoticed as yet. Here has been found an icon of Buddha[35]

assignable to early-medieval period on grounds of palaeography of the inscription incised on its pedestal[36]. The discovery is important in that it points to a Buddhist pocket surviving in this part even after A.D. 1000. Much more material pertaining to the sect might come to light if the site is systematically explored and excavated. The village is a few kms. away from Gaḍhakoṭā.

B. *Badgaon*

A solitary Śiva temple of about tenth-eleventh centuries A.D. is worthy of note. Save for the sanctum and a part of the *Śikhara* all else is lost and still littered around. The *sikahara* shows six *karṇa-āmalakas* indicating arrangement of seven *bhūmīs* originally. Facing the temple is a large sheet of water enhancing the beauty of the place. The village lies about 30 kms. north-east of Nohatā.

The description, given above does not tally with Badgaon figuring in the survey report of Cunningham. He speaks of having noted ruins of about thirty-five temples at the place, some affiliated to Jainism and others to Brāhmaṇism. From the Somanātha temple, he recovered an inscription in characters of ninth-tenth centuries A.D. which contained the name of kalacuri King Vigraha Cedi.[37] One simply wonders why this Badgaon could not rise as rival to Khajuraho where the number of temples is much less.

C. *Banvānsā*

This too is a new discovery made during the explorations undertaken for the present work. Situated at a distance of 20 kms. south-east of Nohaṭā, here survives a small Śiva shrine of flat-roofed and single-slab pattern bearing a close resemblance to the early Gupta temples. But it certainly comes of the post-Gupta period as can be made out from the sculptural remains which are devoid of that grace and charm characterising the Gupta art. In addition to this Śaiva shrine, one dedicated to Viṣṇu could also be postulated on the basis of a door-lintel with Viṣṇu in *lalāṭabṁiba* lying near by.

D. *Doni*

This hamlet on a hill-top is about 25 kms. away from Tendukhedā. About eleven temples appear to have been in existence here assignable to 10th-11th centuries A.D. Utterly ruined beyond recognition, they make a moving spectacle. In affiliation they were Jaina as well as Brāhmaṇical though the exact number in either case is difficult to settle. Among the icons, still lying at the place, those of Skanda, Agni and Jain Yakṣī Ambikā merit mention. Inside a *caitya-gavākṣa* a carving of Yogāsana Viṣṇu is also remarkable.

E. *Hindoria*

Located 15 kms. north-east of Damoh town, the village has numerous antiquities. The gateway of the Jugal-Kishore temple in the village consists of door-jambs and door-stills removed from the ruins of Kalacuri temples. At a distance of 2 kms. to the west of the village is Badi Bhuvan or Isarmau, the original site of this old town, Covered all over with ruins of temples, it is surrounded by cultivated fields on all sides. Among the sculptures lying here, note could be taken of Śeṣaśāyi Viṣṇu, Bhairava, Cāmuṇḍā. Hanumāna and a Jina.

Into the open ground in front of the residence of Shri Pratap Narayan Thakur in the village are scattered some more art-relics, taken obviously from the old town. A *Kāyotsarga* Jina, Nṛsiṃhāvatāra, and Śeṣaśāyi Viṣṇu are noteworthy among these.

F. *Khamaria Maujilal*

This too is an unnoticed site. At a distance of 15 kms. from Nohaṭā on the road leading to Tejgarh, the village has a lovely location. None of the ancient temples survive. now but their traces greet us at the very outskirts. Under a Pipal tree on a platform are accommodated two door-lintels with Viṣṇu and Śiva in their *lalāṭabimbas*. Hard by, a broken image of Hanumāna can also be noticed.

G. *Kodal*

Situated at a distance of 17 kms. south-east of Tendukhedā, the village is known for its ruined Śiva temple of Kalacuri times. Only the sanctum and a fragment of the *sikhara* survive now. The sculptural bands of the *jaṅghā* contain figures of *sura-sundarīs* and *parivāra-devatās* of Lord Śiva. The door-frame also has copious carvings. Destitute of any deity and decorative designs is another structure, resting on massive square pillars, standing close to the Śaiva shrine.

H. *Kundalpur*

Words will fail to depict the beauty of this place. Dotted with hills, each of which is crowned by a Jain temple, the charm of this well-known sacred site of the Jainas is further enhanced by a large body of water called Vardhamānasāgar. Secluded and serene, the place must have attracted ancient ṛṣis.

Kundalpur is about 40 kms. north-east of Damoh town. None among the existing temples on the hills could be taken to ancient or early-medieval period. Similar in shape, they possess square body, domed roof and pinnacles at the corners.

Cunningham located here two flat-roofed temples of the Gupta period to the west of Vardhamānasāgar at the foot of the hills.[38] Made on single-slab pattern, these were dated by him in 600 A.D. One of them still stands in situ consisting of square sanctum and a shallow porch (Fig. 9). The icons enshrined within are surely of later period, one of them is Viṣṇu and the other a *Rāvaṇānugraha* mūrti of Śiva.

A two-storeyed structure, of which the upper one has fallen now, locally known as Rukminī Maṭha also merits mention. Devoid absolutely of sculptural carving and destitute of any deity inside, it poses the problem of deciding upon its dedication. A loose stone slab containing representation of the Jaina Yakṣa pair Gomedha and Ambikā, sitting *lalitākdṣepa* under a tree is lying inside. However, we cannot be sure of its Jaina affiliation as the slab does not seem to be belonging to it.

High up on a hill is the famous Bade Bābā temple. The temple itself is of much later period but its courtyard contains some icons representing Jaina deities. Among these one can see Yakṣīs as well as *Tīrthaṅkaras*. On the basis of these art relics alone the ancient association of Jainas with the place could be established, as the temples themselves are of late-medieval design.

I. *Nohaṭā*

Commanding a captivating confluence of the Barma and the Guraiya rivers, it lies 20 kms. south-east of Damoh town on Jabalpur road.

The solitary monument surviving here is a Śaiva shrine standing within an enclosure of modern make and enshrining a *liṅga*. Erected on a low *jagati*, it has a shallow porch, a large *maṇḍapa*, a constricted *antarāla* and a plain *garbha-gṛha*. The *śikhara*, rising above the sanctum, is curvilinear in design, *pañca-ratha* in plan and ornamented all over with caitya-window carvings. The temple has no *pradakṣiṇā patha* (Fig.10).

Near the Police-Station on the outskirts of the village is a small modern temple of Hanumāna, into the *jagati* and walls of this temple are studded with a number of panels. A door-lintel with Viṣṇu in the *lalāṭabiṁba*, a *sukhāsana* Gaṅeśa, and *āmalaka* piece can be easily made out. In every nook and corner of the village we come upon innumerable icons lying under trees or on the mud-platforms or built into house walls. To name a few, Gaṅgā-Yamunā, Sūrya, Skanda and Navagrahas are easily identifiable.

Upon a mound to the north-west of the village are lying several Jina images and six icons of Gaṇeśa. From other indications as well, the site seems to have been sacred to the sect of the Gaṇapatyas. The Kher Mātā Marhia standing on the road also retains a rich collection of relics finely carved. The beautiful boar at Phutera tank in Damoh town is also said to have been removed from Nohaṭā.

J. *Nandchand*

Located on an island formed by the junction of two branches of the Kundo Nālā with the Patna river, this village is about 60 kms., east-north-east of Damoh. Cunningham found here a temple of Mataṅgeśvara and of Aṣṭaśakti. He assigned them to A.D. 700. An inscription of Kalacuri Karṇa was also noticed.[39]

K. *Raneh*

Situated 15 kms. south-east of Haṭā, the village is chiefly notable for its sculptured panels, scattered in and around. A two-storeyed structure does survive resembling Rukminī-maṭha of Kundalpur in design, plan and style. Nothing can be said of its dedication. Heaps of sculptures lying in front under a tree must have adorned its walls in times past. Easily identifiable among these are Viṣṇu and Pārvatī.

Outside the village scattered near the Sagar tank are a number of panels belonging most probably to eleventh-twelfth centuries A.D. Among these we have an icon of Gaṇeśa and a representation of Sapta-mātṛkās. Walking about a kilometre to the east of the village, we come upon a place called Baḍī Devī. Within a brick-enclosure here are placed plenty of art-relics and architectural members. Note may be taken of a panel with Navagrahas, an icon of Gaṇeśa and one of Viṣṇu.

L. *Sakor*

Associated with Alha in tradition, Sakor is about 13 kms. from Haṭā. It must have shot into prominence very early, as the sole surviving monument of our interest here is a Śiva temple of the Gupta period. Save for the doorway to the sanctum, all else is lost. The extremely ornate and artistic door-frame bears the unmistakable mark of the Gupta artist. The enshrined *liṅga* is still in situ. Perhaps the temple has had no *śikhara* and all traces of a *maṇḍapa* are missing, if there was one.

A little further away stands a Hanumāna temple of modern make. Housed here in a corner are a few mutilated icons of early-medieval times, showing thus that the place continued to be of considerable importance even in post-Gupta times.

Our survey of Damoh district is by no means complete. In addition to the sites described above, Fatehpur, Gubra, Bandakpur, Chitrakhera, Kethora, Pancham Nagar, Kaurpura, Ranoda and Tejgarh also retain antiquities of our interest. Finally, Damoh archaeological museum also houses numerous art-relics which include not only icons but door-lintels and door-jambs as well. At a little distance from here is located the official residence of Damoh District Magistrate. The garden attached to it contains a few remarkable sculptures and so also does the garden of S.P.'s bungalow. Buddhist relics are conspicuous by their absence in all these collections.

V DATIA DISTRICT

A. *Chhoti Badoni*

Believed to have been founded about A.D. 300 mainly on the basis of Gupta and Roman pottery recovered from the adjoining Guptesvara or Gopeśvara hills, this small town lies 6 kms. to the north-east of Datia. Hard by the house of the former Diwan is a Jaina temple dedicated to Neminātha. Completely deserted and dilapidated now, it is locally known as Buddha-mandira obviously due to resemblance between a *tīrthaṅkara* image and that of the Buddha.

The hillocks of Gopeśvara, about a kilometre from the town, possessed painted rock-shelters attesting the fact of early habitation.

The survey team of the Deptt. of A.I.H.C. & Archaeology, University of Saugar, collected some clay-sealings bearing representation of miniature stūpa in centre with a surrounding Brāhmī legend in characters of sixth-seventh centuries A.D.

Some traces of stūpas can still be made out on the hill. Heaps of Gupta bricks lying nearby also speak on the point. Possibly the place had a Buddhist centre of learning and worship in Gupta times.

The Gopeśvara Śiva temple is actually a natural cave having a *liṅga* for worship. Nearby scattered are numerous icons and sculptures, assignable to the Pratihāra and Kacchapaghāta periods. Images of Viṣṇu, Sūrya and Śiva *Rāvaṇānugraha* need notice among them.

This hurried account of the antiquities shows that from prehistoric times down to early-medieval, Chhoti Badoni continued to be a place of considerable religious importance. What is further interesting, the relics surviving speak of all the three major religious sects having occupied it. The soil around being rocky and dry with very low water-spring, one wonders wherefrom came the economic support of these centres. The only conjecture that can be hazarded is the possibility of the place having been on a trade-route of early times.

B. *Gujarra*

But for a Minor-Rock-Edict of the Mauryan monarch, Gujarra has nothing to offer. The village is situated 15 kms. south-east of Datia. The epigraph is incised on the face of a granite rock at the foot of a hill hardly distinguishable from hundreds of such rocks around in the vicinity of the village. A four-pillared canopy erected by the Archaeology Department helps us in spotting the rock. The importance of the inscription lies in preserving the personal name of the emperor.[40]

C. *Gharavah*

The find of painted rock-shelters here by a survey team of the University of Saugar places this village on the archaeological map of the district. Located at a distance of about 11 kms. south-east of Datia town, Gharavah has picturesque surroundings characterised by a beautiful sheet of water at the foot of the hills.

D. *Keolari*

About 8 kms. north of Datia on road to Seondha, the village yielded some punch-marked coins. The antiquity of the village is taken back to the Sātavāhana period. The icons found here included those of Viṣṇu, Gajāri Śiva with mātṛkas above him, ten-armed but headless Durgā, Pārvatī, Haragaurī, Gaṇeśa, Varāha, Navagrahas, Kubera and *tīrthaṅkara* Pārśvanātha.[41] Remarkable among these was a massive icon of the monkey-god.

E. *Radhuāpurā*

About 3 kms. off Keolari, the village has a claim to mention for the find of an icon of Buddhist goddess Tārā assignable to early-medieval times. The only other known image from here is that of Ardha-nārīśvara.

F. *Senvai*

About 13 kms. east of Datia on Seondha road, the village has a collection of sculptures, Brāhmaṇical in affiliation. These include carvings of Varāha, Viṣṇu and Gaṇeśa. An interesting find from here was a colossal *liṅga* with representation of divine figures now removed to a museum in Datia town.[42] Oddly enough, the search for the museum proved in vain.

G. *Unao*

Standing on the bank of river Pahuj and famous for its sun-temple, the village is 25 kms. from Datia. The temple appears to have been erected recently but the enshrined sun-dial comes of the time when the deity was represented aniconically. The village people narrate a number of myths and traditions associated with the origin and history of the temple.

The sun-dial itself has nothing remarkable to interest us save its circular shape with raised points at the periphery, standing, perhaps, for the planets.

The shallow niches of the cella contain a *liṅga*, an icon of Durgā and a pot-bellied deity. The sun-dial is embedded in a high platform. Under a Pipal tree in the courtyard lie a few more sculptures indicating that the present temple occupies the place of an old one, most probably of early-medieval period.

H. *Sonagir*

A place of pilgrimage for the Jainas, it must have shot into prominence from the post-Gupta period. The Jaina temples more than seventy-five in number belong to medieval age but an image of Pārvatī, kept in temple No.76 contains an inscription on its aureole in Siddhā-mātṛkā characters of about eighth century A.D.

Kinnargadh near Seondha is also a place of archaeological interest possessing sculptures of some Brāhmaṇic deities. Before concluding we may note a collection of sculptures accommodated in a room of the P.R.O. office at Datia. Among these icons representing Gajalakṣmī, Sūrya, Gaṇeśa and Sapta-mātṛkās and a fragmentary slab bearing the well-known Buddhist theme—a wheel with a dear flanking—is especially noteworthy.

VI HAMIRPUR DISTRICT

A. *Mahoba*

A railway-station on Jhansi-Manikpur railway-line and a seat of Candella government, the location of Mahoba is in latitude 25.38°N and in longitude 79.41°E. Cunningham did not doubt the popular tradition which holds king Candravarman as founder of this city.[43] The king is supposed to have instituted a great festival here, and so, it came to be called Mahotsavanagara, shortening later on to Mahoba.

A lot of evidence bearing on our theme fell victim to religious fanaticism but the little that remains helps us in highlighting the main religious systems flourishing here. Majority of the temples were made into masjids or mutilated out of all recognition. To quote Cunningham, "The only Hindu building now standing is part of the palace of Parmāla or Parmaddi Deva on the top of the hill fort which has been converted into a Masjid." In the Dargah of Pir Mubarak Shah and adjacent grave-yard he counted no less than three hundred ten pillars of earlier temples. Nearby a black stone-bull was lying and the argha of a liṅgam had been fixed as a water spout in the terrace. Obviously a Śiva temple stood earlier here, which could be ascribed to Kīrtivarman on the basis of a record built into the wall of a tomb.

Among the surviving monuments of Mahoba, Kākrā-maṭha may be taken first. Occupying a rocky island in the north-western corner of the Madanasāgar Lake, it is made of granite. In size, it is equal to the largest of Khajuraho temples. The sanctum is empty but the mark of a *liṅgam* having been fixed indicates its Śaiva affiliation. Cunningham speaks of another dilapidated temple to the north of Kākrā-maṭha and known as *Madāri-mandira* connecting it with Lord Kṛṣṇa, though the connection does not appear convincing.

Mahoba was also a subsidiary seat of Mānyadeva, the family deity of the Candellas who are believed to have brought his worship to Mahoba.[44] The temple dedicated to him is of modern make to all appearances and has none of the antiquities found in other Candella temples. It enshrines merely the rude and natural face of a rock.

Mahoba is dotted with hillocks all around. Whichever direction one moves out, rock-cut reliefs greet the eye. Of utmost importance among these larger than life representations is a massive sculpture of *Gajāsura-saṃhāraśiva* depicted in a forceful manner. Not far from this mammoth carving we have full family of Śiva on the face of another primeval rock. The gorgeous sculpture of Gajāri Śiva is locally knows as *Śiva-Tāṇḍava*.

Of Jainism practically nothing has survived at Mahoba, but it did have a hold on Mahoba. Statues of *Tirthaṅkaras* like Ṛṣabhanātha, Padmaprabhu, Neminātha, Pārśvanātha and Mahāvīra have been shifted to Government Museum, Jhansi. The image of Ṛṣabhanātha is dated in V.S.1228 and that of Padmaprabhu in V.S. 1219. Variety of stones has been used to carve out these icons. Such is the sound given by a seated image of first *Tīrthaṅkara* on being struck that it seems to have been made of metal.[44a].

A few rock-cut reliefs behind the temple of Badi Caṇḍikā include figures of the Jinas and Yakṣas. Hard by is a natural cave containing figures of Ādinātha, Neminātha, Pārśvanātha and Yakṣī Padmāvatī. The report of Cunningham also refers to some broken statues of Jain deities, a few with inscriptions. A Jain *pratimā-sarvatobhadrikā* stands in the garden attached to S.D.M.'s Bungalow.[45]

Nothing absolutely survives now of Buddhism though it did flourish on the soil of Mahoba. The first of its traces came to Cunningham when he found a pedestal inscribed with well-known formula of Buddhist faith in characters of eleventh-twelfth centuries A.D. Later on, icons of Buddha, Siṃhanāda Lokeśvara (Fig.11) Padmapāṇi Avalokiteśvara (Fig. 12) and Tārā were rescued from oblivion indicating that Buddhism had a fairly large following at Mahoba in the early-medieval period. It needs to be underlined that the icon of Siṃhanāda Lokeśvara now ranks one of the finest pieces ever produced by the Indian genius. All these relics have since been removed to Lucknow Archaeological Museum.

Śāktism at Mahoba acquired and maintained considerable following. Śakti's Cāmuṇḍā form had a special appeal here and we meet with numerous independent representations of her. Most of them are rock-cut reliefs with varying degree of artistic excellence. Particular note needs to be taken of a loose but badly mutilated icon of the goddess lying in the garden of S.D.M.'s Bungalow. The icon is unique in showing the deity with sixty-four arms (Fig. 13) No such image is reported from anywhere else.[46]

B. *Makarbai*

Located 15 kms. north-west of Mahoba the village is notable for its Jaina temple. Of special significance here is the arrangement of three sanctums round a common *maṇḍapa*. The temple like others of its time, is ruined but *padmāsana* Jinas placed on the door-lintel leave us in no doubt about its dedication to Jaina faith.

C. *Rahilya*

Lying at a distance of 3 kms. south-west of Mahoba the sole surviving early temple here was dedicated to Sūrya. The antiquity of the place is taken back to king Rāhilavarman who is credited with having raised the shrine and from whom the village takes its name.[47] The King was great-grand-father of Dhaṇgadeva and ruled in the ninth century A.D.

Save for the sanctum and the *maṇḍapa* all else has fallen. Devoid of any sculptural carvings and destitute of the presiding deity inside, the temple truly presents a moving spectacle with its crumbling stones and weather-worn walls. A little further on a platform is lying an icon of dancing Gaṇeśa. On the outskirts of the village in a small temple of recent design, two excellent icons of Sūrya and Viṣṇu (Fig.14) have been accommodated. Both are accompanied by their respective *parivāra-devatās* and attendants.

Before passing on to another district the Śiva temple of Urwara may also be noticed. It is remarkable for having an upper storey which few temples of Central India possess. Built entirely of dry granite masonry, it has projecting *ardhamaṇḍapa* in three of its faces. The upper story is merely a sanctum cella with doorway to the south as well as north. Nothing has survived within though its Śaiva affiliation is beyond question. The walls are devoid of sculptural bands. The temple could be included among the earliest of Candella shrines (Fig.15).

VII JHANSI DISTRICT

A. *Baruāsāgar*

The only monument meriting our study here is a Viṣṇu temple within an enclosure standing outside the town beside the road leading from Jhansi to Chhatarpur. Occupying the high ground with sprawling fields all around and lording over the landscape, it casually attracts our attention even while passing in bus (Fig.16).

Though the sanctum no longer possesses the presiding deity, its dedication to

Viṣṇu is doubtless on the basis of his occupying the *lalāṭabimba* of the door-lintel. The tall, curvilinear and majestic *Śikhara* is intact and should be counted among the very few surviving *Śikharas* of Gurjara-Pratihāra period in the region.

B. *Burogaon*

Here is a classic case of chance playing a part in discovering the past. Some cowherds grazing in the vicinity of the village came upon a few sculptures on digging a mound. Systematic excavations at the site followed and were rewarded by the remains of some temples becoming bare. Actually, the site was little more than a small unpretentious mound of bricks and brick-bats on the bank of the revulet Utari-Chiglaua. The relics recovered included representations of Viṣṇu, Kārttikeya and Gaṇeśa. The excavations uncovered outline foundations of two temples, circular in plan with a projection to one side signifying probably the entrance part.[48] Among the antiquities recovered were two door-jambs and two door-lintels bearing figures of Garuḍa and Gaṇeśa respectively in the *lalāṭabimba*. On grounds of style the sculptures could be assigned to tenth-eleventh centuries A.D.

C. *Dariyāpurā*

Practically now a suburb of the city of Jhansi, here was found a hoard of 318 coins of Mahipāla and Madanavarman, bearing a legend on the obverse and Lakṣmī on the reverse.[49]

D. *Sarkar*

The village yielded as many as eighteen sculptures on excavations which now form part of Khajuraho Museum collection. Needing note among these are icons of Skandamātā, Vārāhī and Gaṇeśa.

Before passing on to another district, mention must be made of the palace museum housed in the heart of Jhansi which contains upwards of 500 sculptures and architectural members in varying states of preservation. A good many of them come from the famous Candella sites of Chandpur and Dudhahi located in Lalitpur district. The collection includes icons of all principal Brahmanical deities and Jain *Tīrthaṅkaras*. Hailing from Dudhahi-Chandpur, here we see certain *vyūha* icons of Viṣṇu like Damodara, Keśava, Nārāyaṇa and śrīdhara which are not easily available in North India. An eight-armed image of Viṣṇu in the palace Museum collection is particularly noteworthy.[49a]

VIII JALAUN DISTRICT

A. *Kalpi*

Tradition recognises it to be the place associated with one of the greatest poets of India, Maharshi Veda Vyās whose masterpiece, the *Mahābhārata*, is the longest epic of the world. Agreeing with this tradition, K.D. Bajpai holds that the epic came to be composed at Kalpi.[50] A mound near here known appropriately as Vyāsa mound has yielded numerous icons and art-relics. Among the images we could name are Gaja-Lakṣmī, Sūrya and Viṣṇu who now have an honoured place in the collection of Mahatma Gandhi Hindi Saṅgrahālaya, Kalpi. Note may be taken that terracotta figurines in hundreds are part of this collection but no proper record of their find-place has been maintained. It is difficult to say how many of them come from within the district. Nevertheless, they can not be left out of consideration since, in all likelihood, those coming from beyond must have been found in areas adjoining, thus not very far from the frontiers of Bundelkhand. Worthy of mention among these terracottas are fine figures of Mother-goddess, Mahiṣa-mardinī and Gaṇeśa. Accommodated beside them are two miniature lithic representations of stūpa in round, bearing four Buddha figures one on each side. Two of them sit in *dhyāna-mudrā* one in *bhūsparśa-mudrā* and the remaining one in *dharmacakra-mudrā*.

IX LALITPUR DISTRICT

A. *Banpur*

The village owes its name to the mythical demon Bāṇāsura who is supposed to have selected it as his capital. Situated in latitude 24.43°N. and longitude 78.45°E on the banks of the Jamini river at a distance of about 15 kms. from Mehroni, Banpur is better known now as *Atiśaya-kṣetra* of the Jains. Naturally, therefore, the sole surviving monument of our interest here is a Jaina temple curiously called *Bānpur Ke Liṅga.* As a matter of fact, it is *Sahasrakūṭa-Caityālaya* intended to symbolise 1008 auspicious qualities of a Jina's body. Modest though in size, with richly carved doorways and *jaṅghā* it has an appeal and charm of its own.

In its sprawling courtyard are scattered statues of Brāhmaṇical deities and Jaina worthies. A rare representation among these is that of Ādinātha with one *Caubīsī* on each side. Flanking the chief deity on either side are Pārśvanātha and Supārśvanātha making the whole composition signify the concept of triple *Caubīsī*, those of the past and future alongwith that of the present (Fig.17). At a distance, of 2 kms. to the north-east of this *Caityālaya*, a Gaṇeśa temple stands inside a neighbouring village. Only the chief image has claim to our notice. Endowed with no less than twenty-four arms, and holding a variety of weapons and objects, the god has found here a remarkable representation.

B. *Chandpur*

Forsaken, forgotten and forlorn, this religious centre of the Candellas is situated in latitude 24.30°N and longitude 78.18°E. The surviving monuments of this place stand close by the railway-line. Chandpur is 2 kms. away from the Dhaurra Station of Central Railway between Bina and Jhansi junctions. Bearing a deserted and dismal look, the place is worth-visiting at least once to have an idea of the devastation wrought by the neglect of man and notoriety of nature. Conspiring in collusion with Time, Nature proclaims her victory here.

Standing close to the railway-line and greeting the eye of passing passengers is a Brāhmaṇic temple locally known as "*Chhoti Belmari*". Save for the sanctum, still *in situ,* all else has fallen prey to Powers of destruction. Since the icon inside is missing, it is difficult to decide upon its dedication. Fine figures of Gajalakṣmī, Gaṇeśa and Kubera bedeck its *jaṅghā.*

A few yards to the south-west we come upon the remains of Sahasraliṅgeśvara temple locally called *Hajāriā Mahādeva.* Perhaps it was a *pañcāyatana* temple originally, since two small shrines still survive in the corners of its courtyard. The main temple enshrines a colossal *liṅga* which is beautifully carved with figures of Viṣṇu, Sūrya, Gaṇeśa and Gaurī, one in each side, in addition to the numerous miniature *liṅgas.* Obviously the temple was dedicated to the syncretic worship simultaneously paid to the five principal deities of Brāhmaṇic faith. Our view gets further weightage from the fact that some of the Smārta *liṅgas* (Fig.18) lie outside in the courtyard. The temple is ruined, except for the sanctum and the *maṇḍapa* which have wonderfully withstood the onslaughts of elements.

Facing the temple is a plain *maṇḍapa* in which a beautifully carved and fully caparisoned figure of Nandi is accommodated. The icon is unique since the artist has shown a boy-figure wearing a loin-cloth and *rudrākṣa* ornaments and attempting to climb the deity from its left side (Fig. 19).

The two subsidiary shrines, noted above, were dedicated to Viṣṇu and Gaṇeśa respectively. We need hardly mention that Chandpur must have been a prominent centre of *Smārta-Pūjā.* Mahendra Varma made a special study of the art of Chandpur,[51] and yet has neither noticed the Nandī icon, mentioned above, nor the cult of the Pentad, to which the Sahaśraliṅgeśvara temple was definitely dedicated.

Note may be taken that the Sahasraliṅgeśvara temple is situated near the embankment on a lake. At the end of the embankment stands the Varāha temple of which hardly any trace is left except for the rudely formed figure of boar bearing an inscription on the front of its pedestal. The record is dated in V.S.1205 (A.D. 1148) thus belonging to the reign of Madanavarman.[52] The boar is represented as stand ing on a tigerskin placing four feet over the four paws of the ferocious animal. Underneath the skin is carved a Nāga, Another inscription is engraved on a dedicatory pillar belonging to the temple of Śiva. The document is undated.

Walking a little to the south of this group, one comes upon "*Surru Marhia*", a Viṣṇu temple, identifiable only on the basis of his figure in the *lalāṭabimba* of the door-lintel on the sanctum doorway (Fig.20).

Going still further towards the south, one finds another group of temples locally known as *Baḍī Belmarī.* All of them turn out to be Vaiṣṇava temples. Save for their sanctums and shallow *maṇḍapas* nothing has survived. Chandpur has yielded rare representations of Nṛsiṁha and Vāmana. In one panel the former is shown fighting face to face with the demon Hiraṇyakaśipu. Very few icons of Lord Rāma we get, but from Chandpur several beautiful examples have come to light.

The Jaina group is located across the railway-line (Fig.21). Meriting mention here is only the temple of Śāntinātha, of which only the *maṇḍapa* is in situ. Another temple, dedicated perhaps to Ādinātha, is just a small room and the colossal *kāyotsarga* Jina is studded in the back-well, barely visible in darkness. Outside the room is lying a *lalitāsana* Ambikā. Our survey of Chandpur temples leaves us in no doubt that it was as good a temple-town as Khajuraho even though the temples here are far inferior in plan, elevation and ornamentation. It is not possible to ascertain whether these temples, like their Khajuraho counterparts, came into being through royal initiative only. A good deal of funds must have flowed in to finance the fashioning of these shrines. We are yet to come across the copper-plates or other records by which a part of revenue was made over to the temple priests for their maintenance. Finally Chandpur, like Khajuraho, lacked holiness of location and fails to find a place in the list of accepted *tīrthas* of early medieval times.

C. *Dudhahi*

Buried in a thick forest and situated beside a large sheet of water in latitude 24.25°N and longitude 78.24°E. Dudhahi is 6 kms. away from the Dhaurra railway station of Central Railway. Bearing a deserted and dilapidated look and making a moving spectacle, the remains of Dudhahi eloquently speak of its former glory and grace. Devoid now of an access to communication links, the village is believed to have stood on an important trade route in times past. Al-beruni has referred to it as a big city. A Jhansi inscription mentions a village Dugdhakupyā which could very well be taken for modern Dudhahi.[52a]

The chief group of temples is located to the east of the present village, commanding a fine view of the Rāmsāgar Lake that imparts a unique beauty to the place. (Fig.22) The survivals here consist of two temples with spires, two Śiva temples, one Varāha temple, two Jaina temples and a Brahmā temple. Of the Śiva temples only the sanctum stands *in situ*. The Varāha shrine is merely a pillared-canopy under which a huge statue of the Boar is accommodated. Cunningham speaks of two more Varāha images.[53]

Pārśvanātha was the presiding *tīrthaṅkara* in one of the Jaina temples, the other probably being dedicated to Ādinātha. Of the former only the sanctum survives, whereas in the latter a part of the *maṇḍapa* is also *in situ*.

The largest temple at Dudhahi is built on a peculiar plan, for which no parallel exists elsewhere. In form it is a cross with two long limbs and two short limbs meeting in the middle. The central portion consists of two rooms with a doorway between them and no provision for a back-wall against which a statue could be placed. The casing of the spire has fallen. The lintels, too, are missing and so also the pedestals. Cunningham thought it to be a Jaina temple wantonly wrecked by the hostile Brāhmaṇas but there is hardly any basis for such a conclusion. He, however, was all praise for its architectural design as well as structural symmetry and beauty.

Brahmā temples are very rare in India. The so-called Brahmā temple of Khajuraho, was originally dedicated to Viṣṇu. Dudhahi has one and probably it is the only available example in Bundelkhand. The porch, the *maṇḍapa* and the sanctum have survived. A three-headed, bearded figure of the God riding goose can be made out in the *lalāṭabimba* of the door-lintel, confirming the fact of its dedication to Brahmā. Lending further weight to our assumption is a pilgrim's record in which the Caturmukha and his consort Sāvitrī have been paid obeisance by the devotee. Of Śāktism nothing now survives at Dudhahi but in times past it was stronghold of the Yogini Kaula cult. Very few Causaṭha-Yoginī temples have so far been discovered, one such rare shrine stood at Dudhahi.[53a]

Interesting as it might seem, all the available inscriptions from Dudhahi belong to the Brahmā temple. Barring the one already noted, we get six more records[54] in nāgarī characters of about eleventh century A.D. put up by Devalabdhi, son of Kṛṣna and Āsarvvā and grand-son of the great Candrella king Yaśovarman. Heclaims to have erected the shrine. They give us Candrella, a Sanskritic variant of the name Candella. The presence of a prince of the royal family at Dudhahi marks it out as provincial head quarters of the Candella kingdom. The view gets greater weightage if Kṛṣṇa of the above records be taken identical with the master of minister Vācaspati, mentioned in Bhilsa stone inscription.[55] The minister claims to have killed a Śabara chief Siṁha and restored the local chiefs their lost dominions.

Be that as it may, Dudhahi records demonstrate that a few of the temples owed their erection to royal munificence. The second group of temples is located about a km. to the west of this group in the midst of a dense jungle. An eerie silence hangs around. They are known as *Baniyā Ki Bārāta* or Baniyas's marriage party with reference to the belief that Jaina Baniya Depat-Khepat financed their raising.

One more rare temple we get here is consecrated to the monkey god, Hanumāna, whose huge but headless statue presents a pathetic sight to the on-looker, standing, as it does, amid heaps of sculptures and architectural members that once constituted a shrine for it (Fig.23). A Jaina temple having been here can be clearly made out from the remains. Cunningham noted here a temple of Viṣṇu and a Varāha image in addition to what now survives.[56]

To the north of the main group within a brick-enclosure we come upon some more carvings. An icon of Gaṇeśa is unique in having the figure of Ardhanārīśvara at the top of its *prabhāvatī* flanked by Brahmā and Viṣṇu present with their consorts (Fig.24).

D. *Deogarh*

Located in latitude 24.32°N. and longitude 78.15°E the hill fort was known by a number of names in times long past. Inscriptions preserve at least three of them—*Srī Śāntinātha Tīrtha*, *Luacchagiri* and *Kīrtigiri*[56a]. Lying 30 kms. souh-west of the town of Lalitpur, the fort now is a well-known *tīrtha* of the Jainas who have continuously and consistently maintained their connection with it. Few places own such natural beauty in Bundelkhand as that of Deogarh. The lapping waters of the Betwā flowing with melodious tune, the sprawling verdant woods all round and the charming lofty hills characterising the landscape, create and radiate joy and purity towards the pilgrim searching salvation from worldly worries and woes.

Prominent among the monuments here is the Gupta temple (Fig.25) better known as the *Daśāvatāra* temple or *Sāgar Maṭha*. Known to be one of the earliest *śikhara* shrines of India and hailed as 'a gem of architecture', it was a rich treasure of sculptural art. Panels of indescribable beauty and immortal art depicting *Gajendra-mokṣa* (Fig.26), *Nara-Nārāyaṇa* (Fig.27), and *Śeṣaśāyī* Viṣṇu (Fig. 28) decorate its *jaṅghā*. Excavations carried out in the courtyard have yielded numerous sculptural representations of scenes from the *Rāmāyaṇa* and *Kṛṣṇalīlā*. Matchless in art and magnificent in mythological content, the temple marks out a significant stage in the history of religion being the earliest example of *pañcāyatana* variety.

The Jaina remains occupy the south-eastern portion of the Deogarh fort and are enclosed by an inner surrounding wall, the date of which is not known. The village of Deogarh is a few hundred yards west of the hill. When Cunningham came, the name was applied to the village only, the fort was known as Karnali. The fort is believed to have been built around 997 A.D. during the period of Kīrtivarman. To all appearances about 35 to 40 temples must have dotted the site, though the official number fixes the figure at 31. The size and shape vary greatly. Large temples with tall *śikharas* stand side by side with tiny cells not allowing an adult even to stand erect.

Only Nos. 12 and 15, dating from about ninth century A.D. possess artistic ornamentation (Figs. 29 & 30), the rest being severely plain save for the door-frame which is usually beautifully carved. The concept of North Indian temple architecture finds lithic translation only in case of two viz., No.12 and No.28. All others are what may be called hall temples consisting only of a square or rectangular room. An inscription engraved on the inner door-frame of temple No. 12 records that the place was known after the presiding deity of the temple as *Śrī Śāntinātha Tīrtha* in tenth century A.D.[57]

Earliest among the dated Deogarh inscriptions comes from the period of Bhoja Pratihāra put up on a pillar in temple No. 12. As a matter of fact, upwards of 400 inscriptions lie incised in the area covered by Jaina *tīrtha* complex[58] but a great many of them being dedicatory in nature we can hardly extract anything to our purpose. By far the largest number consists merely of a couple of words not extending upto even a normal dedication.

Of greater importance and deeper significance than the temples or inscriptions, therefore, are one thousand odd images accommodated inside as well as outside temples—a priceless but large legacy indeed. Part of this treasure is made up of Jina-icons and part of lesser worthies like Bharata Cakravarti, Bāhubali, Ācāryas, Upādhyāyas (Fig. 31) and Yakṣa-pairs. In the history of Jaina art and iconography, Deogarh, marks out many a milestone. In one of the Jina-icons, the artist has verily worked wonder. Image No. 13 has been hailed as highest-production of Indian genius to be classed with the world-famous Sarnath Buddha.[59] *Mānastambhas* constitute as good a source of Jaina art as the temples. One of them now shifted to the Dharmashala courtyard, is an excellent piece (Fig. 32). There are three steep flights of steps hewn in the cliff leading to the river Betwā. They are known as *ghāṭīs*. Rock-cut sculpture of Deogarh has been executed here, the earliest dating back to the Gupta period. Nāharghāṭī is notable among them being carved with twelve niches containing *lingas* and other deities. Sapta-mātṛkās accompanied by Vīrabhadra and Gaṇeśa make part of the sculpture here. The *Ghāṭī* also bears a record from Gupta times and two in shell characters.

To the south of the hill is situated the Rajaghāṭi or Kaṭighāti, preserving an inscription of king Kīrtivarman's time[60] and representations of Viṣṇu, Sūrya, Gaṅgā Yamunā, Lakṣmī and *Saptamātṛkās.* The third *Ghāṭī* has distinguishing epithet, Siddha-ki-Guphā and bears an inscription in later Nāgarī characters. The cave contains a few premitive drawings and, hard by, a figure of Mahiṣamardinī is carved. At Hāthi Darvājā figures of Pārśvanātha and a Yakṣa couple have been accommodated in niches. A *baoli* below the south-west corner of the fort also has some relics round it.

Buddhism, too, managed a foothold at Deogarh as is evident from the discovery of a single Buddha icon from the debris lying between the Jaina temples.

In south-west corner of the fort a temple dedicated to Varāha and assignable to the Gupta period struggles hard to survive.

At no stage of her history, Deogarh had the honour to be the capital of a kingdom. A prince of the imperial Gupta family is believed to have lived here and built the Daśāvatāra temple[61] but the evidence allows only of a conjecture. No prince of the Pratihāra and Candella houses had his headquarters here and in none of their copper-plates we have a reference. One wonders, therefore, who financed the making and maintaining of Deogarh shrines. We do have a Candella minister in one record who claims to have constructed the fort as well as a flight of steps but it is not clear if he did so in his private or official capacity.[62] Financing of the construction of fort involved fabulous funds. With Jainism we can walk on surer ground having numerous records to help us on the point. The whole of their huge holy complex owed absolutely to the faith and finances poured forth by pilgrims.

E. *Madanpur*

If name is any indication, the town was fathered by king Madanavarman. But an inscription of earlier period found at the place proves its prior existence.[63] Obviously, Madanavarman only renamed it.

Situated south-west of Mehroni at a distance of 36 kms., the original town of Madanpur stood to the north of the present one now dotted with Jaina temples. Collectively spoken of as *Pāñcamari*, being five in number, the temples offer us nothing save a few icons of ancient times. Walking a little further north, we come upon three Jaina temples known to be the oldest at the place. One of them has an inscribed pedestal with fish-symbol bearing the date V.S. 1212. Another preserves icons of Ādinātha, Candraprabhu, and Saṁbhavanātha and a long record. The document is dated V.S. 1206 and mentions Madanpur. Further, northwest to this trio, we have two more temples.

Brāhmaṇical monuments of Madanpur lie to the north-west of a large sheet of water. Their dedication to Viṣṇu and Śiva seems beyond question as Cunningham saw a colossal boar and a life-size bull lying close by.[64] Of the two, the smaller one has the record referring to the name *Jejākabhukti-maṇḍala* and victory of the Cāhamāna king Pṛthvīrāja over Paramardi in V.S. 1239. Curiously enough, the temples are called "*Alha's Kachahari*". A chief Ālhana Deva does figure in another inscription of the temple, though we cannot be sure of his being identical with the hero in tradition. The temples make a sorry spectacle since nothing survives save their *maṇḍapas*. A little to the north-east we have one more Śaiva shrine housing a ten-armed Śiva and ten-armed Cāmuṇḍā.

F. *Siron Khurd*

Siyadoni of bygone times, the village is situated in latitude 24.50°N and longitude 78.23°E at a distance of 18 kms. west-north-west of Lalitpur.

An early-medieval centre of industry and trade, it also served as seat of a Pratihāra governor at least for four generations as is attested by the solitary stones inscription found here.[65] The lengthy record is indeed a rare document demonstrating, as it does, the economic base and role of the temples in town life. Hardly any professional class of the town is missing in the record that remains a sort of memorial, containing twenty-seven donations made over the decades by traders and artisans providing for the requisite materials of worship in the temples, named in each case.

The second part of the inscription opens with an invocation to Lord Gaṇeśa and a certain Dāmodara is said to have founded a temple of Murāri now identified with a ruined structure at the neighbouring village Sategatto.

X PANNA DISTRICT

A. *Ajaygadh*

Difficult of access and destitute of inhabitants, this hill-fort is located 31 kms. west of Panna. The original name figuring in its records is 'Jayapura Durgga'[66] verily a city of victory.

Even while climbing one can not miss the crude carvings on the wall beside the path. The deities depicted include Hanumāna, Sūrya, Durgā, and panels containing twenty-four Jinas and *sapta-mātṛkās*. Near the Northern gate two large bodies of water bearing the name Gaṅgā-Yamunā greet our eye. Another tank Bhuteśvara is situated to the north-east. Scores of sculptures are piled here, the only notable being that of *śeṣaśāyī* Viṣṇu.

At the southern end is Paramāla Tāl. The chief temple complex of Ajaygadh was constructed here earning the curious local appellation "Chandeli Mahal". All the shrines here face west. Two of them have Lord Śiva as the presiding god and the other two have Viṣṇu. Shorn sadly of much of their majesty and magnificence, these temples consist only of their *maṇḍapas* and sanctums.

Ajaygadh is rich in rock-cut sculptures. Those executed near Tarhaoni Gate represent Aṣṭaśaktis, seven sitting, the eighth standing. They are rudely rendered with names inscribed below. Here we also have the record of Bhojavarman.

Among other sculptures, reference could be made to some Jinas, a cow suckling her young one, the goddess Ṣaṣṭhī holding a child and flanked by the pigs. Symbols of palm, seven in number, need particular note.

B. *Bilhagaon*

Approachable from Saleha in Pabai tehsil, the village stands on the banks of river Siddha. Appropriately enough, a temple of Siddhanātha Śiva attracts our eye to a hill towering the town. *Pañcaratha* in plan and elevation, the shrine with a *śikhara* a surviving, has also a *maṅḍapa*, an *antarāla* and a *garbhagṛha* as its organic parts.

C. *Mohendra*

Set in picturesque surroundings with beautiful backdrop of hills, the village is situated 47 kms. south of Panna town. Not a single shrine survives now but judging from the number of sculptures and architectural members littered in the lanes and by-lanes as well as vicinity of the village, a dozen or so must have dotted the site in times long past. Sorry becomes the spectacle when one comes upon beautiful pieces being trodden upon by the passers-by with utmost indifference and insensibility to their artistic importance or historic worth. A few fortunate ones have the honour to be huddled together under trees exposed to the elements all through the year.

The largest of collections is dumped inside a dark and dingy cell, hurriedly planned and clumsily constructed near a tank. Meriting mention the representations here are *yogāsana* Viṣṇu, *āliṅgāsana* Umā-Maheśa, Vāmana and Gaṇeśa. Door-jambs bearing river-goddesses and door lintels preserving Viṣṇu and Śiva in their *lalāṭabimbas* speak of several temples having been here.

Lying half-buried under earth in a by-lane is a massive but excellent icon of a Jina. Beneath a Neem tree on a mud-platform sit several yakṣa-pairs and other worthies.

To the east of the village inside a Kabirpanthi-*baoli*, some more Jaina relics have been built into the wall. Remarkable among these are a carving of Yakṣī Ambikā and another of *tīrthaṅkara* Pārśvanātha. Hard by stand some Kabirpanthi temples. Peeping out from their walls we see Brahmā, Sarasvatī and Trivikrama. No record of any period is known to have been recovered from here.

D. *Nachna*

Secluded, serene and sylvan in surroundings, Nachna is well-known for the temples of Pārvatī and *Caturmukha* Mahādeva, monumental memorials left by the Gupta architects and artists.

The Pārvatī temple is earlier of the two consisting originally of two stories, it retains now only the lower one. The sanctum is empty but has a highly ornate doorway. A covered *pradakṣiṇā patha* was unusual among the features of this temple. A few of the relics removed to the courtyard include a square pillar-base or capital with bold carving of four Viṣṇu *avatāras*, a *caturmukha*-Śivaliṅga and an image of *sukhāsana* Gaṇeśa. Earlier a door-lintel with Lakśmī in *lalāṭabiṁba* was found here.

The *Caturmukha* Mahādeva is one of the earliest *śikhara* temples of Northern India. We simply wonder at its successful resistance to onslaughts of elements over the ages. In itself this well state of preservation is a tribute to the makers of this majestic edifice (Fig. 33). The *Mukha-liṅga* occupying its *garbha-gṛha* will defy description. Boundless in beauty and matchless in grace, the piece is one of the finest products of Gupta genius (Fig. 34). The *śikhara*, though heavy and mighty, is curvilinear in design carved all over with *caitya*-window theme.

The authorship of the temples is difficult to ascertain. The twin inscriptions of Vākāṭaka feudatory Vyāghradeva of Ucchakalpa line found here hardly help in the matter. The endowment made for the maintenance of these temples is also missing. Most probably some local noble financed their erection as well as ornamentation. At present Nachna enjoys the prestige of being a place of pilgrimage for the people around who come especially to do obeisance to the *Caumukhanātha*.

XI SAGAR DISTRICT

A. *Ābchand*

About 30 kms. west of Sagar town on Jabalpur Road beside the bank of river Gadheri, Ābchand has a large legacy of prehistoric art. High above in hills the caves contain numerous paintings going back to the days before the dawn of history. To quote K.D. Bajpai, "The Paintings can be called prehistoric in the sense that even in historical periods, some of the aboriginal authors of them have been leading a sort of prehistoric life."[67] Of immense interest for us are some religious symbols such as Tree with sun and star, Cross, *Vajra*, *Svastika*, Hand-palm and *Cakra*. (Sketch No. 2).

B. *Bhenswāhā*

This is a new discovery made in course of explorations undertaken for the present work. The village has hardly any inhabitants. It is absolutely abandoned. Here stands a tottering temple, silent and solitary witness to a bygone period of glory and greatness. About 25 kms. north of Bina Railway junction, it was raised right on the bank of river Naren. Built entirely of buff coloured sandstone, and badly ruined beyond possibility of reconstruction, only part of its gateway, *garbha-gṛha* and *Śikhara* survive. Wild trees have shot through its walls and floors and the end of its existence is merely a question of time, unless the Archaeology Department awakes to its importance coming for rescue and relief (Fig. 35).

Though the sanctum is destitute of its presiding deity, its Vaiṣṇava dedication seems certain on the basis of a bold representation of *Govardhanadhārī* Kṛṣṇa occupying a pilastered niche of the outer wall (Fig. 36). Among other art-relics, representations of Viṣṇu, Kārttikeya, Mahiṣamardinī and Śiva within a *caityagavākṣa* are worthy of mention. A Sati-pillar record does survive near at hand but it cannot provide any clue to the date of this temple. On grounds of style and architecture, its tentative period could be eleventh century A.D.

C. *Bhapel*

About 10 kms. west of Sagar town the village is known for its painted rock-shelters. Bearing upon our theme we have here Buddhist symbols *Nandipada* and *Tri-ratna* (Sketch No. 2).

D. *Bharcha*

The village is a new discovery 25 kms. off Bina town. None of the shrines has survived. Only a few sculptures lie huddled on a platform in the heart of the village. Identifiable among them are *Nṛtta* Gaṇeśa, Viṣṇu, Brahmā with his consort and riding his mount. A curious carving is that of Lakulīśa, the Śaiva saint (Fig. 37). In the absence of inscription, the antiquities could be assigned to the end of early-medieval age on the basis of style.

E. *Eran*

Located in latitude 24.6°N. and longitude 78.15°E. on the bank of the river Bina, Eran lies 58 kms. north-west of Sagar town. It is the oldest inhabited among all historical places of the district. Airīkīṇa of yore, it commenced its career in history as a large chalcolithic settlement, sometime in the second millennium before Christ. Excavations revealed an earthen citadel wall that protected the township in those days. A big hoard of punch-marked coins—3268 in number—also came to light. Of immense interest are two inscribed earthen seals assignable to early centuries of Christian era. One bearing a figure of Gajalakṣmī has the legend: *Airikiṇe Gomika Viṣayādhikāra* and the Second has: *Mahādaṇḍanāyaka Siṃhanāndi*[67]a

In historic times it had the honour to become '*Svabhoganagara*' of Samudragupta, of whom it preserved the only record,[68] other than Allahabad *praśasti*. Majority of the monuments was made during the Gupta period and stand upon some high ground near the river. The ruins testify to the existence of numerous Vaiṣṇava temples having graced the complex but nothing survives of them now save the lower courses of masonry and four columns. The solitary surviving shrine has a massive and mighty figure of the Lord. Close by stands the colossal Boar bearing the record of Huṇa king Toramāṇa.[69] Facing the temple has been planted the towering pillar of Buddha Gupta[70] with the figure of Garuḍa crowning it. Among the relics still remaining here is an icon of Nṛsiṃha.

Of breathtaking beauty are two images representing Nṛvarāha and Nṛsiṃha now in the collection of Sir H.S. Gaur Archaeological Museum, Sagar. The former is inscribed showing its dedication by two devotees—Maheśvaradatta and Vārāhadatta.

The earliest among Eran inscriptions comes from a Śaka chief Śrīdharavarman[71] and is incised on a stone pillar memorial now lying under a tree near Pehlejpur.

Interestingly, this very pillar was chosen later to receive the earliest record of Sati in the world[72] when Goparāja, the faithful feudatory friend of Bhānugupta fell fighting here.

F. *Mahuṭā*

This also is a new site. It is actually an island having a lovely location causing cleavage in the river Betwā. It is 10 kms. west of Bina town commanding a wide view.

The place is littered with icons and architectural members constituting temples in times past. Noteworthy among them is a stone slab carved in all four faces with Śaiva deities. Gaṇeśa and Cāmuṇḍā are easily recognisable. A couple of door lintels contain Viṣṇu and Śiva in their *lalāṭabimbas*, Navagrahas and Mahiṣamardinī also make an appearance. The material is roughly assignable to the end of twelfth century A.D.

G. *Mandi Bamora*

It is a small station between Bina and Vidisha on the Central Railway. A couple of yards from the station, a tall but skeletal Śaiva shrine is visible of which the sanctum, *śikhara* and *maṇḍapa* survive though in bad shape. Facing the temple, a Nandi may be noticed. All around lie numerous relics broken away from the parent structure.

H. *Narayaoli*

Lying 22 kms. west of Sagar, the village has a hill in its vicinity which is notable for its painted cave-shelters. The Siddha-Bābā cave has paintings bearing upon our theme.

I. *Rehli*

About 39 kms. from Sagar, the town has an early-medieval temple of Sūrya. Absolutely ruined, no idea can we get of its shape or size. However, the town did yield Brahmanical sculptures such as Sūrya, Harihara, Vaiṣṇavī, Lakśmī-Nārāyaṇa, Umā-Maheśa, Nāga-pair, and Gaṅgā-Yamunā.[73]

In addition to the sites, covered above, Sagar district has many more. Pali, Pithoria, Deori, Piparia, Bina, and Bada Marha are a few more among them needing notice. The lithic record of Kalcuri King Śaṅkaragaṇa was found at Sagar town isself.[74]

XII TIKAMGARH DISTRICT

A. *Budaur*

About 9 kms. off Palera, a village on Chhatarpur—Tikamgarh road, it is a new site from where some *tīrthaṅkara* images were recovered. Remarkable among these are two representations of *kāyotsarga* Ādinātha with a *caubīsī* in *parikara*, and an icon of Neminātha. About a km. away on a hillock is located a shrine known as *Caturbhuja* temple. Here the relics include representation of *Yogāsana* Viṣṇu, *Rāvaṇānugrahamūrti* of Śiva and a four-armed Viṣṇu.

B. *Kundeshvara*

At a distance of 8 kms. from Tikamgarh on Lalitpur road, the place is now a pilgrimage centre. K.D. Bajpai discovered here sculptures representing Saptamātṛkas, Sūrya, Harihara, and Viṣṇu of the Candella times.[75] An inscribed *tīrthaṅkara* icon was also recovered of the year 1196. A small collection of antiquities is housed in Pāpat museum here, named in memory of the artist who carved a good many of the icons inside.

C. *Khumanganj*[76]

About 5 kms. to the north-west of Budaur, the place is also a new discovery. Relics lie littered in the village. A Hanumāna temple on the bank of river Sandani has number of icons, notable being Umā-Maheśa, Gaṇeśa, and Lakṣmī. In Mātā-Mandira are accommodated Viṣṇu and his incarnations. Some more are housed inside a Śaiva shrine outside the village. The material is datable to eleventh century A.D.

D. *Markhera*

Famous for its sun-temple the village is situated on Tikamgarh-Newari road very near to village Bawari. The temple stands outside the village on a *jagatī* facing west. Consisting of a maṇḍapa, an *antarāla* and *a garbhagṛha,* it possesses beautiful curvilinear *śikhara* which is perfectly preserved with all its crowning members (Fig. 38). The sanctum, as also the *śikhara,* are *pañcaratha* in plan as well as elevation. The *śikhara* is ornamented all over with *caitya* window motif. The door-frame of sanctum is profusely ornamented. Sculptural bands bedeck the *jaṅghā* in which are present the figures of Skanda, Kubera, Balarāma, Paraśurāma, Gaṇeśa, and Varāha. In well state of preservation, the temple has been placed in Pratihāra period.[77]

Some very interesting facts come into focus from the brief and hurried survey done above of the religious remains in the realms of our study. Buddhist monuments are few and far between for the ancient as well as early-medieval period. As regards the period immediately preceding and following the Christian era, we should remember that Mahästūpas of Sanchi and Bharhut stood hard by the Bundelkhand boundaries, absorbig much of its fervour and faith and new centres had no chance to survive in their vicinity. As for the early-medieval period we have some isolated pockets of Buddhism when it was well on the way to decline.

Most of the sites show coexistence of Brāhmaṇism and Jainism. Numberwise the appeal of Jainism may have been narrow but even these handful of followers held on to their faith and the sect fared better than Buddhism. The reasons are worth investigating.

A good number of icons, antiquities and edifices cannot be attributed to royal patronage. They owe their fashioning and financing to the lay faithfuls who must have prospered to an unprecedented scale to incur the expenditure. For Jainism we have profuse epigraphic evidence, at least, from Deogarh but for Brāhmaṇism we possess hardly any. Of one thing we could be pretty sure. Trading class was not Jaina invariably and Siyadoni stone record speaks volumes on the point.

A considerable section of society must have belonged to the class of artists and architects in early-medieval period. It must have been a new class since the number required earlier was much less in comparison if we go by the available archaeological remains. There was no differentiation among the sculptors and architects on the basis of sects. The artist used to be master of the iconographic texts, be they Jain, Buddhist or Brahmaṇical. At Khajuraho such is the likeness among temples and their ornamentation that telling a Jain temple from a Brahmaṇical one, solely on the basis of outer facades, is well-nigh impossible.

REFERENCES

1. *Brahmāṇda Purāṇa*, 2.16.19.
2. Kale M.R.: *Bāṇa's Kādambarī*; op. cit., p. 26.
3. E.I., I, No. 20.
4. Agrawal K.L.:

   विन्ध्यक्षेत्र का ऐतिहासिक भूगोल

   शोधप्रबन्ध, सागर विश्वविद्यालय, पृ. 3;

   In B.P., p. 2———Sandravatis of Ptolemy has been identified with Bundelkhand but the basis for doing so is nowhere given.
5. **रघुवंश** 6.48, काशी संस्कृत ग्रन्थमाला 51, चौखम्बा संस्कृत सीरीज, वाराणसी, 1961.
6. Pande, R.B.: op. cit., Ch. IV, No. 17.
7. Ibid. ch. V, No. 48.
8. A.S,R., XXI, pp. 19-20.
9. **श्रीमद्वाल्मीकीय रामायणम्** 54.43. पण्डित पुस्तकालय, प्रथमावृत्ति, काशी, 1951, पृ. 316

   प्रहृष्टकोयष्टिककोकिलस्वनैर्विनोदयंतं च सुखं परं शिवम् ।

   मृगेश्च मतैर्बहुभिश्च कुन्जरैः सुरम्यमासाद्यसमावागामम् ॥
10. A.S.R., XXI, P. 12.
11. Ibid. P. 14.
12. कूर्मपुराण, उत्तरार्ध, 36. । तथा ॥, संस्कृति संस्थान; बरेली ।

    अ. रुद्रकोटिरितिख्यातं रुद्रस्य परमेष्ठिनः ।

    ब. कालन्जरं महातीर्थं रुद्रलोके महेश्वरः

    कालन्जरं भजन्देवं तत्र भक्तप्रियो हरः ॥
13. A.S.R., XXI, p. 21;

    Ptolemy is believed to have known the place Kanagora, though the identification could be farsetched. Similarly Firishta's belief that the fort was founded by king Kedāra stands uncorroborated. Colonel Pogson was of the view that seven gates of the forts indicated the fact of the place having been sacred to the Sauras. The hill was hailed as *Ravicitra* being allied to sun-worship. For all the above views, not worthy of our credence, we are indebted to B.P., pp. 80-81.
14. I.A. XXXVII, p. 135.
15. महोबाखण्ड, अध्याय I, 164, (नागरी प्रचारिणी ग्रन्थमाला-2, सम्पादक: श्यामसुन्दरदास, संवत् 1976.

कहौ महातम विप्रवर, कालिंजर जब कौन ।
जहां होत अस्नान के करत देवपुर गौन ।।

15A R.S. pp. 24 and 37. It is interesting to learn that the place in his time was as much sacred to Viṣṇu as to Śiva.

16. A.S.R., XXI, p. 34 ff.
17. E.I., XIX, No. 2.
18. E.I., I, p. 133.
19. Ajaygadh Rock Inscription of Candella Kirtivarman, E.I., XXX, No, 17.
20. Supra-Note 18.
21. महोबाखण्ड, अध्याय 1, 124 काशिय तजि कालिंजर आइय ।
चार मास सिय तंह विलमाइय ।।
22. M.P. Chronicle, Bhopal, May 14, 1975, p. 5.
23. A.S.R., XXI, p. 18.
24. Ibid. p. 58.
25. Gupta S.P. and Ramchandran K.S. (Ed.) : *Aspects of Indian History and Archaeology*, B.R. Publishing House, Delhi, 1977, p. 126.
26. In fact, a village named Pahra, about 14 miles from Mahoba has the alternative name of Khajuraho.
27. महोबाखण्ड, अध्याय 2,28 तथा 54
पच्चासी मढ़ देवजुत तव तुव पातक जाय ।
निकट-निकट सरसीरचौ निकट निकट पर बाग ।।
पच्चासीमढ़ देव सव वाहन जुत त्रिपुरारि ।
विसुकर्म्मा कौ रचत ही लगी न घटिका चारि ।।
28. Pande, R.B. : op. cit, ch. V, No. 48, V. 43.
29. E.I., I, No. 19(IV).
30. The chronology as well as dating of the Khajuraho temples is based on the conclusions of Shri Krishna Deva, given in his article entitled 'Temples of Khajuraho in Central India' in A.I., No. 15, 1959, pp. 43-64.
31. E.I., I, No. 19(V).
32. A.S.R., II, p. 426.
33. Ibid. p. 428.
34. Deva, Shri Krishna: op. cit., p. 43.
35. The credit for discovering the image should go to the Gajarath Mahotsava Samiti of Jain Society at Damoh. Dr. K.C. Jain and Shri P.C. Singhai, its members were good enough to get the photograph of the icon for my notice.
36. The inscription was read by my teacher, Shri S.D. Misra, Reader, Deptt. of A.I.H.C. & Archaeology, University of Saugar. It contained the well-known Buddhist formula "Ye dhammā hetu prabhavā . . . ."
37. SA..R., XXI, Pt. II, pp. 164-65.
38. Ibid. p. 167.
39. Ibid. pp. 160-63.
40. E.I., XXXI, No. 27, L. 1 Devānampiyasa Piyadasino Aśokarājasa . . . . .
41. I.A.A.R., 1963-64, p. 87.
42. Ibid.
43. A.S.R., II, p. 439 ff.
44. I.A., XXXVII, p. 137.

44A B.P.P. 96.

45. To Shri S.K. Chourasia, a Petrol Pump owner, I owe a debt of gratitude for the study of antiquities and art-relics at Mahoba.

46. A detailed study of this icon I have done in my paper entitled, "A Unique Image of Cāmuṇḍa published in *Prāchya-Pratibhā*, Vol. V, **No. 2, (July. 1977) Bhopal, pp. 43-44.**
47. A.S R., II, p. 441.
48. I.A.A.R., 1965-66, p. 64.
49, I.A.A.R., 1962-63, p. 76.
49A B.P., p. 46.
50. उत्तरप्रदेश की ऐतिहासिक विभूति, लखनऊ, 1957 पृ. 10.
51. वर्मा, महेन्द्रः चाँदपुर और दुधई की चन्देली कला और संस्कृति शोधप्रबन्ध कानपुर विश्वविद्यालय, 1973.
52. A.S,R., X, p. 97.
52A B.P., p. 87.
53. Ibid. p. 93.
53A Sharma R.K.: *Temple of Causaṭha-yoginī at Bherghat*, Agam Kala, Delhi, 1978, p. 32.
54. I. A., XVIII, p. 236.
55. E.I., XXIX, No. 3, p. 21.
56. A.S.R., X, pp. 94-95.
56A E.I., XVIII, No. 15.
57. Bruhn, Clause: *The Jina Images of Deogarh*, Leiden, 1969, p. 70.
58. *Aspects of Indian History and Archaeology*, P. 118.
59. Bruhn, Clause: op cit., p. 87.
60. E.I., XVIII, No. 15.
61. Agrawal, P.K : *Gupta Temple Architecture*, Prithvi Prakashan, Varanasi, 1968 pp. 38 39.
62. Deogarh Rock Inscription of Kirtivarman, V. 7, I.A., XVIII, p. 239.
63. A.S.R., XXI, Pt. II, p. 171.
64. Ibid. p. 174.
65. E.I., I, No. 21, pp. 162-79.
66. A.S.R., XXI, p. 46.
67. Bajpai, K.D.: *Sagar Through the Ages*, Sagar, 1967, p. 1.
67A B.P., pp. 74-75.
68. C.I.I., III (Revised), No. 2.
69. Pande R.B. : op. cit., ch. IV, No. 31.
70. C.I.I., III, (Revised), No. 39.
71. C.I.I., IV, pt. II, No. 119, pp. 605-611.
72. C.I.I., III (Revised), No. 43.
73. I.A.A.R., 1959-60, p. 70.
74. C.I.I., IV, pt. I, No. 35, pp. 174-76.
75. I. A.A.R., 1963-64, p. 35.
76. The Credit for discovering Budaur and Khumanganj should go to Shri Dasharath Jain of Chhatarpur.
77. Deva, Shri Krishna: op. cit., p. 44.

4

Pre-Classical Period

(Save for the solitary Aśokan Edict, Bundelkhand offers absolutely nothing by way of written records. Our study therefore, has to be done in the dim light afforded by the pre-and-early-historic paintings and pottery, punch-marked coins and anthropological research into the life and society of primitive tribes and traditions. Sources, such as these can hardly supply us the data to reconstruct the past in terms of historical certainty but we have no option in the matter. This very paucity and uncertainty of the evidence compels us to cover and condense the long period of a millennium and a half in a single chapter.)

The dawn of history is generally dated to a point at which we can place the first of available written records, naming the period beyond as pre-history. The case of India is classic in having a long period of rich and rare literature without handing down a single written record. The period so intervening is termed as proto-history. Bundelkhand being the central region of India cannot be an exception to this general scheme and the evidence coming down to us speaks of a fairly long period of pre and proto-historic life of man. As we are chiefly concerned with the birth and growth of religious consciousness in him, we should clarify at the very outset what meaning do we take of the word 'religion.'

In common parlance the word is sometimes wrongly equated with its corresponding Sanskrit term 'Dharma' which is richer in meaning and deeper in significance than its English counterpart. Religion stands for certain characteristic types of beliefs, practices, feelings, moods and attitudes[1] whereas Dharma is taken to be a mode of life or a code of conduct that regulates a man's work and activities as a member of society enabling him not only to attend his mundane obligations but also to strive for Final Liberation through it.[2] In current usage, however, the word religion is understood in the sense of a cult, communicating a system of religious belief and worship[3] the practical expression of the religious experience. The belief in a super-human power is basic to the concept and if a section of society offers worship to a host of gods and goddesses, the other visualises Him as One and Supreme suffering no equal. In the present context, Taylor's definition of religion comes very close to our idea—the belief in spiritual being.[4]

The origins of religious consciousness in the early man of our area are difficult to date or describe. No contemporary evidence is avilable or ever likely to be available on the point. At the most we can merely speculate on the subject in the light of anthropological studies done on the present primitive communities dwelling partly in Bundelkhand and partly around.

Surviving from the second millennium B.C. into second millennium A.D. are several primitive tribes, fast vanishing from the face of Bundelkhand with the march of science and technology upto the very outskirts of their settlements, seeking to work a silent change in the mode of their age-old life and merging them in the teeming millions of India. The fact of their hoary antiquity has been adequately established in one of the earliear chapters.[5] A good deal of Hinduism they have absorbed by now and so, a clear clue to the earliest religious consciousness is difficult to obtain from them. Of one thing, however, we could be pretty sure. The present social set-up of these primitive tribes gives ample indication of the special status enjoyed by woman in ages gone by. One could very well postulate that society all over the world was matriarchal as long as the physical fact of paternity was not known. Studies done about Australian aborigines have established a firm foundation for such a postulation since they were found to be ignorant of the relation between paternity and sexual intercourse.[6] That such ignorance should have survived so long is the strongest evidence in favour of the universal priority of female to male descent. The aborigines of Bundelkhand cannot be exception to this generalisation.

Once we accept this hypothesis, Margaret Murray's theory about the origin of religion based on it cannot be lightly dismissed though we have no records to authenticate it[7]. She opined that in the distant past, small societies consisting only of women and children came into existence as a natural corrollary to the difference of sexes—the women requiring safety and quiet during pregnancy period and the infants requiring protection and nourishment until strong enough to protect themselves. The early man failed to understand the phenomenon of woman producing a child from her body without any apparent cause and once the child was born, producing food from her body to nourish it, also without any apparent reason. This Creation or Transmission of Life by women appeared mysterious to him and to this phenomenon may be traced the origins of religion. It is not without significance that in almost all the ancient religions belief in a female deity long precedes the male one and viewed in this context the theory acquires weight and worth.

Coming back to our area of study the conclusion of Marshall, a pioneer scholar-archaeologist, is well worth quoting on the subject, "In no country in the world has the worship of the Divine mother been from time-immemorial so deep-rooted and ubiquitous as in India."[8] Note has been taken already that Śabaras and Pulindas were among the earliest inhabitants of Bundelkhand. R.G. Bhandarkar believed that Durgā was their goddess and resided permanently on the Vindhya mountains.[9] The very name Vindhyavāsinī is enough to drive home the early manifestation and strong associations of the mother-cult with the people and places of Bundelkhand. Earn excavations have yielded numerous terraootta female figurines representing the mother-goddess.

Nevertheless, the theory of Margaret Murray cannot be the sole or whole explanation of the birth of religious consciousness in society. Factors other than Transmission of life must have been at work making the people aware of a super-human power passing their comprehension. To name a few, fertility, fruitfulness and fear of the mysterious nature, the shock of death or rejoicing over the success of killing an animal gradually sowed the seeds of magic and rituals which are regarded the predecessors of human religion[10] and their role cannot be absolutely ruled out.

The origins of magic are traced to the material needs of the primitive man animals in particular. Animals were both the staff of life and the chief adversary of man. An idea arose in consequence that the hunters and the hunted belonged, as it were, together leading to mimesis and dances in which the hunter thought he was assuming the nature and life of the animal. As he was often able to kill his prey by imitating it, so he thought he could turn himself into an animal and thus have power over other animals. Power over images or imprints gives power over the person is a conception observed to be common to the primitive mind.[11]

It is interesting and worth recording in this context that the earliest among the rock-paintings of Bundelkhand contain certain figures wearing animal masks. A painting in Narayaoli rock-shelter shows a horse-rider wearing animal mask closely resembling the face of an horse. At Ābchand we come across human figures putting on animal masks and holding sword and shield.

The fact becomes further interesting and acquires profound significance when we see that the pre-historic practice of putting on animal masks did not die out but maintained a firm hold on human mind well into the historic as well as contemporary times. The war-dress of Rākṣaṣas who went to the battle-field following Rāvaṇa had faces of the tiger, the horse, the camel, the stag and such others of their species.[12] It goes without saying that these were Rākṣasa soldiers wearing various masks to terrify their opponents. To come to the contemporary evidence, the Kui tribesmen continue to wear animal masks representing wild animals on festive occasions and while participating in communal dances. Of course, the connection of this practice with creation of magic intended for acquiring power is long forgotten and might as well be missing in the Rāmāyaṇa reference, but the original association of the two deserves a little of our credence.

Perhaps the practice had another origin also. This we can read into totemistic beliefs of the early tribes, a phenomenon found all the world over prior to the dawn of history. A totem has been defined as a class of material objects which a tribe regards with superstitious respect believing that there exists between it and every member of the class an intimate and altogether special relation.[13] The early totems were not only as a rule edible animals but also the animals eaten by the totem clans which carried their names. Available accounts and studies about the totems of Australian, Red Indians and African tribes reveal that after domestication of animals and adoption of agriculture, totems ceased to be chief means of subsistence and came to be regarded as ancestors.[14] The Bundelkhand tribes offer a curious explanation of the totemistic names of the septs into which they are now divided. Referring to an incident believed to have occurred ages ago in the life of their ancestor or priest while worshipping, they connect the name with the animal, tree or the object from which the sept name is derived. As a matter of fact, the totem animals or plants have ceased to be revered on their own merits as ancestors or kinsmen, so the need arose for rationalising or at least explaining the sept name or sanctity attaching to the totem by associating it with the gods[15]. But the fact of totem animals having in the hoary past been the means of subsistence is clearly reflected in the myths and legends of origin which some tribes narrate and retain the faint memories of their farthest past. Hardly any district of Bundelkhand is devoid of some Gonds and in the myth relating to their origin they disclose—

> Hither and thither all the Gonds were scattered in the jungle, Places and Hills and Valleys were filled with these Gonds. Even trees had their Gonds. How did the Gonds conduct themselves ? Whatever came across them they must need kill it and eat it ; They made no distinction. If they saw a jackal they killed and ate it ; no distinction was observed ; they respected not antelope, sambhar and the like,
>
> ....They devoured raw and ripe things ;
> They did not bathe for six months together :
> They did not wash their faces properly, even on dunghills
> they would fall down and remain
> Such were the Gonds born in the beginning[16].........

Of course, the whole of this Gond myth cannot be taken at its face value since a good deal was added and amplified after they came into contact with the higher Hindu civilization, as can be easily made out from Lord Mahādeva figuring in it. But part of the legend, particularly the wild state that they lived in, could be accepted as genuine memory when supporting evidence from other sources is available. Among the current totemistic names of some Gond septs Netam (dog) and Warkara (wild cat) could be mentioned.[17] Among the Bhils we have Mori (peacock), Matsya (fish) and Ghodmarya (horse-killer) and Sanyan (cat)[18].

When the totem animals came to be regarded as ancestors and a sort of sanctity was imparted to them, the most common features of behaviour towards the totem animal became a prohibition of the species as food and a certain respect for the animal in its natural state. The surest sign of the prevalence of totemism in our area are certain rock-paintings of high antiquity in which human figures wearing animal masks perform ceremonial dances, which are taken to typify sympathetic magic or to dramatize clan legends.[19]

Totemism is specially remarkable for its striking contrast to all anthropomorphism or anthropopathism where the spirits or gods who are venerated, respected or feared are thought of or described as partly or wholly human and with human traits.[20] A good many of the Zoomorphic deities of Brāhmaṇism owe for their birth to the contact between the primitive tribes and Aryans, when the totem animals were given accommodation in the hierarchical scheme of Hindu gods and also an account of their origin and character.[20]

Be that as it may, factors, other than those covered above, must have contributed to the birth of religious beliefs and consciousness in the early society of Bundelkhand but in the absence of evidence pure speculation on the subject would be idle and irresponsible.

Among the earliest cults, the commonest most probably were connected with worship of trees. Here again the element of totemism steps in and we have septs among the Bhils named after Jāmania (Eugenia Jambolana), Rohini (Soymida febrifuga), Avalia (Phyllanthus emblica), Meheda (Terminalia Beleria) and among the Gonds Tekam (Teak) Markam (Mango), Irpachi (Mahua) and Tumrachi (Tendu).[22] It is difficult to say whether the same circumstances motivated the man to adopt trees as totem which worked in case of animals being accorded that status, but this much can be conceded that the trees were the earliest among objects receiving the reverence of people, perhaps the first ones. Various must have been the reasons They offered the early man food as well as fuel and shelter. Shakti M. Gupta, who has done an intensive study of the subject believes that tree-cults of India could be understood not only in terms of food, shade, and medicine that the trees offered but also in inviting clouds and providing water for the agricultural economy.[23] The idea could be true of the historical period but its validity for the earliest manifestation of tree-worship—particularly among the primitive communities—could well be doubted. Just as animal totems of the prehistoric past contributed Zoomorphic deities to Brāhmaṇism, and Buddhism and Jainism at a later stage, so also the tree-totems found accommodation in the Hindu civilization, for, we have number of plants and trees apotheosized by the Aryan ideologues. What precisely was the contribution of Bundelkhand in this regard it is difficult to ascertain but it must have been considerable if we view the subject in the light of anthropological studies which reveal that even now the 'Bura Deo' or the Great God of these aborigines is believed by them to reside in a Saj tree (Boswellia Serrata) and obeisance done to Him is actually done to the tree.[24]

Working by the same logic one could go further and read a few of the earliest religious beliefs and practices in those of the aborigines. A good many of these seem to have survived from the pre-historic past among the Gonds and such of their bretheren as were absorbed over the ages in the expanding empire of Brāhmaṇisation must have carried the old deities contributing to the bulging Brāhmaṇic pantheon. Apart from Bura Deo, already noted, a great many of Gond gods appear to be principally implements and weapons of chase, an animal or two, deified human beings, power presiding over village destiny, crops and epidemics, spirits of forefathers and creatures of chase.[25] The origins of a host of Brāhmaṇic gods and goddesses have to be traced to these pre-Aryan and non-Aryan Lords, for whom were fabricated and invented countless myths and stories emphasising their subordination to the Hindu trinity of historic period.

Gradual must have been the penetration of the Aryans in this region. Long before the birth of Buddhism and Jainism, numerous hermitages of Aryan Ṛṣis sprang into existence along the river banks and up the mountain fastnesses. Alluring and inviting as were the sylvan surroundings of the Vindhyan range. They naturally offerred an ideal seat to the sages in search of the Divine. In one of the Jātaka stories, we come across the name of Śarabhaṅga, a former commander-in-chief of Kāshī, "Who built his hermitage somewhere in the Vindhya region on the Godavari."[26] Identical account we get of Bavari, a chaplain of King Prasenajita of Kosala.[27] The Godāvari of the Lesser Epic has been taken to stand for a stream near Citrakuta in Banda district.[28] A road is known from early Jaina literature which connected Rājagṛha with Pattithāna and must have gone through the region of our study.[29] The ascetics were divided into many classes, most notable being orthodox and heterodox or as the *Kalpasūtra* refers *Bambhannayeṣu* and *Paribbayanayeṣu.*[30] The Ṛṣis may or may not have worked with the zeal of a missionary but the *Paribrājakas* and *Samanas* certainly did, actively propagating the message of their master and a bulk of Bundelkhand was Aryanised in the process with the passage of time. In traditional accounts the time of this interaction is taken to be the end of Kṛta Age when Aryans were "in occupation of the whole of north India including the regions beyond the Vindhyas and the Narmadā down to the Tāpti and the Satpurās."[31] Pusalkar places the colonization of Bundelkhand about the time of Paraśurāma (2550-2350 B.C.). Kauśika, the son of Yādava King Vindarbha and King of Cedi, should in that case be regarded among of the earliest Aryan Kings.[32] But such an early date for Aryanisation of the area is not at all warranted in view of the unimpeachable archaeological evidence. The absence of P.G. ware and the presence of microliths associated with red painted sherds and followed by iron and N.B.P. ware at Eran and Tripuri indicate beyond a shadow of doubt that these parts were Aryanised rather late.

There is another point pertinent to this process of penetration which must not be lost sight of. The geography and topography of the region being what it is, complete absorption and Aryanisation never took place at any time and going by the sizable section of aborigines constituting Bundelkhand people even now, the percentage must be many times more in the hoary past we are working in[33]. What seems fairly probable is that the routes running through the region and settlements coming up beside the river courses must have led to the conversion of the people in the vicinity while a large chunk continued with the old ways. In this perspective we can rightly view the statement of emperor Asoka when he comes out with a sweeping generalisation—"And there is no country except that of the Yavanas where there are not these orders namely, the Brāhmaṇa and the Śramaṇa a section."[34]

A long course of social interaction that followed witnessed the conquest of the conquerors. This fact finds clear reflection in the *Atharva Veda* of which says A.L. Basham, "It possesses an atmosphere of simple animism and sympathetic magic and seems to reflect a lower cultural level than that of the *Ṛgveda* deriving from the plebein religion of the Aryans and containing many non-Aryan element.[35] B.C. law echoes the opinion observing "It was, indeed, through Atharvanic process that an alliance between secular Brāhmaṇism and all primitive cults was possible."[36] We do not mean that this *Veda* reflects only what happened in the area of our study or it came to be composed in course of social interaction we are talking of. Nobody can be that precise on the point since there are plenty of pre-Aryans in Bihar and other parts of Uttar Pradesh as well and the idea might hold good for any of their parts and people. In fact bearing in mind the archaeological data, mentioned above, one could also argue that composition of the last *Veda* was well past by the time the Aryans reached the region. We simply mean that a good deal of give-and-take must have attended the process of penetration as elsewhere and Bundelkhand must have contributed its share to the Brāhmanic beliefs, behaviour and spiritual beings. Many of the pre-historic totems were taken over as can be made out from an oft-quoted passage : "the deity of those who are devoted to an elephant, a horse, a cow, a dog, a crow, Vāsudeva, Baldeva, Puṇṇabhadda, Maṇibhadda, Aggi, Nagas, Supannas, Yakkhas, Asuras, Gandabbas, Mahārājas, Canda, Suriya, Inda, Brahmā, Deva, Diśā is the elephant, the horse, the cow, the dog, the crow.........respectively."[37] In the 'rock-paintings of Bundelkhand bull and bison find frequent representation. The cult of the boar was prominent in some parts and the adjoining ones towards Malwa. The bull later on became the vehicle of Śiva and the boar an incarnation of Viṣṇu.

The totemistic tribes influenced the early Aryans in another respect also. Early Indian Art invented a number of fanciful figures such as Siṃha-Vyāla, Gaja-Vyāla, Aśva, Vyāla.........in which a particular head was joined to a different body. They are regarded as so many *gaṇas* of Rudra.[38] The Gupta temple of Bhumra has yielded numerous representations of these Zoomerphic attendants of the Lord.[39] In a rock-painting at Abchand we have an animal bearing the face of elephant and legs of horse. The painting can neither be dated with certainty nor its religious significance can be beyond doubt but it is certainly the work of non-Aryans of an early date that dwelt in the cave and its cult significance cannot altogether be ruled out.

Suvira Jaiswal has established the theory that Nārāyaṇa was a non-vedic divinity and has Dravidian origins. She has shown the connection of the God with the institution of human sacrifice. The Pañcarātras, who were an important sect offering worship to the deity, behaved absolutely as Brāhmaṇic people showing no respect for the *varṇa* rules and throwing open initiation to all irrespective of any consideration regarding caste or sex.[40] The very name of their sect has been traced to the ritual of human sacrifice. We are not in position to say wtih certainty what contribution to the cult was made by the non-Aryans of Bundelkhand but note may be taken that as late as the year A.D. 1820 Lieutenant Predergast came across a section of Gonds in central India who happened to be cannibals[41]. Whether the practice had any ritualistic undertones we have no idea, but the possibility cannot be totally ruled out particularly in regard to remote past.

The non-Aryan origins of Lord Nārāyaṇa are largely based on the fact of his finding no niche in the structure of vedic pantheon. Identical is the position of Lord Śiva. In the earliest of his manifestation he figures as god of the frontier region being regarded as the protector of animals and acquiring thereby the epithet Paśupati. The Vedic Rudra got identified with him in course of time and allotted the Lordship of thieves, robbers and wild-tribes[42] in the same way as did non-vedic Nārāyaṇa with Vedic Viṣṇu. The fact of wild tribes having inhabited Bundelkhand is too obvious to need mention but the prominence of thieves and robbers bedevilling the local life here looms large in the account of Bāṇa.[43] This is not to say that Śaivism originated exclusively in this region. A number of its features, beliefs, and rituals must have been contributed by the people converted there. Needing special note in this connection are Kāpālikas who are virtually branded as thieves in orthodox circles, so much so that even their company was to be shunned. The antiquity of this Śaiva-sect goes back to the Upaniṣadic age and they figure prominently in an early medieval play of Bundelkhand which gives a graphic account of a Kāpālin in his own words "My necklace and ornaments consist of human-bones. I live in the ashes of the dead and eat my food in human skulls.........after days of fasting we drink liquor from the skulls of Brāhmaṇas. Our sacrificial fires are kept up with the brains and lungs of men which are mixed up with their flesh and the offerings, by which we appease our terrific God, are human victims covered with gushing blood from the horrible cut on their throats".[44] In *Kathāsaritsāgara* also the value of human flesh in Kāpālika sect is referred to.[45] Of course, the descriptions cited above come from sourses of much later period and may not fully hold good for the period we are writing about, but they give us an idea of the people among whom the sect might have originated and flourished. Bearing them in mind, there are indications that this sect of Śaivism was born on the soil of Bundelkhand. The fact of cannibalism among a sept of the Gonds has already been adverted to above. Describing the Śabaras of Bundelkhand, Bāṇa clearly refers to their blood-drinking and flesh-eating characteristics. Even the offering of flesh in religious worship is also mentioned.[46] That Bāṇa was referring to the ancestors of modern backwaters of Bundelkhand society is beyond doubt when we find blood, flesh and liquor constituting chief offerings made by them to their deities. The Bura Deo of the Baigas is so worshipped. What is more significant, even when they adopted gods of the higher civilization, the mode of their doing worship hardly underwent any change.[47] Further the fact of Lord Śiva figuring prominently in Gond myth of their origin[48] should not be lightly dismissed. Thus viewed in this anthropological perspective, the probability of Kāpālikas having originated in the area of our study cannot be ruled out. Bearing in mind the aboriginal background, the status of the sect as Heterodox Pāśupatism or left-hand Pāśupatism in the history of Śaivism can be easily explained. R.G. Bhandarkar was also of the view that Śiva had a close connection with stragglers in the forests, with Vrātyas or those who were not included in the Aryan community and with the wild tribe of the Niṣādas.[49] He further found that the gods of these last were amalgamated with Rudra. Of course, his views were not based on the area and period we are discussing, they strengthen our reading nonetheless, by connecting the deity with forest dwellers. What is further significant, trident, the most characteristic weapon of Lord Śiva, finds depiction in the pre-historic rock-paintings of Bundelkhand.

Of late, an attempt has been made to trace the genesis of Jainism to pre-Vedic times which may be briefly considered. It is argued that Ṛṣabhadeva, the first Jain *Tīrthaṅkara* figures in the *Ṛgveda* and the Vedic literature refers to him indirectly as Arhan, Keśī Vrātya and Vātarṣana *muni*. The ideals he taught find reflection in Vedic literature as also his followers, who are mentioned as *Śramaṇa Muni* and *Yati*. It is further held that the Vedic King Vena embraced that *Ahiṃsā-dharma* of his maternal grand-father Yama and disregarded the *varṇa* rules to uphold the established social system. Origins of aboriginal tribes like the Śabaras, the Puṇḍras and the Vāhlikas are traced to his time among whom he is supposed to have propagated Jainism. The earliest inscription to mention King Vena is Hathigumpha record of Khāravela who was also a Jaina King and a descendant of great Cedi monarch Vasu, also figuring in the record. Vasu doubtless, followed *Ahiṃsā-dharma* since he opposed the killing of animals at the sacrifice he instituted. Among the ancient names of our region Cedi is the earliest making Vasu thereby the first Aryan King of Bundelkhand.[50] Finally it may be added that J.P. Jain who is the chief author of the above theory is not alone in holding the connection of Jainism with a pre-Vedic civilisation.[51]

The theory is unacceptable as it stands at present. Vasu and Vena may have been opposed to animal sacrifice but that alone does not make them out as devotees of the Jinas. Secondly the available anthropological studies reveal the preference for blood and flesh as sacrificial offerings among the aborigines and any mass conversion of their forefathers by King Vena appears obviously unlikely. Expecting them to switch over all of a sudden, or even gradually, from a life of sheer violence to pure non-violence is to o much to deserve our credence in the complete absence of corroborative evidence. Finally if the literary base of the theory is weak and fragile, on the plane of archaeology it has nothing to authenticate even a part of the hypothesis.

But it would be unfair to reject the theory straightway. It is now believed that Jainism was not born with Vardhamāna Mahāvīra. The antiquity of the faith beyond the last *tirthaṅkara* is now fairly established and the historicity of his immediate predecessor teacher Pārśvanātha is accepted with few reservations.[52] Secondly in our area we have a chalcolithic civilization dated to the second millennium B C. whose authors were certainly pre-Aryans and not as barbarous as are the aborigines whom we take as survivors of the Śabaras and Pulindas of yore. The makers of Eran civilization may have had their own religious beliefs and rituals of which purely archaeological evidence can hardly offer an idea. Of one thing, however, we could be pretty sure. Having advanced upto settled life with agricultural economy, their religion may not have been steeped in blood as that of present aborigines. Their successors might have joined the Vaisya and Śudra class of the advancing Aryans. Their antipathy to animal sacrifice on economic grounds can be postulated and so attraction to non-violent faith becomes a fair possibility. But this is all pure postulation and in no way authenticates the antiquity of Jainism in Bundelkhand beyond Lord Mahāvīra.

The archaeology of Bundelkhand offers the earliest manifestation of religious symbols. Rock-paintings reveal a few and so also does pottery recovered from Eran excavations. But whereas the symbols in the former source are datable to the Mauryan and post-Mauryan periods, those from the latter belong to second millenium before Christ. U.V. Singh who did an exhaustive study of the Eran pottery found on it crosses, stars, sigmas, Suns, plants and animals.[53] He took them to be only as decorative motifs attributing no religious character to them at all.[54] Well may he be right but forms which are regarded as purely decorative or artistic might not be so from their very origin and the possibility of their having had some religious or other meaning can not be altogether ruled out.[55] The view may not hold good in regard to most of the symbols but depiction of the Sun and Sigma cannot be dismissed as mere decorative. Again, we understand that pottery is not the proper medium to put religious symbols on but their manifestation at the same time in rock-paintings stamps them with a significance which is much more than ornamental. Bundelkhand rock-paintings offer us symbols with definite religious significance such as wheel, cross, tree-on-platform, Vajra, hand-palm, Nandipada, Svastika, Sun, Star and fertility figure (Sketch No. 2). At Abchand we get the depiction of cross which is taken to stand for a god though his exact identification is by no means easy to establish. About its religious character we could be fairly sure since we have some crosses in Pachmarhi rock-paintings accompanied by worshippers, though the one at Abchand is without them. In any case, the symbol was worshipped independently or stood for a deity. At times we have the symbol in the form of a hollow plus which is taken to represent the Vedi or fire-pit prepared for the performance of *Yajña*.[56] What intrigues us more than the meaning part is the occurrence of this symbolism in the life of rock-dwellers as well as makers of Eran chalcolithic civilization. The socio-economic and cultural complex of the two must be radically different from each other yet they did obeisance to many symbols common to both. The only explanation we can offer in the present state of our knowledge is that man on road to civilization retained and carried many beliefs and symbols born at the earlier stage of his existence.

Svastika is a symbol with definite religious significance commanding respect in many early societies. At Ābchand we meet with its representation. Most probably cross was the primitive form of *Svastika.* It is a little strange to find that nowhere it is associated with worshippers like the cross. Its occurrence on ancient funerary pottery coupled with its name is taken to indicate the auspicious significance attached to it by the simple primitive mind.[57]

What is further interesting, representation of cross in association with trident is also available in some rock-shelters.[58] Trident beyond doubt is the special weapon of Lord Śiva the god of non-Aryan peoples. Contact, between the cave-dwellers and people of the plains below must have resulted in this kind of representation though any explanation in this regard is hardly more than speculation. The cross is thought to be the oldest sign for representing the earth as also the combination of two serpents indicating the male and female principles in nature. But this is all to project our own mind and sense into the life of early man.

Till now we have talked of symbolism in rock-paintings where our chief difficulty consists in dating the evidence with the required amount of exactitude. Our ground becomes surer, once we walk on numismatic plane. Eran excavations have yielded a number of punch-marked coins, the earlier of which have been assigned to the beginning of third century B.C. by K. D. Bajpai.[59] Mostly made of copper, a few have silver coating on them. Rectangular or circular in shape, their importance for us lies in the symbols they have been stamped with. Noteworthy among these are the Sun, Crescent, *ṣaḍaracakra*, hill, taurine, tree-in-railing, caduceus and vajra. All these are doubtless religious in character and carry cult significance. The coins thereby work as a mirror reflecting the popular among the contemporary cults. *ṣaḍaracakra* is believed to stand for six seasons.[60] The hill symbol is identified with mother-goddess[61] which does not make sense. The tree-in-railing may be taken to be derived from tree cults of hoary antiquity. *Vajra* was special weapon of Indra. About others we can not be definite.

We perhaps very little realise that though the earliest representation of religious symbols in our area dates back to pre-historic times, with our notice of numismatic symbolism we have, almost unconsciously, stepped into the Mauryan period. Apart from the punch marked coins, already referred to, only one of the Aśokan inscriptions has been found so far in Bundelkhand.[62] Together, they do not supply us sufficient information to reconstruct the religious life and beliefs of the people. Hence as much of the general information as can be gathered from other records we can use to prepare the picture, since Bundelkhand was very much a part of the vast Mauryan Empire and Aśoka was not addressing to any people in particular, save in the separate Edicts meant clearly for Kalinga subjects.

That Bundelkhand was fairly Brāhmaṇised or Aryanised before his coming to power one can make out from the XIII Rock-Edict where he says,"And there is no country except that of the Yavanas, where there are not these orders, namely—the Brāhmaṇa and the Śramaṇa ascetics, and there is no place in any such country where man have no faith in one sect or another."[63] The Brāhmaṇas of this passage have been understood to be those recluses and mendicants whose speculations and disciplines were in conformity with the *Vedas* and *Śramaṇas* those, whose doctrines and practises were opposed to the Brāhmaṇic scriptures. To speak in simple terms, the former respected and adhered to the Vedic tradition whereas the latter emanated from the heterodox faiths of the Buddhists and Jainas. The geography and ethnography of Bundelkhand must have militated against the easy penetration of these faiths and the first areas to be exposed to the forces of change must have been round about the routes passing through the province. The process must have been characterised by reciprocal influences and a good many of popular cults and beliefs found accommodation in the higher faiths. The phenomenon can be properly understood when we find Buddhist *Mahāstūpas* and *Mahāvihāras* coming up slightly later at Sanchi and Bharhut in the immediate vicinity of Bundelkhand on two sides, standing on ancient routes and preserving a wealth of sculpture projecting the absorption of popular cults, though that is not to say the cults were peculiar to the region. Inside the region we have absolutely no evidence to assert anything with authority, but going by the large segment of aborigines in the society of recent times one could say that the efforts of the Brāhmaṇas and *Śramaṇas* were to bear fruit much later than the Mauryan epoch.

Another among the Aśokan observations applicable to out area pertains to the creation of a new cadre of officials—the *Dhamma Mahāmātras*—that were to work throughout the empire. The relevant portion reads, "Some *mahāmatās* were ordered by me to busy themselves with the affairs of the *saṃgha* ; likewise others were ordered by me to busy themselves also with various other sects. This different *mahāmātras* are busying themselves specially with different congregations."[64] *Saṃgha* clearly signifies the Buddhist order but Nirgranthas have to be taken as Jainas not separately mentioned. These two, together with the Brahmaṇas and the Ājivikas constituted the four principal sects of the times finding specific mention in the record. We could legitimately postulate that adherents to each one of these lived in Bundelkhand though their relative proportions to the total population we cannot make out. The record refers to various other sects which points to the popular cults—majority with totemistic beliefs and background in illustration of which a passage from contemporary canonical literature has already been cited. This view is further strengthened from the fact that the word *Pāsaṃḍa* of the record denotes followers of non-Aryan faith in addition to the Brāhmaṇic and Śramaṇic orders.[65]

As regards the nature of duties these special functionaries were supposed to discharge, the inscriptions do not offer precise information. Romila Thapar took the creation of this cadre as an attempt on the part of Aśoka to provide some system of social welfare[66] but convincing grounds for holding such a view are given nowhere. Social welfare is too general and too vast an area to allow of any clarity or preciseness on the point. To us the key to the work of these officials seems to lie in the mention of various sects with which they were to remain busy. Basically they appear to be religious functionaries though the qualifying word *Dhamma* in their case had a special Aśokan sense. They were firstly to see that all the sects—great or small—got equal opportunity to flourish and secondly to propagate the imperial ideals envisaged by the *Dhamma* among the meanest of such groups. In this promulgation of *Dhamma* Aśoka was attempting to reform the narrow attitude of religious teaching, to protect the weak against the strong and to promote throughout the empire a consciousness of social behaviour so broad in its scope, that no cultural group cou'd object to it.[67] To get his code of conduct approved by all the sects everywhere may have been one of the basic aims behind instituting the order of new officials. He himself explicitly admits the inherent unity of ethical principles inculcated by each a sect,[68] the officials were to merely emphasise this unity as embodied in the *Dhamma* which was Aśoka's invention. In essence it was an attempt on the part of the King to suggest a way of life which was both practical and convenient being moral at the same time.[69] Instructions characterising his code included rendering obedience to mother and father and elders, compassion towards animals, speaking of the turtb, regard of the pupil for his master and suitable behaviour to the relatives.[70] He was right in holding that these principles formed *porāṇa pakiti dighāvuse*[71] or the nature of a man which is ancient and long-standing. To the people of Bundelkhand only the second among his principles namely—compassion to animals—might have proved less palatable, majority favouring blood and flesh offerings to their gods. The emperor himself was probably aware that complete abstention from killing animals was impossible proposition insofar as it could never be enforced. Any attempt in the direction was doomed where blood and flesh played prominent part in the very worship offered to the clan and local deities, as certainly was the case with Śabaras and Pulindas in our region. The actual interaction that must have resulted from the honest attempts of Aśoka at spreading his theocracy without god through *Dharma-mahāmātras* is matter for speculation. His government in the history of Bundelkhand was the first to shape the religious life of the people by active and untiring efforts, helping thereby the process of Brahmaṇisation.

As effective as the appointment of *Dhamma-mahāmātras* was his *Dhamma-yātrā*. He journeyed upto Brahmāgiri since the edict available therefrom was issued on tour. So also was Gujarra record which was incised when the emperor had been 256 days on tour. The very fact that the monarch personally came to Gujarra is enough to indicate the impact that the journey must have made on the people. The record is rare in being the second to contain the personal name of the emperor, the first being that of Maski. At no time Gujarra seems to have been a considerable city or place of pilgrimage. Perhaps it stood on the highway from North to South and so the emperor selected it for putting up a copy of his Minor Rock Edict.

An observation in this brief record is interesting as well as controversial. The King proudly proclaims, "men (subjects) in Jambudvīpa, who had been unmingled with the gods during this period were made (by him) mingled with the gods.[72]" For a clue to the proper meaning of the statement we may also read what follows. The emperor says that the rich men alone are not entitled to a place in the great heaven. If the poor exert themselves in the cause of *Dharma* and discharged duties associated therewith, observing utmost restraint in respect of all living beings, they can as well attain heaven. He exhorts, therefore, both the rich and the poor to effect their association with the gods by practising Dharma and discharging duties associated therewith. The words "commingling of men with gods' have been explained in variety of ways. D.R. Bhandarkar seems to have drawn the right sense of the statement. In his opinion the commingling of men and gods must be so explained as to show that it was tantamount to the achievement of heaven. This is possible only if we say that by following Aśoka's *Dhamma* men became so virtuous that they attained to heaven and were associated with the gods.[73] To be more precise on the point his policy of *Dhamma* had achieved so much good in the country that it was just as it had been in the righteous days of the Kṛtayuga when the gods in their pleasure the visited earth and associated with the people. The Golden Age, as it were, had been brought back.[74] For obvious reasons, the Buddhist emperor was using a Brāhmaṇical value judgement with which average among the readers were familiar. To drive home his teaching forcefully, the emperor introduced the use of edifying spectacles which helped generating and developing righteousness. These were in effect officially sponsored performances woven round symbols and mythology of popular belief. They constituted the material manifestation of the kind of heavenly bliss that good and virtuous people were sure to enjoy in their next birth when they became gods.[75] Thus Aśoka exerted himself a great deal to effect moral upliftment of his subjects without showing undue favour to any sect, putting all at par. To him must be due the credit of inaugurating a policy of tolerance in respect of religion, followed all through to the Candellas. This is not to say that earlier government practised persecution but first positive evidence on the point we possess from Aśoka onwards only.

Brāhmaṇism came to Bundelkhand much earlier than the Mauryans and Buddhism with Aśoka, if not prior to him. About the introduction of Jainism by the first of Mauryan monarchs we may hazard a speculation. The spread of Jainism is considered more a case of successive migrations than continuous expansion.[76] Jaina tradition of high antiquity unanimously holds that Candragupta Maurya abdicated in old age and retired to the South following his teacher Bhadrabāhu, settling finally at Śravaṇa-Belgola. The tradition figures with minor variations in a number of documents, both literary as well as epigraphic.[77]

It is noteworthy that this Jaina migration is the initial fact of the Digaṃbara sect of the Jainas. The order of the Jainas was undivided for long but with Bhadrabāhu the Digaṃbaras separated from the Śvetambaras. It is quite likely that while travelling to the South the Mauryan emperor and his teacher passed through Bundelkhand since routes leading to the South ran through the region. The great teacher and his imperial pupil were certainly not on mission to convert but their passage must have resulted in introduction of the faith winning some adherents.

Of Vaiṣṇavism as such we have hardly any trace in Bundelkhand till the close of Mauryan period but the discovery of the remains of a Viṣṇu temple at Vidisha datable to about 4th—3rd centuries B.C. is noteworthy.[78] Slightly later, we get Garuḍa-Pillar of Heliodorus from here only.[79] Vidishā being in the vicinity of Bundelkhand, it is not unlikely that a few of the followers of this faith lived here as well.

Till now we have treated of the higher religions which found specific mention in Aśokan inscription. The masses down the ages have always held a number of superstitions connected with their mundane matters propitiating primitive powers and deities. Aśoka is forthright on the point in his IX Rock-Edict,[80] "men are practising various ceremonies during illness, at the marriage of a son or daughter, at the birth of a child and when setting out on a journey. On these and other such occasions men are practising many ceremonies. But in such cases women are practising many and various offensive and useless ceremonies. Now ceremonies should certainly be practised. But these ceremonies bear little fruit indeed. But the following bears much fruit indeed, viz., the practice of morality." Of course, the emperor is not specially describing the superstitions peculiar to Bundelkhand but his observations are as much applicable to the region as elsewhere in the empire. They reflect that whatever be the appeal and hold of higher faiths, the bulk of population believed in a number of lesser deities seeking solution to their day-to-day problems and honouring age-old usages and beliefs. The ceremonies point to the continuance of the worship of Yakṣas, *Caityas*, Gandharvas, Nāgas and so forth, of which we get reliable reflection in Buddhist and Pali scriptures.

Travelling down the stream of time beyond the Mauryans we turn once more to Eran which yielded a fairly good number of punchmarked, die-struck and cast coins, bearing a variety of symbols and figures. These include elephant, horse, tree-in railing, *Indradhvaja*, Ujjain-symbol and river with fishes.[81] Of these, the placing of elephant and horse on coins cannot be construed merely for decorative purpose. In the development of iconography the deities in their earliest form had aniconic representation followed by theriomorphic before attaining the anthropomorphic.[82] The elephant on the coins could therefore be taken as symbolising Indra. Our supposition gets solidity when we get a coin with elephant standing before *Indradhvaja*. The tree-in-railing was symbolic of the *vṛkṣa-caityas* or *sthala-vṛkṣas*.[83] The cross of the Ujjain symbol has been taken to mean the union of male and female principles of nature[84] but the view is purely a speculation.

The die-struck coins offer us three new symbols. They are crescent, *svastika* and *cakra*[85]. Of these the *cakra* is the most important. It signified the Sun-god.

Sketch No. 2 : Religious Symbols in Rock-Paintings of Bundelkhand

In various ritual performances, the wheel was employed as Sun-symbol from very early times as it represented the shape as well motion of the Sun.[86]

That Sūrya was represented aniconically is clear from other independent and unmistakable evidence also. The Sun-temple of Unao (Distt. Datia) enshrines a Sun-dial which is aniconic form of the deity. It is said to be of high antiquity and must be so since it comes of a period when the god had not attained anthropomorphic features. The stone is circular in shape embedded in a high platform in the sanctum. Save for the raised points at the periphery which were not sculptured it has no contours. The temple housing the sun-dial is not very old but some stray sculptures scattered in its courtyard belong to the early-medieval period. The original temple must have undergone repairing and remaking several times, since the dawn of Christian era.

Handed down from the same period we have another identical representation of Sūrya. It is a terracotta figurine in which the deity is shown as goddess. Included in the collection of State Museum, Dhubela (Distt. Chhatarpur) the face of the figure resembles the Sun-dial whereas the hands and legs have been humanly rendered. Adorned with armlets and anklets, the goddess is naked except for the lower garment or ornament. Standing with legs apart, she holds her hands high near the head. May be we are mistaken and the figure might most propably be of mother-goddess, but the resemblance of the Sun-dial with head in this figure is striking. Worship of Sun both as father-god or mother-goddess was prevalent.

Our study acquires a new dimension when we find *cakra* and *vajra,* the unmistakable numismatic symbols standing respectively for the Sun and Indra figuring in the rock-paintings of the region. Abchand rock-shelters contain representation of Vajra and Sūrya. The latter is depicted as a hollow circle with semicircular rays issuing out of it and showing thereby the most primitive among its forms. Now the question arises how the Vedic gods Sūrya and Indra found place among the cave-dwellers. Who were these cave-dwellers? How the identical symbolic representation came about between the numismatic and cave art—one developed and technical, the other simple and primitive. It is not easy to answer these questions. At best one could explain the phenomenon as resulting from the contact between the two sections of society but that would raise many more questions. Further research in future only might offer us a convincing explanation.

In addition to containing symbols representing higher gods of the Vedic pantheon, the rock art also preserves those indicating popular deities. We have already noted tree-in-railing figuring among the symbols on coins. Rock-art also provides us with its depiction. At Ābchand the depiction of Sun has taken place in company with tree and star symbols. Trees were among the earliest objects to command worship or veneration and attribution of spirit qualities to them played large part in their apotheosization. A sacred tree with a platform erected at base or enclosed in a railing being an object of worship came to be called a *caitya* or *caitya vṛkṣa.*[87] At Sānchi we do have scenes presenting tree-worship. In Brāhmaṇism the Yakṣas were often the spirits connected with trees and granted worldly desires, especially progeny and wealth.[88] In Vedic Literature figures association of Yakṣa with the motif of tree-of-life.[89] But we have seen that tree-worship had origins earlier than the advent of Aryans in our area and one cannot be sure that tree-symbol of rock-paintings also stands for a Yakṣa. It could have different significance but these parallels between the cave dwellers and their settled contemporaries are intriguing to say the least. Most probably symbols of rock art, even if they happened to be the same as those on coins, had a sense and significance not corresponding to what we know from Brāhmaṇic records.

Of an independent cult of Yakṣa we have no evidence in our area for the period but colossal monolithic statues representing Yakṣas have been found at Pawaya and Besanagar ranking as the earliest cult icons of India.[90] The ruins of Bharhut also yielded some representations. All these places stand close by Bundelkhand. So the prevalence of this folk cult cannot be denied. In fact, Bharhut has handed down a sort of mirror of the contemporary cults. An eminent scholar was constrained to remark. "In the sculptures and inscriptions of Bharhut, we shall have in future a real landmark in the religious and literary history of India and many theories hitherto held by Sanskrit Scholars will have to modify accordingly."[91] The Bharhut sculptures speak of the nāga as well as tree cult besides that of Yakṣa. Buddhism had definitely entered Bundelkhand with Aśoka if not earlier. The Bharhut art leaves us in no doubt that Buddhism had successfully affiliated to it most of the folk cults of central India.

Coming back to the Yakṣas, we have an interesting tradition with a probable bearing on the area of our study. An isolated reference contained in the Jaina *Bhagavatī Sūtra* tells us that the Ājivikas had shifted their centre of activity to the Puṇḍra country at the foot of the Vindhya mountain and that in their pantheon found place many Vedic and non-Vedic gods. Two of these were Punnabhadda and Maṇibhadda.[92] Beyond doubt these are Yakṣas though the Niddesa list quoted earlier distinguishes their devotees from those of the Yakṣa. An inscribed statue of Maṇibhadra datable to about Ist Century B.C. has been found at Pawaya near Gwalior[93] and Puṇḍra country at the foot of the Vindhyas must indicate a territory populated with non-Aryans in our area. Most probably a section of the Ājīvikas settled somewhere in Bundelkhand and accommodated Maṇibhadra Yakṣa in their pantheon.

REFERENCES

1. E.R.E., Vol. X, p. 662.
2. The use of the word in the *Śrimadbhagavad Gītā* could be taken in this sense and the book contains the quintessence of Hinduism and its teachings.

3. *The Advanced Learner's Dictionary of Current English*, O.U.P., London, 1967, p. 238.
4. E.R.E., Vol. X, p. 663.
5. Supra. Ch. II.
6. Russell and Hiralal : *The Tribes and Castes of the Central Provinces of India*, Vol. I, p. 139.
7. Murray, Margaret : *The Genesis of Religion.*
8. Marshall, J. : *Mohenjodaro and the Indus Civilization*, London, 1931, p. 51.
9. Bhandarkar, R.G. : *Vaiṣṇavism, Śaivism and Minor Religious Systems*, Indological Book House, Varanasi, 1965, pp. 143-44.
10. Khare M.D. ' Early Temples with Special Reference to Gupta temple at Marbia—Dist. Jabalpur" J.M.P.I.P., No. 9 (1973-74), p. 13.
11. Dikshit, S.K. : *The Mother-Goddess*, New Delhi, p. 7.
12. I.H.Q., Vol. V, No. 2 (June-1929), p. 289.
13. Russell and Hiralal : op. cit , Vol. I, p 90.
14. Ibid. p. 96.
15. Ibid. Vol. III, p. 68.
16. Ibid. p. 50.
17. Ibid. p. 67.
18. Ibid. Vol. II, p. 286.
19. Pande, S.K. : *Painted Rock-Shelters in Madhya Pradesh*, (thesis), University of Sauger, 1970, pp. 283-87.
20. E.R.E., Vol. X, p. 667.
21. Closely akin to the institution of the totem is the idea of Taboo which is definitely religious in essence. A tabooed object may not be killed, eaten or spoken to as it tends to eradicate its holy but dangerous essence to surrounding objects which in consequence, become a taboo. S.K. Chatterji is of the view that idea of taboo was born at a time when proto-Austroloids (Niṣādas) and Aryans first came into contact with each other. *The Vedic Age*, p. 150.
22. Russell, R.V and Hiralal : op. cit., Vol. II, p, 286 and Vol. III, p. 67.
23. Gupta, Shakti M: *Plant Myths and Traditions in India* Leiden, (Brill, E. J.), 1971, p. 14.
24. Russell, R.V. and Hiralal : op, cit. Vol. III, p. 97
25. These last further highlight how the totemistic beliefs and worship evolved. The relationship of the creature hunted with his hunters underwent a sort of metamorphosis with the ushering in of agricultural stage.
26. Law, B.C. *India as described in the Early Works of Buddhism and Jainism*, p. 217.
27. Ibid. p. 218.
28. A.S.R., XXI, p. 12. Even if we take it to be modern Godāvari, the fact of intra-country communication through Bundelkhand exposing aborigines to the Aryans is easily established.
29. Law, B.C. : op. cit., p. 220.
30. Pande, G.C. : *Studies in the origins of Buddhism* Allahabad, 1957, p. 328.
31. *The Vedic Age* pp. 311-12.
32. Ibid. p. 284.
33. Nigam, M.L. : *Cultural History of Bundelkhand* p. 13.
34. R.E. XIII (Shahbazgarhi version) C.I.I., I, p. 66.
35. *The Wonder that was India*, Rupa & Co., Delhi, p. 233 Cf. Jaiswal, Suvira : *The Origin and Development of Vaiṣṇavism*, Munshiram Manoharlal, Delhi, 1967, p. 121.

36. *India as described in the Early Works of Buddhism and Jainism* p. 206
37. Vide : Bhandarkar, R.G. : op. cit., p. 3; also, D.H.I., p. 77
38. Agrawal, V.S. : *Indian Art*, Pṛthvi Prakashan, Varanasi, 1965, p. 72
39. D.H.I., p. 356
40. Jaiswal, Suvira : op. cit., pp. 32, 33 and 44. It may further be noted that she has nowhere mentioned any people in particular among whom the practice was prevalent
41. Russell, R.V. & Hiralal : op. cit., p. 114
42. Jash, Pranabananda : *History of Śaivism*, Roy and Choudhury, Calcutta, 1974, p. 2
43. Cowell, E.B. & Thomas, F.W. : *The Harṣacarita of Bāṇa* p. 227
44. Vide : Jash, Pranabananda : op. cit : p. 63
45. Ibid.
46. Kale, M.R. : Bāṇa's Kādambarī (A Literal English Translation), pp. 41-42
47. Russell, R.V. & Hirālāl : op. cit,, Vol. II, p. 85
48. Ibid. —pt. IV, p. 48 ff

48.A Jash, Pranabananda : The Kāpālikas — An Obscure Śaiva Sub-sect in *Proceedings of Indian History Congress*, 1973, (Thirty-Fourth Session) Vol. I, p. 152 ff. has given a graphic description of the sect as reflected in ancient literature but has nowhere speculated about the possible area of the origin of the sect. Important among his observation is "Although the Kāpālikas represented themselves as the followers of Śiva, very often the deity of their worship was Cāmuṇḍā". From *Svarnnadrimahodaya* he quotes, "the venerable goddess Cāmuṇḍā garlanded with skulls... ..... is known as Kapālinī." It is worth noting here that Cāmuṇḍā enjoyed special veneration at and around Mahoba, the Candella capital, where her rock,-cut sculptures can still be seen in plenty. A rare Cāmuṇḍā image with sixty-four arms is also lying in the garden of S.D.M.'s bungalow at Mahobā, of which a detailed note will be taken later.

49. Bhandarkar, R.G. : op. cit., p. 3
50. Jain, J.P. : " Rājā Vena aur Jaina Paramparā ki Prācinatā" in *Kṣullaka Cidānanua Smrti Grantha*, pp. 136-38
51. Pande G.C. : op. cit., p. 353
52. A.I.U. p. 411
53. *Protohistoric Pottery of Eastern Malwa* (Thesis), of University of Saugar, 1966 p. 151
54. Ibid.
55. Shah, U.P. : *Studies in Jaina Art*, Banaras, 1955, p. 39; also *Jain Antiquary*, XV, No. I p. 1
56. Pande, S.K. : *Painted Rock-shelters Madhya Pradesh* (thesis), University of Saugar, 1970, p. 260
57. Dixit, S.K. : *The Mother-Goddess*, p. 27
58. Pande, S.K. : op. cit., p. 263
59. I.N.S., p. 7
60. Dixit, S.K. op. cit., pp. 70 and 105
61. Ibid. p. 85
62. E.I,, XXXI. pt. V, p. 209
63. C.I.I., I, p. 66
64. Pillar Edict VII, C.I.I., I, p. 150 ff

65. Bhandarkar, D.R. : op. cit., pp. 153-55
66. Thapar, R. *Aśoka.........*, p. 157
67. Ibid p. 181
68. C.I.I., I. p. 59
69. Thāpar, R, op. cit., p. 149
70. C.I.I., I, 176. Vincent Smith was right in holding the *Dhamma* of Aśoka as a system of theocracy without a god
71. Brahmāgiri Minor Rock Edict—C.I.I., I, p. 175
72. E.I., XXXI, pt. V, p. 209
73. Bhandarkar, D.R. : *Asoka* p. 123
74. Thapar, R. : *Asoka*...p. 155
75. Bhandarkar D.R. : op. cit, p. 124
76. A.I.U., p. 417
77. Mukherji, R.K., : *Chandragupta Maurya and his Times*, Delhi, 1960, p. 41
78. Khare, M.D. : "Early temples with special reference to a Gupta temple at Marhia, Dist. Jabalpur", J.M.P.I.P., No. 9 (1973-74) pp. 13-19
79. Sircar D.C. : *Select Inscriptions Bearing on Indian History and Civilization*, Vol. I, University of Calcutta (Second Edition), 1965, p. 88 : At Tumain (Gunā District) a huge icon of Balarāma datable to 2nd century A.D. has been found.
80. C.I.I., I., p. 60
81. I.N.S., p. 6
82. D.H.I., 108-9
83. Ibid.
84. Dixit, S. K. ; op. cit, p. 219
85. I.N.S., p. 6
86. D.H.I., p. 59
87. Shah, U.P. : op. cit., p. 55
88. Mishra, R.N. : *Development of Yakṣa Cult*, (thesis), University of Saugar, 1967, p. 318
89. Ibid. p. 54
90. A.I.U., p. 517
91. Vide Cunningham A. : *Stūpa of Bharhut*, Indological Book House, Varanasi, 1962 (Introduction) p. 1
92. A.I.U., pp. 463-64
93. D.H.I., p. 97

5

The Classical Age

(The Classic content of Indian tradition and civilization is customarily associated with the age and empire of the Great Guptas. And rightly so, since the period was witness to Indian genius scaling peaks of glory in art, architecture and literature fittingly forming a standard for generations to come. A portion of what survives from this classic creation belongs to Bundelkhand and, being religious in character, offers certainty and solidity to our hitherto conjectural reconstruction of religious life from sources denying definite information. No longer are we called upon to qualify our conclusions with 'must have been' and 'may have been'; no longer we have to work with literary references only; no longer our march is hampered owing to lack of epigraphic and numismatic data. Thanks, indeed, to the Imperial Guptas and some of their central Indian feudatories who have handed down a variety of records and coins as well as statues and shrines reflecting religious cults and consciousness of contemporary north India.

The period is taken to be one of vigorous Brāhmaṇic Revival and Renovation typified in the amalgamation of Vedic sacrificial worship with countless cults of hoary antiquity revolving round personal gods of pre-Aryan following with popular character. Such was the proliferation of popular deities that even a conservative estimate puts their number at thirty-three crores. Obviously the figure is inflated and arbitrary but it reflects the religious freedom enjoyed by the humblest of Indian Society, How many of this heterogenous mass of gods and goddesses had following in Bundelkhand we have no means to make out. Nothing short of a census operation coming from contemporary priests could help us in the matter. But that is wishful thinking with hardly any likelihood of fulfilment from any of the sources.

Acquiring eminence among these innumerable gods and godlings are Śiva, Śakti and Viṣṇu finding temples dedicated and eulogies inscribed to them. Brāhmaṇas continue, by and large, their devotion to the Vedas switching over in certain cases to the worship of these non-Vedic powers.

The temple, though having pre-Gupta origins, becomes an established institution in the political, religious and socio-economic life of the community owing to landgrants made for its maintenance. The available Gupta records from the area of our study being very few, one has to depend on a general survey of Gupta records found elsewhere as well as those of their feudatories in central India. Vindhyāṭavi account in the works of Bāṇa would also hold good for the time and space we are concerned with.

Among the heterodox sects, Buddhism and Jainism continue struggling their way and holding their ground though the masses make move to Brāhmaṇism once their totems and deities get full and fair accommodation in the hierachical scheme of Hindu worship—a fact highlighted in mythological literature and typified in temple architecture. The hermitage of Divākaramitra and Pañcāyatana shrine of Deogarh constitute land-marks in the history of inter-sect relations and could truly be termed golden pages in our account of the Classical Age.

Finally the cow comes into her own acquiring sanctity to such an extent as being bracketed with the Brāhmaṇas in heading the society. The gift of cow, land and gold becomes an article of faith in royal circles, being regarded as the purest act of piety by Brāhmaṇical ideologues, and rightly so, since Brāhmaṇa was invariably the beneficiary of this majestic munificence. Thus the classical period draws the contours of religious map which were to become clearer and sharper in the succeeding centuries.)

Any study of Ancient India is bound to suffer from the fact that all the available records—literary or epigraphic—represent the views of only one section of society. From the birth of Indian civilization, the Brāhmaṇas produced and preserved the written word, projecting all through their own point of view and the position is little better even when a Buddhist record or a Jain document offers us a glimpse. Naturally, therefore much of our description would cover and concern religious life and beliefs of the royalty and the nobility. That the Vedas held the highest place in the realms of religion goes without saying. Acceptance and accommodation of non-Vedic popular pantheon in no way lowered the authority of the divine documents. It was more of an intellectual minority condescending and coming to terms with mediocre majority, effecting a rapprochement by offering to do honour to some prominent gods without in any way breaking their bonds with the Vedas.

The alliance of Vedic beliefs with Purāṇic gods is writ large in records. Samudragupta performed *Aśvamedha*—a Vedic sacrifice—and financed the building of a temple at Eran dedicated to Janārdana—a non-Vedic—deity to augment his own glory.[2] Kumāragupta I, his grandson, too, celebrated the same sacrifice issuing special coins to mark the occasion[3], yet his title *paramabhāgavat* speaks volumes for his devotion to Viṣṇu.[4] By Nālandā copper-plate Samudragupta made over two villages to Jayabhaṭṭa-svāmin, a scholar of the three *Vedas*.[5] Another *agrahāra* he created out of Revatika village by his Gaya copper-plate for the Brāhmaṇa Gopasvāmin.[6] How the Brāhmaṇas were priding themselves on being Vedic scholars and adopting popular gods in the same breath may be best seen in Eran Stone Pillar inscription of Budhagupta in which the local governor Mātṛviṣṇu erects a lofty flag-staff in honour of divine god Janārdana and making a proud mention that one of his ancestors was head of the *Maitrāyaṇi* school of *Yajurveda*, who performed sacrifices and studied his Veda, verily a sage[7]. Mahārāja Hastin, a Parivrājaka potentate, made over the village Vasuntarasaṇḍika to the Brāhmaṇa Gopasvāmin of *Vājasaneya Mādhyamdina śākhā* and several others in order to increase his own religious merit and build a ladder leading to heaven.[8] By another Khoh copper-plate he converted the village of Kerparika into an *agrahāra* for about a dozen Vedic scholars with identical aim.[9] Likewise his Majhgavam copper-plate speaks of village Vālugarta being granted to the students of the *Chāndogaya-Kautham Śākhā* at the request of Mahādevideha[10] and clearly here the merit was to go to this nobleman. A deep-rooted belief in the highest piety being attached to the granting of village to Vedic scholars is clear in all the cases. Nevertheless, the devotion of the king for Lord Śiva—a non-Vedic god—stands out beyond even the shadow of a doubt. In his Bhumara Stone Pillar Inscription he is mentioned as meditating on the feet of the god Mahādeva.[11] The opening invocation to the same deity in Majhgavam copper-plate further attests the fact. Many more records could be cited highlighting this holy alliance between the Vedic and Purāṇic gods but the cases already quoted suffice to prove our point.

D. R. Bhandarkar rightly felt that two unifying principles bound together the heterogenous mass of Vedic and non-Vedic, Aryan and non-Aryan gods and goddesses numbering thirty-three crores as per the popular estimate.[12] One of them was the belief in the oneness of the Ultimate Spirit for which we should be indebted to our early Aryan ancestors : the other was the Doctrine of Incarnation contributed by the non-Aryan faiths of India which helped the process of snycretisation. Indeed, the first principle has its origins going back to the *Vedas* whereas the second shapes out fully in the *Purāṇas* and both together coalasce during the period under review creating a unique religion of the classical age in India.

It is curious that the *Vedas* did maintain their supremacy but not so the Vedic deities. None of the temples is dedicated to them, not even to the mightiest, Indra, among them who has to be content with only the guardianship of one of the quarters and is relegated to a corner on the outer wall[13]. The inscriptional records open with invocation to Śiva, Viṣṇu or Śakti and commemorate in certain cases the construction of temples to them, never to any of their Vedic counterparts. It is not without significance that Samudragupta is often held equal to Vedic gods Varuṇa and Indra but never to Śiva or Viṣṇu. In Tumain record Kumāragupta is well-nigh the great Indra.[14] According to Mandasor inscription of Naravarman, Indra, the Lord among gods of Vedic pantheon could have his festival celebrated only when approved by Kṛṣṇa.[15] The ruling class in any country or period is always hungry for eulogy and acclamation whereas the intelligentsia which can gratify this hunger is always in need of support and patronage. This universal truth with few honourable exceptions is written large in religious literature and epigraphic records of the period under review. Mythical heroes like Pṛthu and Rāghava were outdistanced by Samudragupta in the giving of gold—obviously to the Brāhmaṇas, according to Eran Stone inscription.[16] The fact is further attested by Mathura Stone inscription of Candragupta II which mentions him as giver of many crores of lawfully acquired cows as well[17]. Complete account in this connection we get from Khoh copper-plate of the Gupta year 156 in which Mahārāja Hastin figures as the giver of thousands of cows, elephants, houses, gold and lands and extremely devoted to the gods and Brāhmaṇas. The gift of land in particular acquired such eminence in the scheme of accepted religious ideals for the ruling class that the surviving contemporary copper-plate grants mostly contain the relevant commandments copied from litrature. To quote only one example, the Khoh record cited above says in its concluding portion, "And it has been said by the venerable Supreme Sage, the arranger of the *Vedas*— "O Yudhiṣṭhira, best of Kings, carefully preserve land that has previously been given to the twice-born; verily the preservation of a grant is more meritorious than making a grant ! The earth has been enjoyed by many kings, commencing with Sagar; whosoever at any time possesses the earth, to him belongs at that time the reward of this grant that is now made, if he continues it. The giver of land enjoys happiness in heaven for sixty thousand years; but the confiscator of a grant and he who assents to an act of confiscation shall dwell for the same number of years in hell."[18] As though this was not enough, and visualising the birth of a confiscator in his own family, the king holds out the threat, "This injunction having been given, he who behaves otherwise—him I will consume with a great contempt, even when I have passed into another body." It is clear from the long passage, quoted above, that gifts of gold and cow worth crores of rupees were given invariably to the Brāhmaṇas, the custodians of religious lore and they, in turn, showered praises on the potentates so complying. The landless labourer or cowless carpenter hardly stood any chance to partake of princely munificence when Lords Spiritual could successfully brainwash Lords Temporal through the literature and education that was their monopoly. One of the Mandasor records is frank on the point, in which figures a ruler whose wealth and life had been consigned to the gods and the Brāhmaṇas.[19]

The cow was not merely coveted item of gift. Just as Brāhmaṇas regarded themselves as heading the human society, in the like manner, cow came to be considered heading the animal world. Eran Stone Pillar inscription ends on a significant note, "May it be well to all the people, headed by the cows and the Brāhmaṇas."[20] Thus the sanctity of cow is established on a firm footing from the Classical age downward. The economic background to this apotheosization of the cow has been given elsewhere in this chapter. For the gift of land we have scriptural injunctions as well as encouragement, none for making and maintaining of an alms house. Yet the humanitarian institution did have a place in the religious life of the people and individual contributions towards its maintenance added to the religious merit of the donor in the same way as did the granting of land. Evidence on this score is wanting from the region of our study but not very far we have four documents, coming from the time of Emperors Candragupta II and Kumargupta I, disclosing continued existence of an almhouse.[21] We have no means to ascertain whether the *Sadāsattra* was meant exclusively for the Brāhmaṇas or catered to the genuinely needy, but the fact that people from far off places came and offered generous help for its expenses indicates its measure of importance in matters of religious benefaction.

S. R. Goyal has propounded a theory that religion was an undercurrent in conditioning the approach of the imperial Guptas towards their neighbours. His view is based on the fact that the Guptas were *paramabhāgavatas* whereas almost all their adversaries—the Nāgas, the Vākāṭakas, the Huṇas, the Maitṛkas and Yaśodharman —were staunch Śaivas. Quoting Junagadh Rock inscription of Skandagupta in which the emperor is spoken of having "plucked and utilized the authority of his local representatives who were so many Garuḍas and used it as an antidote against the hostile kings, who were so many serpents, lifting up their hoods in pride and arrogance." Goyal puts the straight question, "was he (Skandagupta) not looking upon his enemies with the eyes of a Vaiṣṇava, while choosing Garuḍa, the mythical enemy of the Nāgas ? and concludes by offering the answer himself that the attitude of the emperor was coloured by his Bhāgavat affiliations.[22]

The view of Goyal is unwarranted on more than one counts. Samudragupta uprooted nine kings of north India and conquered twelve of the south. We are far from sure if all these kings were devotees of Lord Śiva. No body can challenge the evidence of Allahabad Stone Pillar Inscription in which Hariṣeṇa has divided all the contemporary powers into four categories on the basis of a specific policy adopted in each case and reading role of religion in the shaping of that policy would be importing meaning into that document. In the second place, Goyal makes out the Huṇas to be staunch Śaivas on the ground of Mihirakula's unbroken devotion to Lord Śiva and never doing obeisance to anyone save Sthāṇu. But the prime adversary of the Guptas was his father Toramāṇa who was catholic in his approach to religion. In fact in the very first year of his rule in India, his governor at Eran raised a temple dedicated to Varāhāvatāra of Viṣṇu in memory of his elder brother whom he had succeeded in the office.[23] Toramāṇa was equally well-disposed towards Buddhism.[23A] We have no reason to disbelieve the Chinese evidence in which it is clearly stated that Mihirakula was very much interested in Buddhism and wanted to take lesson in its canon. Only after being insulted and offended, he turned anti-Buddhist. Narasiṃhagupta Bālāditya defied his authority on hearing about his persecution of Buddhism.[24] Śaivism or Vaiṣṇavism is nowhere in the picture of their quarrel. In the third place, all the officers occupying the highest position in administrative hierarchy were not Bhāgavata in their religious affiliation. Āmrakārdava, a quarter-master of emperor Candragupta II and a military officer of no mean ability was a devotee of Lord Buddha.[25] Vīrasena Śāba, his *Sāndhivigrahika*, financed the excavation of a cave shrine in honour of Lord Śambhu even when accompanying his master on a campaign of world-conquest.[26] Śikharasvāmin, another among his ministerial functionaries and his son Pṛthviṣeṇa, first *Mantri-kumārāmātya* and then *Mahābalādhikṛta* under emperor Kumāragupta I, were both staunch Śaivas without being discriminated in matter of appointment or promotion.[27] In the last place some of the Gupta emperors were not Vaiṣṇavas at all. Vidiśā Stone Image Inscriptions show Rāmagupta to be a devout Jaina financing the preparation and installation of *tīrthankara* statues under instruction from his mendicant teacher Cella,[28] Goyal himself admits the leaning towards Buddhism of imperial Guptas from Kumāragupta I onwards leading to the decline and disintegration of the empire.[29]

The scheme of sins as laid down by the Manu much earlier, held good during this period also finding occasional mention is land-charters. Five of these were *Mahāpātakas* or mortal sins and the other five minor ones or *upapātakas* and the transgressor of a grant was held to be guilty of all the ten sins. The scheme was so well-known that it does not find full description anywhere, yet in some cases the transgressor was frankly told of a few of the *mahāpātakas* of which he would become guilty such as the slaying of a cow or of a spiritual preceptor or a Brāhmaṇa.[30]

In the cycle of time as contemplated in Brāhmaṇical literature, we all belong to and breathe in Kaliyuga which is necessarily an Age of Sin. Even a discerning writer like Bāṇa harps on the theme which finds frequent mention in the inscriptions of post-classical period. Only a real sage saturated with knowledge of the scriptures and practising renunciation of the world could wash a part of the sin associated with the Age.[31] Such was then the hold of Vedic ideals and rituals that attainment of heaven or securing of salvation was thought to result from performance of sacrifices. To quote Bāṇa directly, "It seemed as if a bridge-like flight of steps, leading to the road to Heaven, was being constructed in that hermitage under the guise of the successive strips of smoke sent up by the Sacred Fires, who, being pleased with the continued offerings of melted butter were as if desirous of transporting all those sages to the world of gods in their corporeal earthly forms."[32] Ṛṣi Jābāli is proudly proclaimed to be the enemy of the Kali Age. Such was the auspicious character of his Āśrama that the Kali Age had never visited it.[33] The *Vedas* which originally resided in the lotus-like mouths of god Brahmā obtained this second additional but suitable dwelling-place. All the lores of the world which had become vitiated by contact with the Kali Age had once more acquired purity on coming to the Ṛṣi. Above all, Dharma, who nostalgically looked back to the Kṛta Age being reduced to one fourth in the present age ceased doing so having obtained entirety in Jābāli's Āśrama.[34] One cannot help wondering and concluding that Brāhmaṇical ideologues had for the sake of convenience offered concession to the massess accepting their gods in the scheme of religious structure but their belief in the efficacy and sanctity of Vedic ritual and ideal was hardly modified. We should have no hesitation in agreeing with D.R. Bhandarkar who thought it doubtful whether Śiva, Viṣṇu, Sūrya and Mahāsena can be considered to be Brāhmaṇical deities even in the Gupta period.[35]

Among orthodox sects Vaiṣṇavism enjoyed supremacy inside Bundelkhand as well as outside. The fact of Gupta emperors adopting the title of *Paramabhāgavata* is too well-known to need mention. Samudragupta is so styled in his Gaya copper-plate whereas, Candragupta II and Kumāragupta I have this title in their respective Gadhwa Inscriptions. If Candra of Mehrauli record is taken to be Candragupta II, this king may be seen planting a *dhvaja-stambha* in honour of Viṣṇu on Viṣṇupada hill. Bhitari record of Skandagupta aims at recording the installation of a Viṣṇu image in memory of his father[37] and his Junagadh inscription opens with an invocation to the same god.[38] The imperial coinage, no less than inscriptional records, reflects this devotion to Viṣṇu containing representations of Garuḍa and goddess Lakṣmī, and the Gupta coins reveal that Vaiṣṇavism enjoyed the status of a royal religion.[39] S.R. Goyal has shown that this affiliation to Vaiṣṇavism was not purely religious; it was practical manifestation of political philosophy. With few exceptions every devotee has some mundane desire which he seeks as a boon from his beloved deity while offering worship. The Guptas had issued out of obscurity in the early fourth century A.D. Carving out an empire from sea to sea was naturally their ambition and contemporary Vaiṣṇavite texts held out this promise, as *cakravartins*, according to them, were born in each age as essence of Viṣṇu. From *Ahirbudhnya Saṃhitā*, a well-known text of the *Pañcarātra Āgama* we learn that Viṣṇu in the form of *Cakra* was held as the ideal of worship for kings desirous of obtaining universal sovereignty. It is significant that *Cakravarti* ideal, which till the Gupta epoch was connected with Vedic Sacrifice, is given a new orientation becoming a boon from Viṣṇu. Against this background Goyal has interpreted the meaning of *Carkravikrama* type of coins in which emperor Candragupta is shown accepting three balls from the *Cakrapuruṣa* of Viṣṇu. The balls represent *Prabhu-śakti, Utsāhaśakti* and *mantra-śakti*.[40] A beautiful combination between religion and politics is established and the love of the Guptas for the Lord of Lakṣmi does not seem to be platonic but motivated by a mundane desire.

Perhaps the theory of Goyal could be seen in broader perspective. The *Mahābhārata* is the earliest work indicating the raise of theistic cults and offering a sectarian account of Vaiṣṇavite divinities—Vāsudeva-Kṛṣṇa, Nārāyana and Viṣṇu. It is fairly clear now that the Great Epic of India is not a patchwork or a motley assortment of heterogenous material piled at one place and turned into a literary monster by unpoetical theologians and commentators but a harmonious work having an organic unity and conscious design.[41] Originally a popular poem and primarily property of the bards, it underwent a unitary diaskeuasis at the hands of Bhārgava poets, the motive behind this diaskeuasis being to educate and initiate the masses into Brāhmaṇical laws of social and religious morality for which the popular epic provided a convenient vehicle of instruction. One should not miss the significance of its dichotomy in preaching the divine sanctity of the *varṇa* system and adopting at the same time a liberal attitude towards Śudras and other lower sections of society. Working further from this plane, Suvira Jaiswal beautifully sums up the socio-economic origins of Vaiṣṇavism which shaped up in early centuries of the Christian era developing all the potentialities to satisfy the need of a feudo-agricultural society and acquiring a deep influence on Indian mind. Many of the legends, myths and rituals described in Vaiṣṇavite canon, according to her, point to a popular origin not being Brāhmaṇical fabrication in all the cases. In fact some plainly reveal their anti-Brāhmaṇical origin such as the Brāhmaṇicide of the god Saṃkarṣaṇa and denunciation of the sacrificial cult by the Upholder of Mount Goverdhana.[42] Thus the role of Vaiṣaṇavism was not purely religious. Having roots in contemporary society and polity it fulfilled a number of needs. The Guptas needed a new political philosophy and Brāhmaṇical support as well as blessings; the priestly class wanted the state power to enforce the the *Varṇa* order preached by it. Each needed the other and obliged naturally in turn. The period wanted Viṣṇu and He was there to play a variety of parts. Indian tradition and culture was enriched for all times to come by his syncretic and sythetic personality. In him were absorbed, according to D.R. Bhandarkar, three deities with a definite but different past. They were puruṣa-Nārāyaṇa, Vāsudeva-Kṛṣṇa and Gopalā-Kṛṣṇa.[43] The process necessitated the birth of new myths making Viṣṇu a wonderful and colourful among sectarian gods. Contemporary records have handed down us four names of Viṣṇu in our region. They are Vidhātṛ,[44] Janārdana.[45] Nārāyaṇa[46] and Keśavapurasvāmin.[47] The significance of this last is much more than meets the eye. Figuring in a brief pillar inscription from Deogarh, it installs Viṣṇu and Lord of Keśavapura—one of the former names of Deogarh. The same god in Gadhwa stone Inscription of the time of Skandagupta is present as Citrakūṭasvāmin and Ananta-svāmin.[48] Conversely it was also possible to identify a local god with Viṣṇu though a recorded example from our region for the period is not available. This tendency of identifying Viṣṇu with local gods of any village or town or installing him as Lord of the place had an important consequence in the future course of religious history. Viṣṇu thereby became the integrating factor and a bewildering variety of deities and their devotees joined the cultural mainstream. By accommodating place-name as component part in the local name of Viṣṇu, the people were made to feel that the Lord belonged to them. Carrying such varied titles, the god could establish countless relationships and yet remain one in reality. Vedic philosophy of monism in essence but pluralism in forms was thus being translated and Viṣṇu became the focal point of unity amid cultural diversity. The Lord God of the Gītā was one having numerous identities at numerous places.[49] Here we have a glimpse into the process that contributed to *Viṣṇu-sahasra-nāma* of the epic and purāṇic literature.

That Keśavapurasvāmin, the presiding deity of the well-known Gupta temple of Deogarh, was Viṣṇu may be made out from his figure occupying the *lalāṭabimba* on the *uttaraṅga* of the sanctum doorway. Its Vaiṣṇava dedication is further confirmed by the representation of myths associated with him in the panelled niches of the outer facades. The temple has been hailed as a gem of Gupta art and architecture by the scholars and is taken to be one of the earliest *Śikhara* temples of north India. Standing on a *jagati* accessible by a flight of steps on all sides, it consists of a sanctum only with a surmounting but fragmentary *Śikhara*. Facing west, the temple has three panelled niches in its outer facades which are breath-takingly beautiful and bursting with life.

A lively controversy rages round the question whether there were four small porches or a covered gallery going round the shrine. Cunningham[50] held the latter view and Percy Brown [51] the former. Disagreeing with both M.S. Vats[52] believed that a deep and continuous flat canopy, effectively shading the reliefs below had been provided all round the temple. P.K. Agrawala, who made a special study of Gupta temple architecture, felt that an architectural expedient protecting the sculptures did exist earlier but what exactly was it could not be ascertained now.[53]

The five-*śākhā* doorway to the sanctum is exqusitely carved and is certainly one of the absorbing features of this temple. In *lalāṭabimba*, Viṣṇu is shown sitting on the serpent coil. The four-armed Lord holds *cakra* and *śaṅkha* in back hands while the front right is *abhaya-hasta* and front left rests on the folded leg. Lakṣmī is seen massaging his suspended right foot and to the right stands four-armed Nṛsiṃha.

The brief record found here being dateless, a controversy was bound to crop up on the period of the temple. Daya Ram Sahani who supervised excavation and discovered the Brāhmi record was inclined to assign the temple to early Gupta period on its basis[54] but Cunningham[55] was not ready to accept any date earlier than A.D. 600. Percy Brown[56] put the date at around A.D. 500 and more or less the same was favoured by M.S. Vats.[57] P.K. Agrawala first identified Bhāgavata Govinda of the pillar inscription (found by Sahani) with Māhārāja Govindagupta of Basarh Seal[58] (figuring there as son of emperor Candragupta II) and then dated the temple to the period A.D. 400 to 430.

The Eran Viṣṇu temple is ruined beyond recognition. Cunningham thought that the surviving shrine is at least two to three centuries posterior to the Nṛsiṃha temple at the same site. Its flat roof is the only feature indicating an early date. He ascribed the fragmentary record of Samudragupta to this 'old temple of colossal Viṣṇu.' How far was he justified in doing so wondered P.K. Agrawala since its massive capitals and mouldings were discarded at a later date for pillars of a more ornamental style.[59] Except a few *adhiṣṭhāna* mouldings of the sanctum, nothing survives now of its body. The portico pillars are sixteen-sided having a height of about 20 mtrs. 61 cms. They are carved with *ghaṭapallava* and lotus design. The four-*śākhā* sanctum doorway is 2 mtrs. 73 cms. high and 1 mtr. 33 cms. wide. A colossal, but beautiful, icon of Viṣṇu is enshrined within.

Of the incarnatory forms, Varāha and Nṛsiṃha were very popular in Bundelkhand. Earliest among the temples dedicated to them is one at Eran of which only the main icon survives. In plan it consisted of a single cell with a portico in front supported on four pillars. The pillars no longer stand now but their position can be defined by chisel marks on the surface of the plinth. The figure of Nṛsiṃha, still in situ, has an elemental strength and vigour. Save for its head and neck, all else is broken. K.D. Bajpai dated the temple to the time of Candragupta II[60].

In the very first year of the Huṇa King Toramāṇa's rule, the local *viṣayapati* of Eran financed the making of a Varāha temple. The massive boar still stands at its original place. Measuring 9 mtrs. 30 cms. from snout to the tail and nearly 3 mtrs. 75 cms. in height, the body of the boar is covered all over with tiny human and divine figures. The Earth-goddess hangs from its right tusk. Over its right shoulder is accommodated a four-sided shrine with a sitting figure in each face. Forming a kind of garland some human figures are carved round the neck. The dedicatory record incised on the neck praises the *varāhavātāra* in the opening lines with the words; "Victorious is the god Viṣṇu who has the form of a boar; who in the act of lifting up the earth out of the waters caused the mountains to tremble with the blows of his hard snout, and who is the pillar for the support of the great house which is the three worlds......" we learn later on that this 'divine temple of Nārāyaṇa' was erected by Dhanyaviṣṇu to honour the wishes of his deceased brother Mātṛviṣṇu and it was a joint deed of religious merit.[61]

One more Varāha shrine we can mention here located to the west of the hill of Deogarh. Nobody has assigned it to the Gupta period but P.K. Agrawala is of the view that several of its sculptures and architectural fragments represent relics of an early Gupta temple at the site.[61A] The image of Varāha enshrined within, he believed beyond doubt to be surviving from the initial establishment. One could validly differ from him since the Varāha panel has nothing of the Gupta style or finish. The figure of Nṛvarāha is crudely executed and is hardly life-like as the touch of a Gupta artist would have made it. Nevertheless, one cannot dismiss the view of Agrawala for this reason since all the three panels, lying around, contain the same subjects with the same details as we meet in the panels of the wellknown Gupta temple of Deogarh.

Apart from erecting temples, the practice of raising dedicatory pillars in honour of Viṣṇu was also prevalent. Belonging to the time of Budhagupta we have a flag-staff at Eran devoted to Lord Janārdana. Having a height of about 16 mtrs. and placed on a pedestal 4mtrs. 30 cms. square, the pillar was planted facing the temple of Viṣṇu described above. The shaft is 1 mtr. square up to a height of 6 mtrs. 70 cms. and then octagonal. Crowing the pillar is a two-armed male representing Garuḍa, about 1 mtr. 50 cms. high, facing both ways and had a radiated halo round the head. The dedicatory record is incised a few mtrs. above the plinth on the side facing the temple. Coming to us from the year A.D. 484-85, the inscription invokes Viṣṇu in the opening lines with the words,[62] "Victorious is the lord, the four-armed god Viṣṇu, whose couch is the broad waters of the four oceans; and who is the cause of the continuance, the production and destruction of the universe; and whose ensign is Garuḍa."[63] The flag-staff was financed by the brothers Mātṛviṣṇu and Dhanyaviṣṇu with the object of increasing the religious merit of their parents.

The institution of temple having been firmly rooted, iconographic texts were bound to follow containing elaborate injunctions regarding the representation of various gods and goddesses. The Classical Age witnessed the composition of the earliest among them. It would be worth our while to examine how far the theory in iconography corresponded to practice in Bundelkhand.

According to *Bṛhatsaṁhitā*, "The worshipful god Viṣṇu may be represented either as eight-armed, four-armed or two-armed; his breast should be marked with *Kaustubha* gem. He should be yellowish green in colour like the lin blossom, be clad in a yellow garment and should have a serene expression; he should wear earnings and a topped-crown (*Kiriṭa*) and his neck should be thick (full and fleshy). The right hand of the two-armed god should be in the *ābhaṅga* pose, the left one holding conch-shell; in this manner the image of Viṣṇu should be made by those who desire prosperity."[64] *Viṣṇudharmottara* enjoins that Vāsudeva should be four-armed, prossessing a charming appearance and beautiful body, ornamented with *kuṇḍala, aṅgada keyūra, vanamālā, kaūstubha* and *kiriṭa.* His loin-cloth and *vanamālā* should go up to knees and *yajñopavīta* should hang up to navel. A fine lotus should be carved as his *śiraścakra* and he should have long arms. Below, between his legs should be shown the earth-goddess. Flanking him should be shown Gādādevi and *Cakrapuruṣa.*

We have a couple of Viṣṇu images from Eran being the earliest in our area, but the artist has not fully adhered to the above injunctions in shaping them out. One of the icons is massive in built with full and fleshy body. Standing *samapādasthānaka*, the god is ornamented with a *Kirīṭa*, flat torque, a fine *vaijayantīmmālā* and armlets in accordance with *Viṣṇudharmottara* directions. The left arm of the deity seems to be *Kaṭyavalambita* contrary to the injunction of *Bṛhatsaṃhitā* which prescribes the showing of *saṅkha* in it. In another image the god stands *samabhaṅga* flanked by the *Saṅkha-puruṣa* and *Cakra-puruṣa* whereas *Viṣṇudharmottara* enjoins the placing of Gadādevi on one side.

In the realms of religious history Bundelkhand artist has gifted some of the rare representations of Vaiṣṇava myths, literally translating them into lithic medium from literature. It may be noted here that in most cases the artist was to exercise his own judgement and so arrange the facts and minute details as to make the story come alive in a single panel. It was indeed remarkable feat and nothing less was expected of the classical artist. We could briefly survey some of these shining stories in stone.

The myth of *karivarad* has found pictorial description in a single panel still studded in the northern niche of the Deogarh Gupta temple. The elephant stands helplessly in a lotus pond, being tightly bound by the coiled-tails of a nāga-pair. He is rescued from this painful condition and fast-nearing end by the grace of God Viṣṇu who hastened to make timely intercession. The elephant is shown proferring lotus flower to the deity held in his uplifted trunk. The Nāgapair is rendered in *namaskāra-mudrā*. (Fig. 26)

In the eastern niche has been accommodated the theme of Nara and Nārāyaṇa sitting on a rock under trees in their hermitage. The abode is unique in having lions as well as deers among its inmates enjoying close companionship. Seated *lalītākṣepa*, four-armed Nārāyaṇa is on proper right. Bearing an *akṣamālā* in upper right hand, the lower right is shown near chest in *vitarka mudrā*. We cannot make out the object of the upper left whereas in lower left he holds a long-necked flask. Sitting to his left in a similar posture is the figure of Nara, of course, with two arms only. Holding rosary in right hand, the left one is suspended with palm towards the onlooker. Both are depicted with matted hair tied into different chignons over their heads. Each wears a deer-skin thrown across his left shoulder and arm while their loin-cloth is secured by a waist-band. A bearded anchorite is carved behind them and so also garland-bearing celestial couples above their heads flying in the air. Crowning the whole composition Brahmā sits on a lotus (Fig. 27).

The southern niche of the temple shows us an elaborate rendering of Śeṣasāyī Viṣṇu. We have seen above that Eran record of Budhagupta describes four oceans as the couch of Viṣṇu. Such was the popularity of this form that the god came to have a number of names, obviously associated with it. From Varāhamihira we learn that Viṣṇu was known as Kamalanābha, Abjanābha Padmanābha and Padmadhana, which relate to the myth of the lotus, issuing from his navel and giving birth to Brahmā.[65] According to *Viṣṇudharmottara*. "Padmanābha should lie on the Śeṣa which floats on the primeval waters. The eye of the onlooker should be dazzled by his face which is brightened by the precious stones on the hoods of the Śeṣa. One of his hands should rest on thigh, second on navel, third below head, fourth with *Santāna mañjarī* :Brahmā be shown sitting on the lotus issuing out of his navel near which should stand demons Madhu and Kaiṭabha. The *āyudha-puruṣas* of Viṣṇu should be shown near Śeṣa."[66] In the *Śeṣasayai* Viṣṇu panel of the Deogarh temple, Viṣṇu has been depicted four-armed. Lakṣmī may be seen massaging his legs. Brahmā is carved sitting on a lotus the stalk of which issues from the navel of Nārāyaṇa. Flanking Brahmā are figures of Śiva-Pārvatī, Indra and Skanda riding their respective mounts. All these figures are shown hovering in the sky. The reclining body of Viṣṇu is slightly raised in its upper-half. T.A. Gopinath Rao, an authority on Hindu iconography, remarked, "The whole body has the outline of a bow which is described in the *āgamas* as appropriate to the reclining images of Viṣṇu."[66A] One of the left hands supports the head while the other rests upon the bed : of the right hands one is held in *kaṭaka* pose and the other stretches out parallel to the body so as to rest upon the thigh. Adorned with *kirīṭa-mukuṭa, kuṇḍala, hāra, keyūra, kaṅkaṇa* and *vanamālā* the Lord is close to life testifying to the high talent of the Gupta artist. The demons Madhu and Kaiṭabha have been shown in the lowermost-section of the panel alongwith *āyudha-puruṣas* (Fig. 28). Suvira Jaiswal has interpreted the myth of Śeṣasāyi Viṣṇu as subordination of non-Brāhmaṇical divinity snake worshipped by agricultural classes to Brahmanical god Viṣṇu.[67]

Varāhamihira has noticed some of the Viṣṇu incarnations such as Varāha, Vāsudeva, Vāman-Trivikrama and Rāma, the son of Daśaratha. It is, however, noteworthy that he nowhere describes them as *avatāras.* Even the name Rāma he uses in three senses, indicating his awareness of the three Rāmas viz.. Paraśurāma, Dāśarathi Rāma and Balarāma.[68]

In course of excavations at the Gupta temple of Deogarh, P.C. Makherji came upon sculptural representations of all the ten incarnations of Viṣṇu. Naturally, he named the shrine as Daśāvatāra temple.[69] So fruitful proved the process of prying around the temple, that the lives of Lords Rāma and Kṛṣṇa in their lithic translations came to light in a series of beautiful panels beyond words. These art-relics that once adorned the temple-*jagatī* include Ahalyā-*Uddhāra* ; *Vanagamana* of Rāma with Sītā and Lakṣamaṇa; visit of Rāma, Lakṣamaṇa and Sītā to the hermitage of sage Atri ; Rāma and Lakṣamaṇa learning the art of archery; Lakṣamaṇa deforming Sūrpaṇakhā; Lakṣamaṇa garlanding Sugrīva; Sugrīva under intoxication; Rāvaṇa threatening Sītā, Hanumāna carrying hill with Sañjīvani all from the Rāmāyaṇa. Episodes from Kṛṣṇa's life include Devakī handing over the child Kṛṣṇa to Vasudeva; Kṛṣṇa hurling a butter-cart; Nanda and Yaśodā fondling Kṛṣṇa and Baladeva; Kṛṣṇa welcoming his pauper friend Sudāmā; Dhenukāsura-vadha; Kaṃsa-vadha and Vasudeva fondling Kṛṣṇa. Going by the score given above, which by no means may be complete, one may legitimately conclude that the makers of Deogarh temple aimed at executing lives of both the heroes into stone, preparing a sort of pictorial gallery around the temple and offering visual spectacles of epic stories to the illiterate masses.

The *Varāhāvatāra* seems to be a special gift of Bundelkhand to Vaṣṇavism.[70] From early times the cult of the Boar found deep devotion in the local tribes. Its totemistic past can be made out from the cave art in which it has earliest manifes tation. Sir H.S. Gaur Archaeological Museum, Sagar houses an icon of Nṛvarāha belonging to the classical age. The pedestal inscription speaks of its dedication by Maheśvaradatta and Varāhadatta, apparently brothers. Bursting with vigour and vitality, the deity is ornamented with a *hāra,* Vanamālā and bracelets. His waist-band is finely knotted in front. The raised left leg is placed on the pedestal. With head turned to left, the earth-goddess is shown hanging from the snout. Interestingly, a lotus flower is carved on the head, probably to clarify that the god is just emerging out of the bottom of the Sea. Measuring 1 mr. 70 cms. in height and made of red sand-stone, the image is a wonderful work of art.

Śrī or Lakṣmī, the wife of Viṣṇu, believed to have been a fertility goddess of pre-Aryan origin, was taken over in the Vaiṣṇava pantheon in the process of rapprochement between the Vedic and the folk religions. Her Gajalakṣmī form is connected with tribes of nāga stock, since she is represented between the two nāgas (elephants). This connection is based on the Mahābhāratan legend according to which Śrī originally lived with the Asuras and abandoned them on their degradation, turning to live with Indra, the Vedic god.[71] The Gajalākṣmī scene is taken to refer to the fertilising of a female divinity of nāga genesis. It is quite possible that a mother-goddess with simple agricultural background was saturated with symbolism, once admitted to intellectual worship. Testifying to this transformation we have a record from the area adjoining to ours. By khoh copper-plate of Mahārāja Śarvanātha, half the village of Dhavasāṇḍika was made over to a non-Aryan priest Chhodugomika for meeting the cost of repairs in the temple of a non-Aryan goddess Piṣṭapurikādevī as also to perform normal rituals. The goddess has been taken by Fleet to be a form of Lakṣmī.[72]

We have a couple of Gajalākṣmī icons coming down from the classical Age. According to *Viṣṇudharmottara* a pair of elephants should be made behind her upturning the contents of two jars. Symbolically, the elephants stand for two *nidhis*—*Śaṅkha* and *Padma* which the goddess can graciously grant to the devotees. Placed within a semi-circular panel and adorning the pilaster of the southern niche of the Gupta temple, Deogarh, we have an icon of Gajalakṣmī. In the collection of Śir H.S. Gaur Archaeological Museum, Sagar, we have another datable to A.D. 400. Measuring 35 cms. high and 32 cms. broad, the image shows her seated *lalitākṣepa.* Ornamented with *kuṇḍalas* and *hāra* and flanked by one elephant on each side, pouring contents of their upturned jars over her, the goddess is clad in a garment up to her ankles. From Nachna, an *uttaraṅga* with the figure of Gajalakṣmī in the *lalāṭabimba* was recovered. On grounds of style it could be assigned to the period under review.

Among the chief Vaiṣṇava doctrines that of *Bhakti* had sociological significance. Originally, the word *bhagavat* denoted primitive tribal group owning tribal wealth and *bhakti* was a share thereof. In course of time with emergence of personal gods resulting from long interaction with non-Aryan masses, *bhagavat* signified god and *bhakti* stood for faith in him.[73] A devotional cult with unquestioned faith of the devotee was the supreme need of the time immediately preceding and suceeding the Christian era and the Gītā reflects this while preaching devotion to a god who incarnated himself repeatedly for the good of his devotees and assured the maintaining of social and religious laws. In the *Gītā bhakti* does not mean mere enjoyment of ecstatic trances by fancying the nearness of the deity ; it actually stands for carrying out one's caste duties and other social obligations in a spirit of renunciation. This theory of desireless action had definitely a social significance since in religious records of the age we see the worshippers raising temples and pillars in honour of Viṣṇu with the specific desire of increasing religious merit of their parents or themselves.

Ahiṃsā was another of the chief Vaiṣṇava doctrines.[73A] It also had socio-economic background dating to the time of Lords Buddha and Mahāvīra. Taken literally, it stands for non-killing of all beings—human and sub-human. But in actual practice it meant abstinence from animal killing and vegetarianism. We have already seen how Vaiṣṇavism held before Kings the ideal of *Cakravarti* status that necessitated waging of numerous wars and killing of innumerable soldiers. Thus the principle of non-violence was confined in its application to protecting cattle for agriculture. We have earlier pointed out how cow reached her apotheosis by this period. The bull was accepted as vehicle of Śiva. The role of *Ahiṃsa* in fixing rules of food can be seen even in contemporary eye-witness accounts.[74] Even the concept of sin conceived by Manu reflects the impact of this doctrine. He frankly admits that a householder has five slaughter-houses : the hearth (*culli*). the grinding stone (*pesaṇī*), the broom (*upaskara*), the pestle and mortar (*kandani*), and the water-vessel (*uda-kumbha*) by using which he is bound with the fetters of sin.[75] In order to expiate these inevitable offences Manu, on the authority of great Sages, prescribed five great sacrifices for the householder. That all this was not theoretical position we may easily judge from the contemporary epigraphic records which frequently refer to these sacrifices. The chief object, with which grant of land was solicited, in Damodarpur copper-plate of Kumāragupta I of the year A.D. 446-47 was the institution five great sacrifices.[76] In any case, this analysis of the Ahiṃsā doctrine as advocated and practised by the Vaiṣṇavas brings them very near to the Jainas.

Whereas Vedic literature gives very little data for framing some idea of the way in which the character of Viṣṇu was formed and one has to infer its existence as a popular religion,[77] it has preserved some intimations in regard to his rival Śiva. His final form emerged from Rudra, Bhāva, Śarva, Kāla, Iśāna, Iśvara and Mahādeva. But of Śaivism the surviving evidence does not speak as much as of Vaiṣṇavism. The available Eran records coming from imperial Gupta family or that of local *visayapatis* commemorate the construction of temples or erection of pillars and turn out to be Vaiṣṇava. Obviously any such act of piety or devotion demands surplus funds which worshippers of Śiva lacked. Thus going by this negative evidence we cannot help concluding that Śiva continued to command devotion of lower orders and, having a background of original association with fertility and agricultural operations, this was but natural.

Nevertheless, royal support to Śiva was not altogether wanting. Mahārāja Hastin, whom we have already seen offering generous grants to Vedic scholars, was a worshipper of Lord Śiva as reflected in the phrase *Mahādeva pādānudhyato* in the opening invocation of Bhumrā Stone pillar inscription.[78] That Kālañjara contidued to be the chief centre of Śaivism can be ascertained from evidence found not far from the frontiers of Bundelkhand. At Bhita two seals were discovered containing *liṅga* representation and bearing the legend *kālañjara-bhaṭṭārakasya* in one case and *kālañjara* in the other.[79] In all likelihood they seem to have been issued from the Śaiva shrine or monastery over there rather than royal establishment. Any more speculation beyond this would be unwarranted. The surviving Śiva temple of Kālañjara cannot be dated to this period, though some Gupta panels at the place point to one having been here.[79A] We do have some remains of a Śaiva shrine of this period at Sakor (Dist. Damoh). A partly preserved sanctum containing a *liṅga* and possessing a richly sculptured doorway is all that has survived of this shrine. Standing on a high *jagati*, about 79 cms. high, it is a *nirandhāra-prāsāda* facing west. The *triśākhā* doorway to the sanctum measures 1 mr. 71 cms. in height and 85 cms. broad bearing unmistakable stamp of Gupta artist. The *liṅga* inside the sanctum is 151 cms. in diameter and 81 cms. above the earth. Theoretically, the *Mānuśa* or man-made *liṅgas* are made up of three parts, known as *Brahmā-bhāga*, *Viṣṇubhāga* and *Rudra-bhāga*. The first is the square lowest section ; the second is octagonal middle one while the third or the topmost is cylindrical *Rudra-bhāga*. This last section is also called *Pūjā-bhāga* since it received offerings of water and flowers.[80] Remarkable, as it might seem, the *liṅga* of Sakor temple is made perfectly in accordance with the injunctions noted above. Its *Brahmā-bhaga* is inserted in the *pīṭha* whereas the octagonal *Viṣṇu-bhāga* and cylindrical *Rudra-bhāga* are clearly visible above. A few fluted lines carved on the *pūjā-bhāga* seem to be intended for draining off the water offering.

The non-Aryan and non-Vedic mode of worship in Śaivism is clear in the account of Varāhamihira who refers to the consecration of Śambhu image by the besmearing Brāhmaṇas.[81] It seems doubtful if Veda-studying Brāhmaṇas would have accepted the assignment. In fact D.R. Bhandarkar clearly stated that no Brāhmaṇa officiated as priest in temple of Śiva, Viṣṇu or Ambā.[82] Like the god, his mode of consecration also appeors to be of non-Aryan origin. The Pāśupatas observed the practice of besmearing the body with ashes thrice a day and sleeping on ashes. Describing Kāpālikas Varāhamihira says they were so called since they used human skulls as receptacles of food and wore garlands of skulls.[83]

Before passing on to another cult we could refer to a Śaiva record found close to our area. Tumain inscription refers to a shrine of Lord Pinākin as lofty as the peak of a hill and bearing the lustre of the moon. It is interesting to note the temple was raised by five brothers from the mercantile class.[84]

Of an independent cult of Skanda as such we have no evidence. Elsewhere in North India he enjoyed considerable following and has been held as popular as Śiva and Viṣṇu by D.R. Bhandarkar.[85] With non-Aryan past, like his father Śiva, he found full accommodation in Brāhmaṇical worship as we can make out from Bilsad Stone pillar inscription where he is hailed as Brāhmaṇya.[86] Interestingly, we have a record from the area adjoining to ours in which the consort of Kārttikeya finds consecration. Ṣaṣṭhī is otherwise little-known. Six-headed like her husband, she gets good coverage in the Greater Epic.[87] In the Meghadūtam of Kālidāsa, the cloud-messenger is to cover a place called Devagiri in course of his journey, where the permanent abode of Lord Skanda is located. Fleet identified it with Deogarh[88] and if that be so, we have here a centre of Skanda-worship. But all this is hardly more than speculation since out of the religious remains at the place we can not cite even a single piece showing the connection of Skanda with Deogarh. Srīdhara-vaman, the Śaka potentate, was certainly a devotee of Svāmi Mahāsena as is evident from his Kānākherā Stone inscription[89] Some area of Bundelkhand being part of his dominions, he might have financed the erection of a shrine there devoted to Skanda, but that also is merely a possibility.

If we were to name any cult which was earliest in origin and held ground through the ages consistently and continuously, we would mention the Mother-goddess. She came to be known by numerous names by now like Devī, Mātr, Ambikā, Āryā, Durgā, Bhadrā, and Khemā.[90] Propitiation through offerings of flesh and wine pointed to the pre-Aryan past, on epigraphic plane we have the solitary record of Svāmibhaṭṭa from Deogarh assignable to this age in which he claims to have constructed Avanīśvara temple in honour of the Sapta-Mātṛkās.[91] The shrine apparently is none other than Nāhar Ghāṭi in which the Mātṛkās are accommodated inside eleven niches alongwith Vīrabhadra and Gaṇapati. According to *Bṛhatsaṃhitā* the mothers should be made with the forms and cognisances of the individual gods whom they are named after.[92] At Deogarh first to find representation is Vīrabnadra holding *vīṇā* followed by three-headed Brāhmī. Next may be seen Māheśvarī seated on lion and holding Gaṇeśa. Kaumarī and Vaiṣṇavī ride their respective mounts peacock and garuḍa. Then we have Vārāhī and Indrāṇī on tortoise and elephant respectively followed by four-armed Cāmuṇḍā riding on human corpse. Last in our list is Gaṇapati. It is interesting to note that apart from animal head, Vārāhī has been endowed with a human face as well.[92A]

A free-standing temple of the goddess we do have at Nachna known as Pārvatī temple. Though it is placed in the period between A.D. 470-90 on the basis of a record of Mahārāja Vyāghradeva,[93] P.K. Agrawala holds that the inscription possibly marks the rebuilding of the monument with a cloister and a *maṇḍapa.*[94] The *garbhagṛha,* is enclosed by a larger chamber serving the purpose of a *pradakṣiṇā-patha* thus rendering the temple a *sandhāra-prāsāda.* Having a *maṇḍapa* in front, the interesting feature in this temple is that it is double-storeyed. The gloom of the sanctum is relieved by a doorway in the west and stout trellises in the remaining three sides. Similar trellises had been fixed in the corresponding part of the cloister wall. The ceiling of the sanctum consists of flat monolithic slabs. The *pancaśākhā* doorway to sanctum consists of a meandering creeper, geometrical pattern consisting of diamond-shaped ornaments ; a pilaster and a superimposed row of half-opened rosettes. Two of the *śakhās* have been carried over the lintel. Needing special note here is the fact that the difference between the height and breadth of the temple, 2 and 1 mr. respectively, corresponds to the one prescribed in the text.[94A]

Of the Sun-cult we do not possess any positive evidence assignable to this period. But the fact that the Sauras did constitute a part of population could be postulated since evidence of sun-worship from earlier period we have cited and already discussed. Deserving of mention here, however, is a curious fact.

The Nachne-Ki-Talai inscription of Mahārāja Vyāghradeva contains the carving of a wheel.[95] The exact sense of the symbol could be a matter of dispute but earlier we have seen that the wheel represented Sūrya in the rock or pottery art.

Before turning to heterodox sects we should notice a land-mark in the history of orthodox, Hinduism highlighting the unity emerging out of diversity which Bundelkhand has preserved for posterity. The Gupta temple of Deogarh had four subsidiary shrines attached to it. We shall never know, perhaps, to whom were they dedicated. But their mere existence renders the temple a real *pañcāyatana.* Normally the four subsidiary shrines are occupied by the four principal gods of Hinduism, other than the god of the main temple. The concept was that of offering all the five great deities simultaneous worship. The ideal perhaps found literal translation into stone at Deogarh and if our surmise is held valid, the Gupta temple here has to be taken as the earliest example of a *pañcāyatana* shrine.

In sharp contrast to the wealth of archaeological evidence attesting the hold and sweep of orthodox sects, the religious remains of Buddhism and Jainism are few and far between. But that in no way reflects the reality. Such was the irresistible appeal of Buddhism that even Vedic scholars of very high merit sometimes switched over their allegiance to it abandoning orthodox views and studies. The fact is testified to by no less an authority than emperor Harṣavardhana. While wandering in search of his sister among Vindhyan wilds—in all likelihood somewhere in the area of our study—he is on record having heard about Divākaramitra and reflected, "I have heard that a follower of the *Maitrāyaṇī Śākhā,* the boy friend of the deceased Grahavarman of auspicious name, having abandoned the three *Vedas,* when he was a leading Brāhmaṇa teacher, though still young in years, turned his studies to the Buddhist doctrine and assumed the red dress."[96] The very fact that the emperor himself and queen Rājyaśrī also desired to be initiated into Buddhist order[97] further shows that the example cited above cannot be treated as isolated and exceptional. Freedom of conscience and creed that it reflects is in sharp contrast to the persecution and intolerance characterising the religious life elsewhere in the world at the time. Only a true intellectual could exercise such option and Divākaramitra was certainly one, having reached even the teaching stage and then veering away from the Vedic doctrine.

But the change did not make of him a Buddhist bigot. His disciples came from a wide variety of philosophical and religious affiliations and, if Bāṇa is to be believed, were all equally welcome to his hermitage which permitted free exchange and fair interaction. Among the inmates of the Āśrama, the emperor saw Buddhists from various provinces seated in different situations,—perched on pillars or lying in thickets, or in the shadow of the branches or squatting on the roots of trees,—devotees dead to all passion, the Śvetāmbara Jainas, Hindu ascetics who had abandoned Buddhism, the Bhāgavatas, ascetics who pulled out their hair, students of philosophical system of Kapila, Kaṇāda, Upaniṣads and *Nyāya,* Lokāyatikas, assayers of metals, students of legal institutes, students of the *Purāṇas,* adepts in sacrifices requiring seven ministering priests, adepts in grammar, Pañcarātras and others besides, all diligently following their own tenents, pondering, urging objections, raising doubts, resolving them, giving etymologies, disputing, studying and all gathered here as his disciples.[98] This long and almost endless list of religious sects, subsects and philosophical systems together with a few secular branches of khowledge makes out the hermitage verily a university for which a parallel is difficult to search particularly in respect of religious catholicity that it reflected. If Divākarmitra could attract students of Upaniṣadik, Paurāṇic and Dharmaśāstra literature coexisting with Lokāyatikas and Jainas even after his open switch-over to Buddhism from Brāhmaṇism, it is a golden page in the annals of our country that records it. In all likelihood his *Āśrama* stood somewhere in Bundelkhand and so it can be treated as another land-mark in the religious history of the region, coming appropriately from the Classical Age. But Buddhism now had a lot in common with Brāhmaṇism. The Buddha is now verily a creator like Brahmā of

Hindu trinity. The Sammatiyas looked upon Śākya-muni not only as perfectly Enlightened One but also as God and Creator of the world.[99]

On the plane of archaeology, the prevalence of Buddhism can be postulated from the traces of fast-vanishing *stūpas* that once flourished at Chhoti Badoni (Dist. Datia). They had a radious of about 15 mrs. and were constructed of bricks of Gupta character that are still scattered at the place. Local traditions do speak of Mahāyāna Buddhism having been associated with the hillocks of Gopeśvara in the vicinity of chhoti Badoni from the early centuries of the Christian era.[100] Confirming further our assumption are a few backed clay-sealings collected from the place bearing the miniature representation of a stūpa and inscribed with the usual formula.

Bundelkhand Chhatrasal museum (Banda) displays among its antiquities a sculptural representation of a stūpa possessing a square base crowned by a cylindrical dome. Carved fully in round, and measuring 18 cms. side at bottom, on each of its faces, the stūpa contains representation of a miniature shrine within which a seated Budda is accommodated. In two of the three representations, the Budda has been depicted in *dhyāna-mudrā* whereas in the other two he is shown in *dharmacakra-mudrā* and *bhumisparśa-mudrā* respectively. The *stupa* is inscribed on three sides below with the Buddhist formula. Exactly similar sculptural representation of a miniature stūpa is included in the collection of Mahatma Gandhi Hindi Musem, Kalpi. Like the earlier one, it is also carved out of state-coloured stone. Unfortunately findplaces in both the cases could not be ascertained, otherwise they have pointed to two more centres of Buddhism in Bundelkhand.[101]

Positive evidence we do not possess proving hold of Jainism during the Gupta period However, B. C. Jain made out a case for assigning temple No. 15 and the *Mahāmaṇḍapa* attached to temple No. 12 at Deogarh to the Gupta period. He relied on the resemblance between the Gupta temple, described above, and temple No. 15 of the Jaina group surviving there. He came to the conclusion that either of them must inspried the conception of the other, [102] implying thereby that temple No. 15 could be earlier than the Gupta temple or at least not far removed in date from it. His views with regard to Jaina architecture and sclupture merit discussion.

He thought temple No. 15 took on its present from in coures of four centuries with *Mahāmaṇḍapa* as the earliest component part datable to fourth century A.D. Is was originally planned as the centralmost section of a *Samavasaraṇa*. This section has 12 compartments and here also they are three in each direction. *Gandhakuṭi* occupies the cetralmost position with a square form and contains the seat of the *Tīrthaṅkara* on three circular platforms. Though this *vedi* is lost now, but an inscrption found on its place is now studded in the southeast corner of the *mahāmaṇḍapa*. This inscription is known as *Jñānaśilā* record, containing lines of letters from different alphabetical orders starting with Brāhmī. It symbolises that the sermon of a Jina is delivered in 18 chief languages and 700 dialects and so, it was placed in the centre of this *mahāmaṇḍapa*.

We have some difficulty in accepting the views of B.C. Jain. Of course, there is some resemblance between the temple No. 15 and the Gupta temple of Deogarh, since both hove an arrangement of panelled niches in outer facades. But the latter has one cella whereas the former has three. The Gupta temple definitely had a *śikhara* whereas the Jaina temple is crowned by a pavilion. The Gupta temple was provided with a deep and flat continuous canopy to protect the panelled niches whereas no such expedient can be made out in case of the Jaina temple. Moreover, epigraphic evidence found within the temple is not assignable to the Gupta period. Hence the resemblance between the two noticed by the scholar is not great enough to warrant us in dating the Jaina temple to the time of the Imperial Guptas or even the middle of the 7th century A.D.. H.D. Sankalia also felt that Jainism flourished at Deogarh in pre-Gupta and Gupta period but could not cite any evidence.[103]

As regards temple No. 12, it is true that its making was spread over some centuries and its component parts come gradually into existence. But here also no ground has been cited for placing its *mahāmaṇḍapa* in the 4th century A.D. The earliest dated inscription of Deogarh, which incidentally come from this temple, belongs to the time of Bhoja Pratihāra.[104] Klaus Bruhn, who has done a monumental work on Deogarh remains of the Jainas, thought that among the component parts of temple No. 12, *vimāna* with porch was the earliest to appear and the hall belongs to later period. As a matter of fact, he categorically remarks, "there is no evidence which would lead us to suppose that important Jaina temples and sculptures were in existence before the middle of the 9th century A.D."[105]

But the influence of Jainism in our area cannot be altogether ruled out in the absence of positive evidence. *Mahārājādhirāja* Rāmagupta who financed the carving of three Vidisha stone images representing Candraprabha, Puṣpadanta and Padmaprabhu was very likely the governor as well as ruler in the Eran part of the empire. [106] Jainism must have flourished under him and the earliest of Jaina establishments coming up at Deogarh in his time appears a fair possibility though nothing survives to substantiate it.

We could very well close our account of Jainism with reference to another example of religious harmony based on mutual respect among not only the cults of Hinduism but between orthodox and heterodox sects. The record does not come directly from our region but as it belongs to adjoining area we could legitimately quote it to show the intersect-relations. Kahaum Stone pillar inscription is distinctly Jaina in character commemorating the setting up of five *Ādikartṛ* images. [107] The donor here is Madra who is mentioned as exceedingly affectionate towards Brāhmaṇas, religious preceptors and ascetics. The remarkable fact here is the honour harboured by a devout Jaina towards Brāhmaṇas as distinct from Srāmaṇas.

Till now we have referred to the raising of many temples and related in some cases their architecture as well as sculpture. One wonders in what way the state figured in the management of these religious institutions. No record of our area has anything to reveal on the point. Fortunately close to us were found Bamhni plates of Pāṇḍava monarch Bharatabala which mention an officer—*deva-vārika*, who was entrusted with the task of superintending temples and holy places.[108]

In concluding our coverage of the Classical Age, we may notice a curious religious practice prevailing in central India for which there is no parallel either in the preceding or succeeding period elsewhere in India. Even scriptural injunction is not easy to come by imparting vailidity to it. Supia Pillar inscription of the time of Skandagupta is in fact a memorial planted by Varga grāmika to commemorate the death of his father, grandfather and brothers. The pillar is mantioned as *bala-yaṣṭi* called *gotra-śailikā,* [109] Interestingly *gotra* is nowhere mentioned and the family was clearly of *vaiśya varṇa.* Since the object of the record is stated to be increase in the religious merit of the donor it has direct bearing on the theme of our narrative. One more instance of such a memorial handed down from another husbandman family is the well known Bhurma Pillar inscription,taken for long to be a boundary pillar between the Parivrājaka and Ucchakalpa kingdoms of central India under overlordship of the imperial Guptas.[110] D. C. Sircar removed the wrong impression pointing out that it was a memorial raised by Śivadāsa in honour of a dead raltive.[111] The records being irritatingly brief and instance elsewhere, even in immediate vicinity, absolutely wanting, one is left wondering where rose the ritual and why did it vanish so soon ?

REFERENCES

1. C.A., p. 14
2. C.I.I., III (Revised), No. 2
3. C.A., p. 23
4. C.I.I, III (Revised), No. 17
5. Ibid., No. 3
6. Ibid., No. 4
7. Ibid., No. 39
8. Fleet, No. 21
9. Ibid., No. 22
10. Ibid., No. 23
11. Ibid., No. 110
12. C.I.I., III (Revised), p. 124
13. Ibid., No. 1
14. Ibid., No, 20
15. Ibid., No. 14

16. Ibid. No., 2
17. Ibid. No., 10
18. Fleet. No. 21
19. C.I.I., III (Revised), No. 14
20. Ibid., No. 39
21. Ibid., Nos.—8,17,26 and Fleet No. 66
22. Goyal S.R. : *A History of the Imperial Guptas* Central Book Depot, First Edition, Allahabad, 1967, p. 135 ff.
23. Fleet. No. 19

23.A Goyal, S.R. : op. cit, p. 345

24. गुप्त, परमेश्वरी लाल: गुप्त साम्राज्य विश्वविद्यालय प्रकाशन प्रथम संस्करण, 1970 पृ. 151 also Goyal S.R., op. cit., p. 345
25. C.I.I., III (Revised), No. 9
26. Ibid., No. 11
27. Ibid., No, 21
28. Ibid., No. 5 A.B.C.
29. Goyal, S.R. : op. cit., p. 293
30. C.I.I., III (Revised), No. 30. It is noteworthy that the life of a Brāhmana and a cow is held to be of highest value and is in tune with the class legislation of *Dharmasāstra* literature advocating discrimination on the basis of *Varṇa*.
31. Cowell E.B. : (Tr.) : *The Harṣa-carita of Bāṇa* Royal Asiatic Society, London, 1897, p. 238, Thomas F.W.
32. Kale M.R. (Tr.) : *Bnua's Kādambari* Vaman Yashwant's Co., Bombay, 1924, p. 51.
33. Ibid., p. 53
34. Ibid., p. 60
35. C.I.I., III (Revised), p. 125
36. Ibid., No. 12
37. Ibid., No. 31
38. Ibid., No. 28
39. Altekar, A.S. : *The Coinage of the Gupta Empire*, Numismatic Society of India, B.H.U., 1957, p. 92
40. Goyal, S.R. : op. cit., p. 136
41. Jaiswal, Suvira : *The Origin and Development of Vaiṣṇavism*, Munshiram Manoharlal, Delhi, 1967, p. 9
42. Ibid., p. 31
43. C.I.I., III (Revised), p. 127
44. Ibid., No. 39
45. Ibid.
46. Fleet. No. 36
47. A.P.R., 1915-18, p. 29.
48. Fleet. No. 66
49. *The Bhagvad Gītā*, X. 19 हन्त ते कथयिष्यामि दिव्या ह्मात्म विमूलय: प्राधान्यत : कुरुश्रेष्ठ नास्त्यन्तो विस्तरस्य मे ॥
50. A.S.R., X, p. 106
51. Brown, Percy : *Indian Architecture* (Buddhist and Hindu), D.B. Taraporewala sons & Co., (Seventh Reprint), Bombay, 1976, p. 50
52. M.A.S.I., No.70, p. 6
53. Agrawala, P.K. : *Gupta Temple Architecture*, Varanasi, 1968, p. 36
54. A.P.R., 1915-18, pp. 28-29

55. A.S.R., X, p. 110
56. Brown, Percy : op. cit., p. 50
57. M.A.S.I., No. 70, pp. 9-10
58. Agrawala, P.K. : op. cit., pp. 38-39
59. Ibid.
60. *Sagar Through the Ages*, Sagar, 1967, p. 5
61. Fleet No. 19

61A. Trivedi, S.D. also echoes this opinion. (B.P., p. 23) we fail to understand on what grounds he took it to be of *Śikhara* style as the surviving remains hardly warrant such a supposition.

62. Agrawala, P.K. : op. cit., p. 32
63. C.I.I.. III (Revised), No. 39
64. B.S., 58, 31-32, 35
65. Shastri, A.M. : *India as Seen in the Bṛhatsaṃhitā of Varāhamihira*, Delhi, 1969, p. 128
66. *Viṣṇudharmottara Purāṇa*; 81, 2-8; Venkatesvara Press, Bombay, V.S 1992

66A. E.H.I., Vol. I, pt. 1, p. 110

67. Jaiswal, Suvira : op. cit., p. 58
68. Shastri, A.M. : op. cit., pp. 127-29
69. M.A.S.I., No. 70, p. 2
70. Jaiswal, Suvira : op. cit., p. 121
71. Ibid., 89 ff.
72. Fleet. No. 29
73. Jaiswal, Suvira : op. cit., p. 110 ff.

73A. Ray Choudhuri, H.C. : *Early History of the Vaishnava sect*, Orient Reprint, New Delhi, 1975, Preface, p. VII

74. C.A., p. 579
75. Manu, III, Bharatiya Vidya Series, Vol. XXXII (II), 68-71 : C. I.I., III (Revised), p. 290, Note-9
76. C.I.I., III (Revised), No. 24
77. Barth, A. : *Religions of India*, S. Chand & Co., (Sixth Edition), New Delhi, 1980, p. 165
78. Fleet. p. 110 ff.
79. Jash, Pranabanand : *History of Śaivism*, p. 48

79.A A.S.R., XXI, p. 32.

80. D.H.I., p. 458
81. Shastri, A.M. : op. cit., p. 138
82. C.I.I., III (Revised), p. 138
83. Shastri, A.M. : op. cit., p. 138
84. C. I.I., III (Revised), No. 20
85. Ibid., P. 123
86. Ibid., No. 16
87. Supia Sati Pillar Inscription, *Proceedings and Transactions of the All Indian Oriental Conference*, XII Session, Vol. III, B.H.U., 1943-44, p. 587
88. Shastri, C. Sankara Rama : *Meghasandeśa of Kālidāsa*, Sri Balamanorama Series, No. 38, Mylapore, Madras, 1947, p. 42
89. C.I.I., IV, Pt. I, No. 5, pp. 13-16
90. C.I.I., III (Revised), pp. 125 and 137
91. E.I., XVIII, No. 15
92. B.S., 57, 65.

92A. B.P., p. 51
93. C.I.I., V, No. 20
94. Agrawala, P.K. : op. cit., p. 72; S.D. Trivedi has dated the Pārvati temple to 5th century A.D. but has not given any grounds for doing so. (B.P., p. 31)
94A. B.S. 56.12; Some of the medieval texts such as *Mānasāra*, *Mayamata* and *Gurudeva paddhati* have idential recommendation. See-Mallayya, N.V. : Studies in Sanskrit texts on Temple Architecture, 1949, pp. 235-236
95. C.I.I., V, No. 20
96. Cowell E.B. : op. cit., p. 233
Thomas E.W.
97. Ibid., p. 258
98. Ibid., p. 236
99. C.I.I., III, (Revised), pp. 141-142
100. साप्ताहिक भारती, सम्पादकीय—'संस्कृति के सूत्र' दतिया, वर्ष 12, अंक 47, पृ. 28
101. The clay-sealings were collected by a team of the Department of Ancient Indian History, Culture, Archaeology, University of Saugar, in course of a survey undertaken in the district of Datia,
102. जैन भागचंद: देवगढ़ जैन कला का सांस्कृतिक अध्ययन, शोध प्रबन्ध सागर विश्वविद्यालय 1970, पृ. 127 और आगे
103. Sankalia, H.D. : *Aspects of Indian History and Archaeology*, p. 118
104. E.I., VI, No. 44; A.S.R., X, p. 10
105. C.I.I., III (Revised), No. 5, A.B.C.
106. Bruhn, Klaus : *The Jian Images of Deogarh*, Leiden, 1969, pp. 52-53
107. Ibid., No. 29
108. E.I., XXVII, No. 24
109. C.I.I., III (Revised), No. 32
110. A.S.R., X, p. 8 ff.
111. E.I., XXXIII, p. 171

6

Early Medieval Period

If we were to sum up the characteristic quality of religious life of this period just in one word, we would do so with—DYNAMISM. Whichever way we look at the area and the evidence it offers, early medieval Bundelkhand is bursting with life and activity, change and novelty, power and prosperity. And religion becomes a force in this multi- dimensional revolution of that rocky region which is brought about by the sons of the oil – the Candellas. Whether one wants to study contemporary polity or society or even economy, the role of religion can hardly be ignored. The very fact of this triple role renders religion a dynamic force, which quickens and enlivens the land lying asleep for centuries. With the Brāhmaṇisation of the Candellas, a local centure of power emerges for the first time imparting political unity to the province, converting aboriginal masses into cultivating classes, raising an army equal to those accompanying alien invaders, offering impetus to trade and industry and transforming, for a while, this peripheral' region into a 'core' one.

The territory now teems with temples of whom the tally runs into several dozens. If the ruined ones were also to be Included, the number would go well over a couple of hundreds. The making of temples and carving of sculptures verily grows into an inde- pendent and prosperous industry with obvious specialization of labour in the working classes. In the fore-going period only emperors or high officers could finance the building of a shrine. Now the commercial classes come forward with their new-gotton prosperity. Even a single merchant can be seen financing several shrines. A regular management of these holy institutions emerges, not imposed from the above but developed from below. A new priesthood is the obvious concomitant of this proliferation and it isthere to take charge with assignment of immense wealth. However, Vedic scholars maintain their supermacy and all the available land-grants with few exceptions, go in their favour. A massive influx of these immigrants into this inhospitable region can legitimately be postulated, as, in a couple of cases, the number of donees runs into hundreds.

Hinduism is hard to define. Whatever sense we attach, the period reveals it in all its aspects—its Vedic foundation and Paurāṇic superstructure, its modes of worship and prayer; it beliefs, rituals and even superstitions, its strength as well as weakness. Apart from five Great Deities, a few lesser ones also find independent cults built around them. Buddhism maintains a few precarious pockets whereas Jainism grows much stronger and spreads wider sharing a lot in common with contemporary orthodox cults. Throwing a welcome light on all the major cults we have an eye-witness account, perhaps a bit prejudiced one, in the shape of a drama—Prabodhacandrodaya—definitely datable to this period as well as province.

Religious consciousness finds remarkable manifestation in art and architecture so it is natural that the period hands down to us some rare gems in sculpture and architecture. We verily have here Bundelkhand 'mind materialised into stone'. In grace andexcellence, some of them have hardly any match elsewhere in the country. Indeed, Bundelkhand comes into her own during the Early-Medieval Period.)

We were badly handicapped in our study of the preceding period since written records were simply not there or very few. An air of uncertainty naturally hung thickly over many aspects of religious life that we could touch. With the commencement of Early-Medieval Period, we can walk on tolerably sure ground getting plenty of epigraphic and archaeological evidence. Available inscriptions are from royalty as well as nobility but mostly they come from orthodox faiths. No doubt, Jaina records from Deogarh number 400, and together with those from other places, they certainly outnumber Brāhmaṇical documents, but they do not put us wise on the inside structural or doctrinal changes in Jainism. Perhaps they had reason to be reticent. Jainism did not flourish on royal support as did Brāhmaṇism and so, returning praise for patronage was never needed. Coupled with this may be seen the section of Jaina laity, which mostly came from commercial classes of urban areas, content with their names figuring in the records and hardly concerned about doctrinal description. The situation thus forces us ro give greater coverage to orthodox sects.

Our period of about 600 old year from the death of Emperor Harṣa Vardhana to the termination of Candella rule witnessed the accentuation of those very beliefs and tendencies that came to the fore in the preceding period for the first time. The concept of the Kali Age solidified and a nostalgic longing for the lost Kṛta Age leads the religious thought in the epigraphic records. The picture in both the cases was painted by the Brāhmaṇas and coloured by their values. Any power adhering to these values and offering their translation in life was most welcome to them. Part of our period was dominated by the Pratihāras and part by the Candellas. Both were of obscure origin and shot suddenly into prominence. They would not have found easy acceptance. Legitimation by a recognized religion has always been decisive for an alliance between politically and socially dominant classes and the priesthood. Integration into the Hindu community provided such religious legitimation for the ruling stratum. It not only endowed the ruling stratum of the barbarians with recognised rank in the cultural Hinduism but through assumption of Brāhmaṇic *gotras* and *pravaras* secured superiority over the subject classes.[1] The Princes promised to practise the Brāhmaṇic values of the Golden Age and agreed to exterminate the vices of the Kali Age. The fact comes clearly home from the Candella records. In the very opening account of their origin occurring in a Khajuraho inscription the family is admired inasmuch as 'they practised the conduct of the golden age.'[2] The conduct of individual Candella Kings created a wrong impression that Kali Age had ended untimely. Dhaṅga is credited in the same record accomplishing his purposes by means of such conduct as to make people believe that the Kali Age had, out of season, come to an end.[3] One of his descendants, Vijayapāla is likewise spoken of in the Mau Candella inscription as purifying the earth with his virtuous conduct. Exterminating the wicked and gladdening all good men he put an end to the Kali Age.[4] Further the Poet of this record makes out King Kīrtivarman as Virtue Incarnate descended on the earth to destroy the sin of the Kali Age. Not satisfied with one mention in this case, the poet once more refers to his extirpating the multitude of thorns together with the strife induced by the impurity of the Kali Age. Appropriately enough the ministers were not to be outdone in the matter and since the record is ministerial one, the conduct of Gadādhara, a minister, is described good enough to cheat the people into believing that with him Kali Age had come to an end. One wonld naturally ask what distinguished the Golden Age and what defiled the Kali one ? Since the records—whether literary or epigraphic—are Brāhmaṇical on the subject, the value-system applicable here was also of their making. Fortunately in a couple of records we do have some idea into what constituted the Golden and Iron Ages. Mau Candella record of Madanavarman, while eulogising king Pṛthvīvarman says. "who, hating the ill-behaved and greatly delighting in worthy people, desirous of taking lawful wealth and then expending it according to prescription sacred objects, carefully protecting all beings and wholly intent on securing propriety of conduct, thus practised here—a noble art—the conduct of the golden age.[5] If any elaboration of above-mentioned features of Golden Age is required, Ajaygadh Rock Inscription of Kīrtivarman settles the matter beyond the shadow of a doubt with just one phrase. This epigraph is an eulogy of another ministerial family in which Maheśvara, the incharge officer of Kālañjara gates, was born who restored the golden age of virtue by establishing the laws of Manu.[6] Thus the establishment and administration of *varṇāśrama dharma* and allied Brāhmaṇical ideals as laid down in Manu's scheme constitute the main features of the Kṛta age. Any deviation therefrom was indicative of the advent of the Kali. The fact that many of the Candella kings earned the merit of having inaugurated the Golden Age and ending the Kaliyuga highlights the ideals that they upheld and shows the extent to which their conduct approximated to Manu's scheme of values. Reverence for the Vedas was fundamental to this conduct of the Golden Age. So the Pratihāras as well as the Candellas, who dominated the period for the most part, withheld nothing in their support for the *Vedas*. The records do not speak of their having celebrated an *Aśvamedha* like the Guptas but with few exceptions almost all the available copper-plate grants aim at sustaining and encouraging Vedic scholarship whereas the genealogical accounts abound in references to the cult of sacrifice. To take the second point first, such was the hold of sacrificial religion that the volume of smoke sent by sacrificial fires rose in the shape of a cloud in the sky cheating peacocks who used to dance on seeing it—a fact we learn from Mau Stone Inscription of Madanavarman.[7] Interesting as it might seem, even the warfare was also viewed in terms of performing sacrifice. Rahila, an early Candella ruler, is thus spoken of in Khajuraho Stone inscription:

"Who never tired, at the sacrifice of battle, where the terribly wielded sword was the ladle, where the oblation of clarified butter was made with streaming blood, where the twanging of the bowstring was the exclamation *vaṣat* and at which exasperated warriors marching in order were the priests, successful with the counsels (as with sacred hymns) sacrificed, like beasts, the adversaries in the fire of enemity : made to blaze up high by the wind of his unappeased anger."[8] This literal likeness between the priestly and princely sacrifices, seen and described in all its aspects by the poet, fully drives home the hold of Vedic sacrifices on the upper classes. If any more instance is required, Baṭesvar inscription of a Candella minister admires an earlier minister thus : " "The lines of smoke of whose bright sacrificial fires, with their numerous clearly visible undulating lines, assumed the beautiful appearance of braids of hair put playfully on the big breasts of the women of the quarters."[9] Thus the three beautiful pen-pictures in which the irresistible appeal of Vedic sacrifice is amply reflected should convince us that Vedism stood at the top of all other contemporary cults.

Closely allied to it was Vedic Scholarship that found unprecedented welcome in the region. With few exceptions almost all copper-plate grants aim at assigning revenue for its maintenance. By Barah copper-plate, Bhoja Pratihāra made over Valākāgrahāra to the Brāhmaṇas born of the family of Bhaṭṭa-kācara-Svāmin, students of Vājasaneya Śākhā.[10] Likewise Candella monarch Devavarman by Charkhari Plate gave away village Bhūttapallikā to Paṇḍita Kikkana who had emigrated from Kumbhaṭibhaṭagrāma. The donee was scholar of the *Vedas*, the V*edāṅgas*, *Itihāsa*, the *Purāṇas* and *Mīmāṃsā* and devoted to *Ṣaṭ-karma*. We also have Charkhari plates of Paramardideva which record the grant of Sagaudo village to a number of Brāhmaṇas whose forefathers had emigrated from Mutautha

Bhaṭṭāgrahāra, making an exception of five *halas* of land already gifted to a Buddhist Shrine.[11] One more Charkhari plate we have, this time from Hammirvarman, recording the grant of Kikaḍgrāma to two Brāhmaṇas,, though in this case full details of the donee are wanting owing to the fragmentary nature of the document. Many more copper-plates could be quoted to prove the practices of assigning villages and lands to Vedic scholars but as our point is well-established by now, we would conclude with Semra Plates of Parmardideva which are without parallel in respect of the number of villages assigned as well as donees favoured and details offered. The number simply surpasses those known so far from other records of this class in the area. The villages figuring in the inscription include Khatauda-dvādaśaka, Tāṇṭa-dvādaśaka, Hāṭa-aṣṭā-daśaka, Śeṣa-igrāma, Pilikhiṇa-Pañcela, Itāva-Pañcela, Isarahāra-Pañcela Uladana, Kakarādaha, Nasohahathidaha and Paṭha. It is fairly probable that a few of these names stand for a group of villages as can be easily made out from the suffixes dvādaśaka, aṣṭādaśaka and Pañcela indicating the figures of 12, 18 and 5 respectively. Thc beneficiary Brāhmaṇas number 309 here representing every Vedic school of the time reflected in the titles —Dvivedin, Trivedin, Caturvedin Agnihotrin, Śrotrīya, Paṇḍita, Dikṣīta, Thakkura, Rājaputra—that they carried.[12] Of course, the last two titles do not pertain to Vedic studies but official position that they or any of their ancestors enjoyed. What is more significant, all the beneficiaries had emigrated from various *Bhaṭṭāgrahāras* like their counterparts in other copper-plates. If anything, this mass influx of the Brāhmaṇas indicates intensive and extensive Brāhmaṇisation of Bundelkhand on the one hand and warm welcome offered by the reigning family for its own legitimation on the other. This newly-imported intellectual minority together with surviving one of the earlier times stood at the apex of social and religious and, to some extent, political structure of the times.

The second class of beneficiaries sharing this manifestation of royal and official munificience were the temples and priests attached to them. Proliferation of temples we have already seen in the chapter on Archaeology. An interesting fact is worthy of note in this regard. Of all the characteristics qualifying the Kṛta Age in Brāhmaṇical literature, the most striking is frequent manifesting and free mixing of deities with their devotees with no need of instituting the temples.[13] We fail to understand when Kṛta Age had been truly restored by the kings, as mentioned above, where was the need of raising temples ? Were not the Brāmaṇical ideologues contradictory in their statement ? Perhaps they implied that Golden Age had gone for good and Kali had come to stay; only the conduct of kings and ministers approximated to the values of the Kṛta Age creating a false impression of its having been restored ! The masses had neither the mind nor the courage to question the contradictory position of their leaders.

In the preceding period we did have some copper-plates aimed at endowing the temples, though from the adjoining area. Curiously enough, copper-plates of the period under review are largely devoted to the maintenance of the Vedic scholars and in few cases, of secular functionaries. Temples seem to have taken back seat in this regard. Even the world-famous Khajuraho temples do not figure in any of the available copper-plates though thereby the fact of their having been endowed is not denied. None among the Khajuraho records is a copper-plate. Hardly a couple of the stone inscriptions refer, that too in the vaguest possible terms, to the provisions for meeting the financial expenses of the priests and the rituals, and one is left wondering how such a large complex of some 35 temples was maintained, especially when the town was not a place of pilgrimage and so, the cash generosity of the pilgrims was out of question. Such a conglomeration anywhere would have required revenue of a good many villages for its upkeep, rituals and priests. Elsewhere in the area also, the few references to temple maintenance we get are all from stone inscriptions never couched in as clear and legal a language as the copper-plate grants. The relevant portion of Khajuraho inscription of Dhaṅgadeva dismisses the financial management of temple dedicated to Pramathanātha just in two verses, referring only to the residential quarters for the Brāhmaṇas to whom donations were made of land, grain, money and cows.[14] Another inscription from the same site condenses the matter in one verse only—which is badly mutilated—to the effect that certain buildings close to the temple of Vaidyanātha were erected for pious Brāhmaṇas.[15] The Ajaygadh rock inscription of the time of Bhojavarman devotes one sentence to the making of a temple but none to financial provision thereof.[16] According to the first Vaillabhaṭṭasavāmin temple inscription at Gwaliar, Alla, the Gopagiri Koṭṭapāla of Ādivarāha, built a temple of Viṣṇu but the record is silent as regards its endowment. He also financed the construction of another shrine—this time of Nava-Durgā. A piece of land is assigned to it in the second record, which also refers provision of two fields for the former temple. Arrangment of oil and flowers is separately made by the town-administration in conjunction with guild-chiefs of respective commodities.[17] A couple of more such inscriptions could be cited but they would hardly improve upon those already covered.[18] Our conclusion obviously is that in comparison with Vedic scholars, for whom villages by the dozens were assigned, the financial position of temple priesthood was less secure and sufficient. Even when raising of shrines by the royalty is recorded, revenue assignment for their running expenses is hardly made anywhere. This must have been further so since, on social plane. the temple priest stood much lower than the Vedic scholar though both belonged to Brāhmaṇa Varṇa. In the contemporary classification of the Brāhmaṇas into ten groups, the latter has been placed in the first category and the former in the sixth, qualified by the epithets Deva and Śūdra respectively.[19] Incidentally the classification also reveals the variety of professions the Brāhmaṇas had taken up to earn their living.

Various were aims that prompted people to build temples in honour of their favourite gods and goddesses. Increase of religious merit is implied and understandable but that being too abstract and remote a return, in very many cases people were motivated by gratification of worldly desires. From Unchahra fragmentary inscription we learn that a temple of Vindhyeśvara was constructed and consecrated by a lady Uddalladevī with a view to obtaining wealth including sons and grandsons. A secondary aim appears to have been salvation of the twenty one past generation of her family. Lastly she confesses that she was inspired to the pious deed by the god Vindhyeśvara Himself who commanded her to construct a Temple dedicated to Him.[20] Nana, a Candella minister, financed the making of a Hari image in honour of his ancestors and for love of fame. His aim in raising a temple to the same god is stated to be, again, salvation of his ancestors.[21] Alla, the hero of the Villabhaṭṭasvāmin temple inscriptions wanted his deeds to be worthy of the Kṛta Age and one of his deeds was the making of a Viṣṇu temple which was thought in terms of an even path of beatitude, a greatship for crossing the ocean of existences, the seed of the tree of spiritual merit which bears endless fruit and a receptacle of his fame.[22] Likewise, Kokkala also aimed at crossing the deep ocean of existences when he financed the building of Vaidyanātha temple at Khajuraho.[23] Gadādhara, the Chief Minister of Pṛthvīvarman, had no such worldly or other-worldly aims in erecting a shrine of the Lord Nārāyaṇa. For him it was merely a pious deed as any approved beneficial act. The relevant verse of the Mau-candella record is well-worth quoting :" Always anxious to engage in pious and beneficial acts and other good deeds, he caused this edifice to be erected, endowed with...in it there is here the god Nārāyaṇa : for the wealth of the great is employed in acts of piety."[24] Kṛṣṇadevī, the queen of Rājaputra Deuka had the religious merit of her parents at heart when she caused the construction of a temple dedicated to Śiva.[25] Hindu doctrine conceives of a choice of three apparently exclusive holy ends in the beyond. They are 1. Rebirth to a new temporary life on earth in circumstances at least as fortunate as the present ones or rebirth in a paradise 2. Unlimited admission to the blissful prescence of a supramundane God (Viṣṇu Śiva) 3. Cessation of individual existence.[26] It will be apparent from the records cited above that the first and third of the ends weighed with the worshippers inspiring them to erect shrines for their deities. Increase in religious merit could contribute to Liberation of the Soul as well as secure higher birth.

Closly connected with the idea of religious merit is the concept of sin and consequences following therefrom. Since every record of ours is either a land-grant or temple dedication, we meet mostly with one kind of Sinner—a man who in ony way interferes with lands or money donated. Siyadoni record makes an interesting reading of the curses or consequences with which such a sinner was sought to be visited. The usual formula which saddled the sinner with Five Great Sins is, of course, first to figure. Next follows the fear of the Great Hell. Then comes the warning that the meddler would live the life of a worm in excrement for 66000 years. As though the curses for the sinner only were considered not sufficiently deterrant, we find his near and dear ones also covered by the contemplated consequences. Towards the end the record says that anybody meddling with the benefaction would drag his dear ones to hell.[27] It might seem senseless to us that innocent relatives should suffer for the crime with which they were not, at all connected but the idea might have been to terrify the offender, should he, have any feelings for his friends and relatives. Far more interesting scheme of curses we come across in Charkhari Plate of Devavarman. Being a lang-grant, it threatens the confiscator first with the usual torture of hell for 66000 years, prescribing then rebirth as dog for hundred times ending with birth among the Cāṇḍālas. Even if the donor happens to be confiscator, habitation into waterless dry hollow of a tree in Vindhyana wilds or birth as snake in a desert is his fate.[28] His deed was deemed so black that the stigma attaching to him would not be washed even by digging of thousands of wells or performing of hundred *Aśvamedhas* or gifting of millions of cows. Viewed from the opposite angle digging of well constituted a pious act alongwith other two which were already well-estblished in this regard. The formulas might appear merely customary with very little practical effect but their variety and frequency conveys that the cases of infringement may not have been rare.

With regard to the role of temple in contemporary economy, we have already seen that none of the land-grants was made to maintain a temple. Whatever references we do get in stone inscriptions cannot account for the overwhelming number of temples springing and still surviving in pathetic neglect throughout the lenght and breadth of Bundelkhand. However, at least one record throws welcome light on the role of these religious institutions in urban economy. Coming from Siyadoni (Lalitpur Distt.) it is a long document containing[27] donations, all by private individuals. Invariably they were either merchants or artisans. Richest among the local merchants were those dealing in salt. Specifically mentioned as "*Nemakavaṇika*", they financed the making of temples to which even the royal representatives made donations assigning tolls and taxes. They dominated the local council which naturally made liberal endowments to these temples. They invested money with almost every professional class of the town securing permanant endowment of materials for worship and money for maintenance. Of course, the temples may not have been as majestic and artistic as those raised under royal patronage at Khajuraho and Mahoba, but by establishing and endowing them the salt-dealers devised a mechanism to control the economic resources of the town. Every detail from the document would demonstrate how the temples grew into heart-throb of economic life of an urban settlement.

First part of the record consists of[27] donotions made at different times. The whole town assigning a field figures in the first endowment made to the temple of Śri Nārayaṇabhaṭṭāraka set up by Cāṇḍuka, *Nemakavaṇik*. Next the local Pratihāra governor Uṇdabhaṭa secures daily payment of a quarter of a Pañciyaka-ḍramma and one Yuga to the temple of Viṣṇubhaṭṭāraka, also erected by Cāṇḍuka.

Next Cāṇḍuka himself, alongwith his brothers assigns an *āvāsanikā*. Then Nāgāka, his son, is seen investing money with potters but fixing up with liquor dealers to give liquor worth half a *Vigrahapāla-dramma* on every cask of liquor. He also endows daily payment of a *Varāhaviṃśopaka* by investing money with certain sugar-boilers. Now we have another *Nemakavaṇika*, Vāsudeva, erecting and endowing a temple of Viṣṇubhaṭṭāraka adjoining to the one set up by Cāṇḍuka. He separately arranges for worship of the the sacred fire by assigning a house in favour of god. In the context of the Viṣṇu worship in epigraphic record, this object is uncommon. Next assignment is by Cāṇḍuka consisting of one Vīthī in Prasanna-market and four elsewhere. Then Keśava, a seller of betel, but belonging to Grahapati family makes over a *Vithī* in Catura-market. Nāgāka, now grown to be *nemakavaṇika*, gives two *vithis* in the next gift. We have third salt-dealer, Sīluka assigning a *vithi* to Nārāyaṇabhaṭṭāraka. Next follows another donation by Nāgāka who invests a huge sum—1350 *Śrimadādivarāhadrammas* with distillers of liquor binding them to pay half a *Vigrahatuṇgīyadramma* on every cask of liqour. Even Mataṅgas, the lowest of social sections, appear with whom Nāgāk, invests money for edowment realizing regular payment of two *Kapardakas*. Then we have another salt-merchant Bhail assigning a Vīthī. Dhamāka, a Brāhmaṇa betel-seller, gives an *Uvaṭaka* to the temple of Umā-Maheśvara. Śavara, also from his class, endowed the payment of a *Vigrahadrammaviṃsopaka* on every palikā of leaves to the Viṣṇu temple set up by Cāṇḍuka. Next Nāgāka gives a palikā of oil from every oil-mill of the town, of course, by investing money with their guild-which is not clearly mentioned. Then the Mahājanas of Dosi market decide upon a monthly payment of 1/3 dramma to Sri Bhailsvamideva. In all probability, this shrine must be the work of *Nemakavaṇika* Bhail, referred to earlier. The masons are not to lag behind in this march to divinities. Sūtradhāra Jejapa and some stone cutters, being of one mind, assign a payment of 1/3 of vigrahapāladramma on every *bharaṇa*. Next we have donation of one palikā of oil from every oil-mill, to the Viṣṇu temple of Cāṇḍu. Again we have a *nemakavaṇika* Pappa putting up a temple dedicated to Cakrasvāmideva and endowing it with three houses. Next we have assignment of a Vīthī from Catuṣka-market. Once more we meet a merchant of salt, Mahāditya by name, and the maker of Viṣṇubhaṭṭāraka shrine. Thus the hurried survey done above, amply reflects how the temples came to acquire vast property in real as well as monetary terms and this must have been at the disposal of the management in which the maker of the temple must have lorded over others. All the professional classes from the mighty Mahājanas, dominant distillers to meek Nātāṅgas figure in the provisions made with regard to the worship and expenses of the temples. Hardly any market was left in which the temples did not have some share in real wealth.

If Vaiṣṇavism dominated the religious life of the preceding period now it was supplanted by Śavism. This should be evident from the variety of names, no less than thirty, with which iva is mentioned in our records. He was known and hailed as 1. . Hara 2. Rudra 3. Śūladhara 4. Digambara 5. Maheśvara 6. Vaidyanātha 7. Śaṅkara 8. Śarva 9. Indumauli 10. Śambhu 11. Sthāṇu 12. Ked ra 13. Śūlapaṇi 14. Purāri 15. Iśvara 16. Candraśekhara 17. Bhavāniyā 18. Tryambaka 19. Tripurāntaka .0. Viśveśvara 21. Bhavānipati 22. Somanātha 23. Paśupati 24. Markateśvara 25. Candramaull 26. Girijābhartuḥ 27. Nīlakaṇṭha 28. Sadāśiva 29. Pañcānana 30. Srīgura.[29] Viṣṇu, his rival. has only 18 names in our inscriptions. They are 1. Vāsudeva 2. Vaikuṇṭha 3. Hari 4. Madhuripu 5. Vaillabhaṭṭasvāmin 6. Viṣṇubhaṭṭāraka 7. Nārāyaṇa-bhaṭṭāraka 8. Vāmanasvāmi-deva 9. Cakrasvāmideva 10. Tribhuvanasvāmideva 11. Trivikrama 12. Murāri 13. Śridhara 14. Gadādhara 15. Nārāyaṇa 16. Śauri 17. Viṣṇu 18. Puruṣottama 19. Kaiṭabhāri.[30]

The list in both the cases shows that normally names were based on iconography and mythology of the god in question rather than the place or person as we remarked earlier. In fact stray examples we do come across even during the period under review as in the case of Vaillabhattasvāmin and Vindhveśvara. It is also possible that the need for associating the god with any particular town or village was no longer felt, once the process of absorption and expansion of the cult reached the optimum level.

On the political plane the cult of Śiva had the support of Emperor Harṣa even in the foregoing perid. He styled himself as Parama-māheśvara[31] and the deity is depicted on his coin alongwith his consort.[32]

Of all the Śaiva shrines of this period, Caturmukha-Mahādeva temple of Nachna (Dist Panna) is the earliest. Its importance lies in the fact that it still retains its typical north-Indian *śikhara* taken to be earliest of the type available to us. Together with Viṣṇu temple of Baruāsāgar (Dist. Jhansi) and Sun-temple of Merkherā (Dist. Tikamgarh.) it registers a distinct advance on the Gupta temple architecture and presupposes the marvelous and magnificent shrines of Khajuraho, constituting as it were, an architectural link between the Guptas and the Candellas. Having a severaly plain interior and richly carved exterior, the temple stands on *jagati* with door-way in the east and trellis widows in the remaining sides. possessing a high *adhiṣṭhāna* which consists in ascendiding order of *khura* mouldings with *patrāvali* at angles ; *kumbha* and *kalaśa* mouldings, *kapotas* decorated with *kuḍus* having plain *vajanā* and *valabhī* below. A projecting *paṭṭikā* is the last member of the *adhiṣṭhānā*. *Pañcaratha* in plan as well as elevation' the sanctum exterior is marked by a *bhadra* on three sides, containig the lattice window. The *bhadra* as well as *karṇa-ratha* niches are all formed by pilasters of square section and canopied by a *kapota*. We have earlier remarked that some of the Vedic gods were reduced to to the status of *dikpālas* with the rise and popularity of paurānic deities. Here we have their actual representation in their reprentative corners though only Agni and Kubera among them now survive. Niches of the *karṇa-rathas* were allotted to them. A prominent *chādya* separating the *śikhara* from the *jaṅghā* is also noticeable. Rising into five *rathas*, all of which extend beyond the *grivā*, the entire surface of the *śikhara* is characterised by *Caitya*-window design. The arrangement of 5 *Karṇa-āmalakas* indicates the division of the *śikara* into six *bhūmis*. The *Śikhra* is appropriately crowned by an *āmalaka*, a *vijapuraka* (Fig. 33), Into the interior we find *antarāla* having been partly renovated. The sanctum is a plain square cell measuring 4 mrs. side and having a *samatala* ceiling consisting of plain monolithic slabs supported by lintels and architraves. It still enshrines the originally and beautiful *caturmukha* Śiva-*liṅga*. Its a pity that we have no inscriptional evidence giving clue to the date of the temple. A controversy was bound to crop up and dates ranging between 6th to 8th centuries A. D. have been suggested by the scholars. Cunningham brackted it between 6th-7th centuries A.D.[33] and Shrikrishna Deva favoured the 8th century A.D. But reasons for so dating in either case are not convincing. S. K. Sarasvati placed the temple in the 7th eentury A.D. on the ground that *śikhara* becomes a regular feature of Indian temple therefrom.[34] We are in absolute dark about its authorship or assignment, if any, for meeting maintenance expenses.

Among other early Śaiva shrines 1. Siddhanātha Mahādeva temple, Bilhagaon (Dist. Panna), 2. Lalguan Mahādeva, Khajuraho 3. Gopeśvara Mahādeva Chhoti Badoni (Dist. Datia) 4. Śiva temple, Kodal (Dist. Damoh), 5. Śiva temple, Banavānsā (Dist. Damoh) and 6. Śiva temple, Badgaon (Dist. Damoh), deserve mention. They are in varying states of preservation and even a brief description of any of them would be little more than monotonous repetition of what we have said about Caturmukha-Mahādeva Temple, Nachna, which is an important link between the simple and modest Śikhara shrines of the Classical Age and ornate and imposing temples of Candella times.

Śaivism scaled new peaks of popularity during the Candella period. Of course, some of the Candella monarchs were devotees of Viṣṇu and the *Prabodhacandrodaya*, a contemporary drama, has also Vaiṣṇava philosophy as its message and motivation, Śiva maintained his supremacy with princes as well as masses. Khajuraho is regarded as the religious capital of the Candellas and temples raised there are a class by themselves meriting special treatment. But books on Khajuraho, ever since its discovery, number much more than shrines surviving there. Every centimetre of their sculptural beauty and architectural planning has been minutely photographed, colourfully presented and competently studied. Any description on our part would, therefore, be sheer wastage of valuable words, time ānd space which we can purposefully devote to covering their less fortunate and unnoticed counterparts elsewhere in the area. We would, however, note a few details of our interest. Mataṅgeśvara is taken to be the earliest among Śiva temples at Khajuraho. It is built entirely of sandstone. The colossal *liṅga* enshrined within is the highest among all the *liṅgas* found in Bundelkhand. Shrikrishna Deva ascribed it to Harṣa Candella.[35] Viśvanātha, Kandariyā and Dulādeo temples are of finer variety bearing a wealth of sculpture and beautiful contours. Kandariyā, in fact' is beyond description having an intricate arrangement of 84 subsidiary *śikharas*, consisting of which and crowing them all, its grand, lofty and majestic *śikhara* truly resembles Kailāśa, the Himalayan abode of the Lord.

Sankalia made a small but special study of Khajuraho offering a sort of socio-economic background to the making and location of temples. He felt mere land-revenue or vassal tributes would not have sufficed to embark on such a stupendous and sustained raising of temples. Barring a couple of early granite structures, the rest have the body of sandstone available in the immediate vicinity. In close proximity, the Candellas also found diamond mines. The Panna diamond permitted the rulers not only to finance rearing of temples but mint in gold as well. The only expense the kings were required to incur was payment to sculptures, which may have been in kind or gold or even diamonds[37] The theory of Sankalia explaining the economic background to the conglomeration of temples in an out-of-way forested region might hold good for Khajuraho but hndreds of shrines that sprang up throughout the region had their sources in general property under the Candellas, generated by a sort of economic revolution which we have elaborated in the second chapter.

Turning now to other Śaiva Shrines of the Canella times, three we find standing at Ajaygarh in which Śiva can be seen occupying the lalāṭabimba on the door-lintels. In plan and elevation they are slightly different from Khajuraho temples. In two cases we have figures of Camuṇḍā and Gaṇeśa also in addition to the orthodox Brāhmaṇical tried represented on the lintel. This indicates not only rise to greatness and prestige of the two in the Śaiva pantheon but their enjoying independent position otherwise as well. Whatever their origins, since long were they treated *parivāra*-deities of Śiva.

A fact needing special note is survival of pedestals in the sanctums of these temples clearly indicating image of the god being object of worship. The Śaiva Shrines of Khajuraho burst with human forms of Śiva on the exterior or interior but the holiest of the holies placed within the sanctum is always an aniconic symbol of the god. Anthropomorphic representation in the *garbha-gṛha* at Ajaygadh indicates existence of a sect other than those flourishing elsewhere.

Among othere Śaiva Shrines, one standing at Nohaṭā is entirely intact though deserted. Another, fully developed and standing on lofty *jagati* survives at Gairaha (Dist. Jhansi). It is dated to the time of Kirtivarman. The socalled Kākrāmeṭha of Mahoba was also a Śiva temple Remains and ruins of Śaiva temples of the period lie scattered at Bandakpur, Banvānsā (Dist. Damoh) Pithoriā (Dist. Sagar) and Madanpur. At Mahuṭā (Dist. Sagar) and Burogaon (Dist: Jhansi) as well as in Damoh and Jhansi Archaeological museums we have door-lintels bearing Śiva or Gaṇesa in the *lalāṭabimba* attesting the existence of Śiva temples. Sometimes we come across a lintel in which Śiva occupies the *lalāṭabimba* fanked by both of his sons and the remaining member of the orthodox Brahmanical triad. One such fragment we have in the collection of Khajuraho museum in which all the five gods have been shown within the pilastered niches standing *samabhaṅga* and endowed with four arms (except Gaṇesa). Identity of the fourth figure being Kartikeya may be doubted and disputed but cannot be denied off-hand outright. It is also intersting to note that the only surviving hand of Viṣṇu (lower right) holds a *mālā* (Fig. 39).

The Sahasraliṅgeśvara temple of Chandpur (Dist. Lalitpur) is devoted more to the cult of the Pentad than to worship of Śiva. The huge *linga*, it enshrines contains carvings of innumerable miniature *liṅgas* on it. Besides, figures of Sūrya, Sakti, Viṣṇu and Gaṇeṣa are also represented on it, one on each side. Thus it was meant for syncretic worship or *Smārtā-pujā*. Perhaps Bundelkhand possesses only one such *linga*. In preceding chapter we have referred to the *pañcāyatana* temple of Deogarh which was dedicated to Viṣṇu, one could interpret that it was an attempt glorifying Śiva or Viṣṇu showing the other four as subsidiary, but more probably the motive was to offer simultaneous worship to all the five and emphasise the unity of Hinduism. Bargaon Temple inscription in area adjoining to ours mentions a god Saṇkara-Nārāyaṇa which demonstrates the tendency to syncretise the two great gods of Paurānic pantheon. Another possibility is that of devotees and deity being combined in the name.[38]

Śiva had a multi-dimensional personalily. He meant whatever the worshipper wanted to read. Interestingly, in our of our records he is conceived as Lord Physician, an effective and consummate cure-all all for any and evrey malady. But in the relevant portion of the record we also notice insistence on the part of the devotee to conceive of Śiva as one Reality manifested in numerous orthodox and heterodox divinities. The 3rd line of Kokkala's Khajuraho inscription says, "Adoration be always to that Śarva, who causes all (gods) to be comprehended in (his) one person ! —he, whom those aquainted with the end of the *Veda* call Śiva, the desire of the mind, while people of true knowledge call him the one supreme *Brāhmaṇ*, the idestructible, ageless, immortal, others verily auspiciuos Buddha, (and) others again the spotless Vāmana, the trtumphant (Jina)." As though it was not enough, Śiva is also regarded remover of those afflictions that are normally sent by 'mischievous' gods like Indra and Viṣṇu. To quote again, "People overcome with severe distress brought about by violent fever sent by the great Indra or by Viṣṇu and those seized again and again by goblins and by evil spirits that show themselves day by day and those afflicted with leprosy, which displays its fierce might by sore thumbs and fore-arms—all these are freed from evil whey they set eyes on thy clearly shown uncouth twisted tresses of hair." [39] From Dhaṅga's Khajuraho record we learn that he erected a magnificent temple for god Śambhu with two *liṅgas*—one of emerald and the other of stone. The latter still survives and the former is understandably missing. But we wonder how they were enshrined in a single sanctum.[40] Saugar stone inscription opens with an invocation to Śiva and refers to the erection of a Śiva temple by a noble lady Kṛṣṇadevī for the increase of religious merit of her parents.[41]

In Śaiva sculpture, the earliest form to find representation from mythology is *Rāvaṇānugrahamūrti*. At Gopeśvara hills near Chhoti Badoni (Dist. Datia) a panel bearing the theme is lying. The demon is shown on the pedestal, possessing five heads and eight hands. He is flanked by four figures on each side Śiva in the company of his consort sits above in *lalitāsana*. Their mounts bull and lion appear below. Gaṇeśa and Skanda have also been included in the composition. Another *Rāvaṇāugraha-mūrti* we have from khumānganj (Dist. Tikamgarh). *Umāsahita-mūrti* among art relics of Mohendra (Dist. Panna) may also be noticed. *Gajāsura-saṃhāra* of Śiva is no less popular than *Rāvaṇānugsaha*. One panel was found at Keolary (Dist. Datia) alongwith an Ardhanārīśvara icon of Śiva.[42] Lakulīśa is taken to be the originator of certain austerities and religious practices called the Pāśupata or Māheśvara Yoga which his pupils disseminated.[43] By the period under review he was already a Śaiva deity in his own right finding frequent representation. One of his icons we have from Lokhri (Dist. Banda) and another in collecton of Jhansi Museum. But by far the most interesting, yet unnoticed and unpublished. is his icon from Bharcha (Dist. Sagar). Indeed it is unique in our area. Seated *padmāsana* the god is slightly potbellied and was endowed with two arms which are mutilated now. Destitute of any ornaments and possessing a divine calm on his face, the god gives the impression of being a Jaina *Tīrthaṅkara*. But his ithyphallic character is unmistakable though neither his club has suavived nor any trace of it which is his special cognisance (Fig. 37).

Independent icons of Pārvatī could also be noticed here. An image of Skanda-mātā was found at village Sarkar (Dist. Jhansi) now housed in Khajuraho Museum. The goddess has a *jaṭā-mukuṭa* and a bull is carved below as her *vāhana*.[44] Temple No. 76 on the Sonagir hill (Dist. Datia) contains an icon of Pārvatī with a Sanskrit inscription in Siddhā-mātṛkā characters of 8th century A.D.[45]

The Candella artist of Khajuraho broke all the records by offering an unprecedented variety in Śaiva sculpture. Such was the sway of Śaivism that even the Vaiṣṇava and Jaina temples standing there bear a numder of *Śiva-mūrtis* on their exterior. He seems to premeate the place. Dancing figures of the seven mothers together with Gaṇeśa and Vīrabhadra or Pārvatī occupy the prominent niches projecting from the *adhiṣṭhāna* facades of the Viśvanātha and Kandariyā temples. Identical arrangement was made on the Śiva temple at Nohaṭā (Dist. Damoh). An Ajaygadh temple accomodates them in the *maṇḍapa*. The three developed Śiva temples of Khajuraho exhibit a uniformity in the representation of images on the *bhadra niches* of the sanctum. Andhakāntaka, Naṭarāja and Tripurāntaka icons occupy such niches in case of the Duladeo and the Kandariya respectively on South, West and North while the northern niche of the Viśvanātha contains a figure of Ardhanārīśvara in place of Tripurāntaka. Khajuraho has supplied us with two Sadāśiva images which have been correctly identified and interpreted by Rāmāśraya Awasthi. One of them is included in the collection of the local museum and the other is placed in an interior niche of the *mahāmaṇḍapa* of the Kandariyā temple. The former is four-legged, six-headed and twelve-armed. With front two legs in *padmāsana* and the remaining two in *paryaṅkāsana*, the deity is adorned with various ornaments. The six heads are arranged in two tiers and topped by a *liṅga* at the rear. Only two arms survive of which one rests on the thigh and the other merely hangs down. Between the *paryaṅkāsana* legs, a bearded and three-headed figure of Brahmā in *padmāsana* is present. An inscription on the pedestal referring to the image as that of Sadāśiva is also noteworty (Fig. 40). The like of these icons being not found so far elsewhere, they are regarded unique in the art of iconography.[46]

Of Saṃhāramūrtis, a hill-size panel of Gajāri Śiva we have from Mahoba which, though lacking in life and lustre, speaks for the accomplishment of Bundelkhand artist in working on such a high and wide canvas. Being painted with gaudy colours by the devotees, it needs an effort to recognise the hand of Candella artist in hewing it out.

A Kalyāṇasundara icon of Śiva we have in the collection of Bundelkhand Chhatrasal Museum of Banda. In the Palace Museum collection, Jhasi, we have another showing *pāṇigrahaṇa* and *āliṅganāsana* together with Brahmā as officiciating priest and eight *maṅgala-ghatas* depicted on either side. The Nahar-ghati and Raj-ghati of Deogarh fort contain representation of *Śiva-liṅga* in *Eka-mukha* form. An identical but excellent *Eka-mukha liṅga* we have from Nachna also. Kālañjara has yielded a variety of *liṅgas* such as normal *mukha-liṅga* and Sahasra-*liṅga* the last bearing 1001 tiny replicas on its body. A rare representation of *Matsyāvatara* bearing a *Śiva-liṅga* is also available to us.[46] A Śiva representated in his Bhairava form is available to us at Kālañjara and on a rock behind Baḍi Caṇḍikā temple at Mahoba. Some more such images we can see in the museum of Damoh, Jhansi and Sagar. A rock-representation of Śiva-parivāra is carved near Mahoba. Sapta-mātṛkās are associated with Śiva in mythology. We have numerous panels depicting them. One on display in Jhansi collection is very beautiful.

Cāmuṇḍā, a minor deity of Śaiva pantheon, seem to have become particularly popular at Mahoba and must have enjoyed somewhat independent status. Roaming in and around the town among hillocks we casually come across numerous rock-representation of the goddess. Nowhere in India we get a sixty-four-armed image of the deity. Mahoba offers us one, though badly mutilated. Carved fully in round this unique icon is lying in the garden of S.D.M.'s Bungalow who had hardly any idea of its importance till we chanced upon it. Most of the hands are now missing but a tally is possible. Her open mouth, protruding eyes, web of ribs and *naramuṇḍa-mālā* around the neck are still intact answering very well to her emaciated and awe-inspiring form in thc texts (Fig. 13). One of the outer niches of Nohata Śiva temple contains a beautiful representation of the goddess. Standing in *atibhaṅga* pose, the four-armed *pretāsana* devī has been perfectly rendered by the artist. Her ferocious form is brought home not only by ribbed and emaciated physical structure but by snake-ornments and scorpion creeping on her sunken belly as well. In curious contrast, we could note her *preta vahana* sleeping quite comfortably and fairly healthy. One of her left hands is held near lips whereas the other must have held a *khaṭvaṅga* which is now broken. Of the objects in right hands, only a dagger can be recognised.

Nandi, the vāhana of Śiva, was never so popular as now. At Khajuraho he has been represented theriomorphically as well as anthropomorphically. Human form of the deity has generally been accomodated in the upper register of the sculptural bands constituting a distinctive trait of these temples. Endowed with four hands and bearing attributes of Śiva, the bull-headed god is accompanied by his own theriomorphic form as mount. The Duladeo temple is unique in showing a crocodile Vāhana of the deity. Normally Nandi was represented in theriomorphic form placed inside a four-pillared pavilion facing the Śaiva shrines.

Unique icons of Lakulīśa and Cāmuṇḍā we have already described above. Now we have a rare representation of Nandi. It comcs from the ruins of Chandpur (Dist. Lalitpur). In all respects the deity appears to have been rendered in normal way being in bull form. But the unique feature here consists in the presence of a boy-figure who is trying to mount the god. Wearing wristlets, armlets, and mālā of rudrākṣa, the boy is clad only in the loin-cloth and is slightly mutilated. We are left to guessing only about the identity of the boy, the texts being silent on the theme. He could be taken as boy-skanda teasing and playing with the mount of his father (Fig.19).

Before concluding our survey of Śaiva sculpture we must make a brief mention of the mode of worship current in the period under review. We have some panels presenting scenes of *Liṅga-pūjā* from Khajuraho. A large sculpture lying on the bank of Śiva-Sagar lake shows twenty men in all—eleven on one side of the *liṅgam* and nine on the other. The *liṅga* is occupying a high pedestal and the nearest man holds a kalaśa from which he seems to be pouring water on it. The two men next to him also carry *kalaśas*. The fourth man has folded his hands in *añjali-mudrā*, probably muttering a prayer. The fifth man carries offerings in a big basket and the man next to him plays on the clarionet. A man with drum astride his knees and a female dancer follow him. One more man with drum and another with symbals can be made out. The last man has one hand *kaṭihasta* and another in *vyākhyāna-mudrā.* Likewise the men on the other side also carry various materials of worship i.e. garland, bell and censor-pot' bag of money, conchshell, drums, *ghaṇṭikā*. The last man of this group holding sword must be taken as *Mahāpratihāra* just as female dancer of the former group is most likely the *Mahānācanī*. Both these temple functionaries had become regular by now and are known from a Kalañjara record.[47] Fortunately an epigraphic transcription of the pūjā materials, partially of course, we get from Siyadoni stone inscription in the phrase—अवलेपनसम्भाज्र्घंनाङरात धूपप्रदोपनेवेद्यार्घर्थे[48] More *Liṅga-pujā* pictures we have from Khajuraho—one at the right back of the Lakṣamaṇa temple, another in the small frieze at the back of the same shrine and few in the inner *pradaksinā-patha* and right belcony of the *ardhamaṇḍapa* of the Viśvanātha temple. What to talk of humans, even the super-humans have been shown by Khajuraho artist offering, worship to to the *Liṅgam* in a scene from the Kandariyā, located in small front freize of the *maṇḍapa*.

Our survey of Śaiva shrines and sculpture shows not only the spread and sweep of the cult throughout the region and its undouted ascendancy during the period under review but also the contribution Bundelkhand has made to ancient Indian art and iconography. The mass base of Śaivism is as much a fact as its apeal to the ruling class. The conception of Śiva as multi-dimensional deity had as much to do with his popularity as the affiliation of local and aboriginal godlings to the expanding Śaiva pantheon. Curiously enough, Śaivism did not utilise the theory of incarnation which was one of the prime factors contributing to the popularity of Vaiṣṇavism. Lakulīśa may have been regarded as one but none of our records makes reference to the fact, whereas in case of Viṣṇu we would shortly mention an inscription invoking him in almost all of his established incarnatory forms. Part of the popular appeal of Śaivism seems to have emanated from its ability to absorb Tantric modes of worship which originated in long interaction between the higher and lower cults of Hinduism. The occult and the esoteric dominated the Śaiva sects of our region. A Kālanjara record mentions kīrtivarmans as patron of of Pāśupata Śaivism.[49] The worship of Lakulīśa also points to the prevalence of the sect. The Pāśupatas and Kāpālikas disregarded the caste system in admitting people to their orders. The Kaulas were avowed sensualists.[50] The aboriginal masses of the area, being free from puritanic rules and regulation could hardly be averse to the appeal of Kaulas and Kāpālikas who came to the fore in Śaivism. It is significant that the range of Śiva was set against the caste system making the untouchables.[51] We can bring home the point better with the word-potrait of Śaivism in a drama authored by its staunch opponent. In the Third Act of the drama *Prabodhacandrodaya* we meet a Kāpālika introducing himself as one who, "wears the garland of human bones, lives in cremation ground and takes his meals in a human skull."[52] It it significant that of all the Śaiva ascetics, a Kāpālika has been selected to represent the sect hinting thereby the hold of Kāpālikas on Śaivism. He holds the view that Siddhis can be achieved even by keeping oneself attached to the *Viṣayas*.[53] He is represented as drinking wine and persuading others to dring, too.[54] Frankly he declares, "The inner self does not desire the dry state of *mukti*. One should, therefore, enjoy the embraces of his beloved consort as has been said by Śiva himself."[55] Exaggeration of the evils of Śaivism by Srikriṣṇa Miṣra is not ruled out and it may also be conceded that Kāpālikas did not enjoy eminence all through the region but their practices could not be as revolting to the primitive communities as to the puratanic society. In any case, their hold at Khajuraho is highlighted in the concentration of erotic sculpture over there with hardly any parallel elsewhere in Bundelkhand. In fact, we frequently meet with sculptural representation of kāpālika teachers on the walls of Khajuraho temples (fig. 41). They aimed at obtaining different Siddhis and as a means to it indulged in most dreadful and hateful practices such as offering bones, blood and flesh to the fire.[56] The aboriginal background of the ruling line which financed the making of most of the khajuraho temples was additional factor in their easy acceptance and undoubted eminence in that forested territory. But this is certainly not the whole and sole explanation for the accommodation of erotic sculptures on the auspicious abodes at Khajuraho.

We must view the problem in larger perspective with Khajuraho as our natural and immediate concern. Intriguing indeed are the obscenities accommodated on the walls of Khajuraho temples posing a puzzle alike for the art-critics and historians. Evoking universal interest and inviting a number of explanations as regards their aims and accommodation on sacred sanctuaries, these 'postures of pleasure' constitute a mysterious chapter of Indian art, eluding agreement among scholars on their exact import. Love has a thousand postures and at Khajuraho one may discover as many. [57] Here is eroticism galore ! what could be the justification of this farnk, vivid, uninhibited and unabased display of things humanity now hides away ?

Not that any justification is needed, for those who put it on the temple-*jaṅghā* do not, at all, seem apologetic about what they carved so freely and frankly. Indeed, one cannot dismiss it all as the hurried and mischievous coat and chalk scribble of a school-boy. Much of the *mithuna* carving is superb art, is such exquisite and delicious carving that there is hardly any consciousness of its bearing on sex. The spiritual bliss, the beatific expression, the joy of intermingling, of being one and not two, of reaching a stage where each is both—all that has been caught by the chisel with surpassing excellence and only the crudest mind will see in those representations anything but beauty, the evil would lie in the eye of the beholder himself.[58]

Sex was never a taboo in Indian Society though it is so now. Varāhamihira clearly states that the whole world right from Brahma to the minutest worm is based on the union of the male and female principles and illustrates it by telling us that the greed of having a look at woman made even Śiva assume four faces.[59] In fact Vidya Prakash frankly admits that Indian culture like its European counterpart did not attach a feeling of guilt to sex. Indian literature is full of sexual allusions and symbolism. Sexual desire was a positive religious duty and sexual symbolism had religious connotation. Sexuality and religion were closely interlinked.[60]

Yet, we wonder how this sexual scroll came to be carved in stone under those very Candellas in whose court Srīkṛṣṇa Miśra was staging an anti-sex and puritanical drama *Prabodhacandrodaya* barely 75 kms. away at Mahoba ? Various are the approaches and answers to this problem. We may briefly review them.

Hemavatī, the Brāhmaṇic ancestress of Candellas in folk-lore is said to have committed a faux pas with the moon-god and in expiation the son was to hold a *Bhāṇḍya* sacrifice, part of which consisted in sculpturing indecent scenes with a view to holding up one's foibles to the disgust and ridicule of the world.[61] To say the least, the explanation is naive even when applied exclusively to Khajuraho. Another view takes the presentation as protection of the shrine against evil eye. Even textual injunction is cited in support and *Bṛhatsaṃhitā* certainly prescibes placing of *mithunas* on temple facades.[62] One still wonders why Khajuraho temples alone were required to adhere to the injunction and what actually is displayed is much more than *mithuna* couples of Varāhamihira. After decades of discussion one is compelled to feel that the answer to this puzzle of passions has been lost in the mist of time.

Interesting as it might seem, one view takes this mithuna manifestation as advertisement to attract the people who would eventually worship within.[63] Another regards temple precincts to be the teacher's class-room and the walls his black-board—meaning thereby that the erotic carvings were aimed at satisfying the the curiosity of the people and teaching lessons in sex hygiene. We wonder whether this riddle in romance had propaganda value or preaching mission in sexology, the fact of its being confined to one place in the whole region negates either possibility.

Religious significance is altogether denied in one view whereas the other attaches medical sense to this sculpture. It is argued that all aspects of this game of love to meet the desires of all types of devotees were purposely and conspicuously placed on the temple walls so as to produce a sense of satiety in the beholder. He could enter the shrine free from carnal thoughts thereafter. It could as well be the test of his mind which, if disturbed by the erotic scroll, rendered him unfit to usher himself in the Holy Presence.

It is also contended that Indian deities are modelled on human devotees never detached from the material aspects. But it is difficult to agree that the couples figuring in erotic art represent any of our gods or goddesses. Taking the representation as visual plates illustrating *Kāmasutra* of Vātsyāyana is also unconvincing. One view holds the panels to be portraying the process of evolution. Travelling successively from the vegetation to the animals, higher animals and lower-humans, our eye rises to elegant *mithuna* scenes of men and women, reaching the semi-divine and the divine and meeting finally the *Parabrahma*—the *śikhara* or the finial or pure abstraction. The view is far-fetched and does not merit disscussion.

As a matter of fact, the practice of placing erotic couples on temple facades seems to have originated out of a variety of factors acting conjointly and so this 'phenomenon in flesh' cannot be studied in isolation merely on the basis of symbolism underlying it or treating it only as decorative motif. Among such factors Tantrism was certainly one. Erotica in Indian art owes it origin to the Vajrayāna in which the monks made woman the centre of their yogic exercises, and as they came from the lower classes they did all that was opposed to the tenets of orthodox Brāhmaṇism. The excommunicated Brāhmaṇas formed sects like that of Kāpālikas and indulged in horrible and obscene exercises. A situation developed in which "what was *dharma* for the Brāhmaṇas, was *adharma* for them, and what was *adharma* for the Brāhmaṇas they regarded as *dharma*.[64] The completely shaven or bearded and long-haired ascetics of Khajuraho sculptures are most probably Tantrics. The Vaikuṇṭha icon of Lakṣamaṇa temple was a Pañcarātric image coming from Tantric regions. Much later even Ibn Batuta also speaks of long-haired jogis at Khajuraho knowing and practising magic.[65]

Devangana Desai has done monumental work on erotic art of India. She is of the view that the practice of *maithuna* as makāra is based essentially on the concept of magical power of sex. The pavcamakāras are actually offerings to the deity and form the most essential part of Tantrism. So the sculptural depiction of erotic couples near the deities may be taken as offering of *maithuna* for the propitiation and for fertility purposes. The fertility deity needs to be refreshed by sexual acts in the sanctuary.[66] This ritual had ramification in the inauguration of Devadāsī institution. The sexual act creates the power for auspicious and defensive purposes. It gives Siddhis.

Recognition of the magical power of sexual depiction has been explicitly made in one of the *Śilpa* text of *Kaulā-cāras* written between the 9th and the 12th centuries A.D. It mentions *Kāmakalesvara yantra* which was a symbolic representation of six for magico-propitiatory and magico-defensive purposes. The placing of this *yartra* iu the temples dedicated to Rudra and Śakti has been made mandatory. Then the monument will stand unmoved. This *Yantra* is utterely secret and must not be known to everyone. For this reason it is enjoined that *Kamabandhas* erotic couples should be carved to delight the people from whom the actual Tantric *Yantra* symbolising the sexual act has to be hidden.[67] At least one example we can quote from our area—Nohata Siva temple, where only a single mininature sexual panel is fixed which one cannot easily locate.

Two basic factors in Indian culture are germane to the representation of sex in art. These are magico-religious aspect of sex which is *raison-d'etre* for the existence of sexual depiction in religious art and the worldly interest in sex which leads to the secularization and sensualisation of the original sacred nature of the sexual depiction. The apparent contradiction between this 'labyrinth of love' and lofty goals of Hinduism stands resolved when we see that alongwith sublime ideals like *tapas*, *vairāgya* and *mokṣa* Hinduism continues to hold beliefs and practices connected with fertility and vegetation cults. This primal connection between sex and religion partly explains the presence of erotic element in the art of Khajuraho because the views and analysis of Devangana Desai has only general applicability to our case.

Sankalia devoted himself solely to Khajuraho when he wrote on the socio-economic background to the temples standing there. He felt that the shrines seem to have been meant exclusively for the king and his small group of courtiers. With their *ardhamaṇḍapa, maṇḍapa* and *mahāmaṇdapa* being unusually small, they are compact in design. The *mahamaṇḍapa* of the Lakṣamaṇa and that of Kandariyā measurs only 3.5 metres side. It would hardly accommodate 10 persons comfortably and would leave little room for the dancer to move freely. That the dances did take place is beyond the shadow of a doubt. Sankalia concluded therefrom that the temples were built primarily for the king and his nearest courtiers and certain sects which indulged in esoteric rites now regarded as questionable.[68] Absence of any large town or city near Khajuraho further strengthens the view. Sankalia also accepts the impact of Tantrism and association of Kāpālikas with the place. For depiction of unnatural sexual act he traces early origins.

Once the exclusive character of Khajuraho shrines is accepted, some other points become worth pondering. A distinction is also made between pornography proper and sexual symbolism in iconography. The longing of the individual soul for the universal is believed to be typified in the union of male and female which on philosophical plane become cosmic principles—*Puruṣa* and *Prakṛti.*[69] This intellectualisation of the erotic art can be acceptable at Khajuraho since the shrines were meant for chosen few and not public at large.

We can now better understand the silence of contemporary writers in this regard who never breathe in a word about erotica on temple walls. They found nothing contradictory in the situation. We should not miss the point that Khajuraho with its character of a pure temple-town and religious-capital of the royalty and the nobility never attained the status of a *Tīrtha.* It does not figure in the *Tīrthakāṇḍa* of Laksmīdhara of Kanauj and *Tīrthacintāmaṇi* of later date.[70]

Thus the erotic sculpture belongs to a category of art which is not Tantric but art as influenced by Tantrism without being functionally related to Trantic *Sādhanā.* The depiction of scenes containing Tantric rituals could not, theoretically, have been the work of genuine Tantrikas. The true Tantric art is functionally related, to *Upāsanā* and *sādhanā.* The original Tantric *pīṭhas* in the borderland of India are not associated with erotic display. The prevalence of sexual motifs in religious art before the documented Tantric period shows that factors responsible for their existence were deeply ingrained in Indian Culture and were brought to the fore by the influence of Tantrism.

We may close our long analysis with words of Vidya "Prakash, "Perhaps the final word of explanation of the erotic sculptures of Khajuraho would be that they could not have been forced on an unwilling on-looker......... They must have been required. The artist was bound to carve them. His age demanded it; his religion sanctioned it; he was equipped by the age-old tradition and he was inspired by the writings of *Kāmaśāstra.*"[71]

Vaiṣṇavism remained a rival of Śaivism though could never supplant it from the first position. The royalty and nobility of the period were not consistent in their support of any particular cult god whereas in the earlier period Viṣṇu had virtual monopoly on their conscience. The Pratihāras and the Candellas were so free in matter of cult affiliation that often we have a son subscribing to a sect different from his father's. The Pratihāra potentate Devaśakti was a Vaiṣṇava, his son Vatsarāja and grandson Nāgabhaṭa were Śaiva and Śākta respectively. Rāmabhadra and Bhoja, the son and grandson of Nāgabhaṭa were Saura and Śākta respectively.[72] This is as much an example of catholic spirit and broad outlook as of complete absence of a royal cult. We feel, therefore, that prominence of any cult rested much on mass support and its ability to enlist the popular deities in its pantheon. Vaiṣṇavism could do so earlier, Śaivism succeeded now. It is not without significance that three of the great Gods of the period—Śiva, Śakti, Gaṇeṣa, belong to Śaivism. Viṣṇu in this respect is not only alone but Sūrya who had intimate association originally with him came to have an independent cult. Proliferation of deities must also have worked against Vaiṣṇavism particularly when it had already exhausted its absorption potential.

Going by the much-publicized *Viruda Srīmadādivarāha.*[73] We may safely hold Bhoja to be *Parama-Vaiṣṇava.* But he also assumed the title Mihira.[74] The two *virudas* if taken literally would make him out a devotee of Viṣṇu and Sūrya. But in actual fact he subscribed to Śāktism and styled himself *Paramabhagavatī-bhakta.* This religious spirit is unique in the history of Bundelkhand. Political motive behind this extra-liberal stance cannot be ruled out. In response to the sentimental needs of an expanding empire, the king must have adopted plurality of cult affliation. His coins contain Boar incarnation of Viṣṇu as well as the legand *Srīmadadīvarāha.*[75] The anthropomorphic form of the theriomorphic deity corresponds in its representation very nearly to the icon from H.S. Gaur. Museum, Sagar, we have already described. But here he is shown accompanied by his usual weapons and a reptile below his feet.

Variety of names with which Viṣṇu figures during the period in our inscriptions we have noted earlier while listing Śiva's names. In Gwalior records of the time of Bhoja, he is named Vaillabhaṭṭasvāmin after the name of Alla's father who financed the making of the shrine. Here, again, we have an example how, like their lords, the officers also had plurality of cult affiliation. Apart from the Vaiṣṇava temple, Alla also financed the construction of a Navadurgā temple and out of four donations recorded, first was exclusively for the latter whereas the remaining three jointly for both.[76] Recorns there are many more reflecting Pratihāra affiliation to Viṣṇu but neither they come from our area nor that adjoining to it. As regards Bundelkhand the earliest among important Pratihāra records is Siyadoni stone inscription to which we have already given good coverage while discussing the role of the temples in contemporary urban economy. In it Viṣṇu virtually monopolises religious fervour and figures under the names Viṣṇu-bhaṭṭāraka, Nārāyaṇa-bhaṭṭāraka, Vāmansvāmideva and Cakrasvāmideva. Possibly Tribhuvanasvāmideva and Bailasvāmideva of the record also stand for him.[77] Bates'vara Candella inscription of Paramardideva refers to the erection of a temple dedicated to Visnu. Interestingly, the inscription also mentions making of a Śiva temple which stood beside it, both being financed by the same minister.[78] Likewise Mau Candella inscription of Madanavarman refers to the building of a Vaiṣṇava shrine by another Candella minister. Longest epigraphic description of Viṣṇu's personality and his incarnatory forms we get from Ajaygadh stone inscription of Nana. The first ten verses of this record constitute beautiful prayer to Viṣṇu and his *avatāras*. They are well worth quoting coming, as they do, directly from our area and containing an account of Vaiṣṇava mythology.[79]

"Salutations to the illustrious V sudeva.

May Deva (Viṣṇu), the preserver, the enemy of the sons of Dīti (Asuras) afford you joy, who generally does not feel physical weariness, being in the constant happy embrace of the bold Lakṣmī and who signifies amazingly consummate love (for the consort) with his restless rolling eyes intoxicated with delight; and whose *śrīvatsa* (breast-jewel) shines like the Cupid's arrows shot by the expanded bow of its blazing rays.

May Murari (i.e. the enemy of Mura), of ardent beauty, bless you, who, while being looked upon by his herd of cows, held upon the tip of his hand the mount Govardhana like a lump of mustard cake, and whose wonderous lustre was enhanced by the love-stricken wives of the cowherds.

May Hari who is, as if in pleasant sport, thwarting in jest the diversions of the licentious deer with their consorts by an (array of arrows whose beauty has been blunted by the stiff breasts of the milk-maids,enhance your knowledge.

May Deva, the fish-transformed husband of Śrī (Lakṣhmī), the restorer of the set of the *Vedas* buried in the ocean, the refulgent, the destroyer of the burdens of the world, and the slayer of Śaṅkhāsura destroy your sins.

May the tortoise, who revelled in abstract in the watery ocean with its shores destroyed by the Saṃvarta (one of the seven clouds at the dissolution of the universe), the refuge of the world constant in refulgent beauty, prosper you.

May Mādhava, (in the form of a boar) who, by the mighty thrust of his long cruel tusks delivered the earth in the shape of a muddy lump of clay and who extended the fixed order of religion and duty; the abode of intelligence and the habitat of the universe, and who is ever-ready to destroy the mental agonies, increase your blessing.

May Nṛsiṃha, resplendent like the rays of thousand Suns resting on the tip of the peaks of the Sumeru, and appearing with drawn nails for the destruction of the demon (Hiraṇyakaśipu), destroy your sins.

May Vāmana (dwarf), of metchless glory, bless you; who by the pretext of smashing the eye of Śukra denounced the very statesmanship of his enemies; who expanded himself proportionate to the arrogance and haughtiness of Bali.

Victorious be that renowned Parasurama, of great intelligence, the abode of victory and fame, who placed the earth in the hands of the Brāhmaṇas after acquiring its governance, and who made the wives of the enemies sad.

May Rāma, too, the slayer of demons, whose deeds of valour gladden the hearts of the magnanimous and serve as the protection of the body, save you from all miseries."

The opening verses of Khajuraho inscription of Yaśovarman and Dhaṇga also describe Vaiṣṇava mythology, though the coverage given here is much shorter in comparison with the Ajaygadh account. After invoking holy Vāsudeva the record goes on :

"May that Vaikuṇṭha protect you, who frightening the whole world with his roaring, as boar and man-lion, slew the three chief Asuras, Kapila and the rest, (who were terrible in the world (and who) possessed one body which by the boon of Brāhma enjoyed freedom from fear (and) could be destroyed (only) by (Vaikuṇṭha) having assumed those forms.

May the three strides of the god Hari, (made) when he was cheating Bali (and) at once praised by the astounded gods and demons, protect the three worlds ! Even now that one father of the three worlds, Hara, bears on his head the holy water which, respectfully then offered by Brahmā fell on (Hari's) lotus foot.

May that god protect you, on whose famous breast, broad like the well of the Anjana mountain (and)......marked with scars by the swords of the Daityas, fell, withdrawn from all (other) inhabitants of heaven, many glances of Lakṣmī, agitated with confusion at the proximity of the Mandara mountain ! "[80]

Taken together, the two records prove how Vaiṣṇava mythology was getting transcribed from books to the inscriptions claiming far larger coverage than in the records of the earlier period. The tendency to compare kings with gods and combine in their character, qualities and excellences of more than one god is also noteworthy here. Only one example from the above inscription would suffice.

"Deep like the oceans, pleasing like the moon, radiant with brilliancy of the sun, firm like the Creator, great like the noblest of mountains, munificent like the trees of Paradise,—tell me truly, if anywhere there has been another lord charming with a multitude of spotless excellencies unchangeable to the end of the world, equal to Yaśovarman ! "

One wonders naturally if there is any scope left for improvement and if the king was verily a human in flesh and blood. The Lords Spiritual pale into insignificance confronted here with a single Lord Temporal. We fail to understand why the Candellas did not follow the practice of dedicating temples into themselves as did the Kuṣāṇas. With heavenly potential packed into their person the practice would have been more than warranted in their case. In Marxist perpective the comparison might sound an echo of feudalistic tendency in realms of religion. But shorn of all the overtones and undertones, the element of sycophancy is little more than poetic praise for Princely patronage. The inscription aimed at commemorating the construction of Viṣṇu temple in which a rare image of Vaikuṇṭha was to be consecrated. The icon was unique in having a long and splendid past. We learnt that "the Lord of Bhoṭa obtained if from the Kailāśa and from him Ṣāhi, the king of Kīra, received it as a token of friendship; from him afterwards Herambapāla obtained it for a force of elephants and horses, and Yaśovarman himself) received it from Devapāla, the lord of horses and the son of (Herambapāla)." The temple figuring in the record is identified with Lakṣamaṇa temple of Khajuraho and most probably the much-sought-after image is still enshrined within. Either the image was believed to bring fortune and fame to the owner or it was connected with Tantric *Sādhanā* since it came from the region of Tantrism. Alternatively, perhaps its possession carried political prestige so the princes desired to have it even at high cost. In any case, Khajuraho proved to be the terminating point in icon's journey and the Candellas never parted with their proud possession. Such a celebrated icon certainaly deserves description. The god has three faces, four arms and usual ornaments. The front face bears a benign look and the right and left ones are those of Nṛsiṃha and Varāha respectively. Standing *Samapādasthānaka* and flanked by *Cakrapuruṣa* and *Śaṅkhapuruṣa* to his right and left respectively the god is accompanied by figures of the orthodox Brāhmaṇicaltriad with Sūrya in middle (in place Viṣṇu), Srī, Puṣṭī, and Śaṅkha-bearing attendents. An ornate *makara-toraṇa* enclosing the composition contains 8 *Vyūha* forms of Viṣṇu in miniature niches. They are Govinda, Aniruddha, Nārāyana, Keśava, Vāmana, Śrīdhara and Dāmodara.

It is curious that a theistic record should also contain doctrines of philosophy. The Khajuraho insciption briefly mentions main ideas of the Sāṃkhya philosophers while tracing the origin of the Candellas. We are told, "From Nature unmanifested and changeless there proceeded here the Great one; from that was born Self-consciousness which engendered the group of the organs; from that in due order the Subtile Elements took their origin and from them the Gross Elements; from them afterwards proceeded the world.

Then, when the whole world had come to an end, there was first here by his own greatness the migtly Creator.........From that Creator of the universe... sprang those early sages of holy conduct, Marici and the rest. Atri, one of them, beget the sage Candrātreya......"[81] Its an interesting example of philosophy coming at the service of polity.

We have noted above how Yaśovarman nas been likened to various gods in the record. But nowhere he is said to be equal to Viṣṇu of whom he was staunch devotee. His successors do not hesitate in proclaiming even that equality. Deogarh rock inscription refers to Kīrtivarman as Viṣṇu without his gadā.[82] In Mahoba stone inscription Madanavarman was regarded as Gadādhara incarnate by the people.[84] Ajaygadh rock inscription of Vīravarman credits Trailokyavarman with having lifted the earth like Viṣṇu.[85] Apotheosization is almost reached by the Candellas when we are told that sublime appearance of Viravarman made people wonder whether he was Viṣṇu riding his Garuḍa or Śiva roaming on his bull.[86] The devotion of Jayavarman to Nārāyaṇa is recorded in a Kālañjara stone inscription.[87] Thus we see that successors of Harṣa and Yaśovarman did not confine themselves to worship of Śiva only. In fact they seem to be equally well-disposed towards Vaiṣṇavism since they accommodated Lakṣmī and Hanumāna on their coins. Instead of a Śaiva deity, needing further note in this connection, is the figure of Gajalakṣmī carved in the copper-plates of Devavarman, Vīravarman and Hammīravarman. The four-armed goddess sits in *lalitasana* on a double-petalled lotus or on a stool, with an elephant on an expanded water-lily standing on either side and holding an upturned pitcher over the head of the goddess.[88] Crowning all this evidence is the drama *Prabodhacandrodaya* written with tne specific purpose of glorifying the Vaiṣṇava cult and staged in the court of Kīrtivarman. The dramatist assures that mere recitatation of Viṣṇu's name was enough to end the miseries of the people and devotion to him liberated one from the bondage of the world. On the mundane level Viṣṇu-worship warded off the attacks of evil forces. Indeed, an evil character of the play puts it point blank." The Yoginī named Viṣṇubhaktī commands great influence......we have litille influence on those who she looks favourably."[89] Devotion to Viṣṇu was the chief means to the achievement of Siddhis. Thus all the transcendental values held high in Hinduism are offered by Vaiṣṇuism.

Earliest among the Vaiṣṇava shrines of the period is one standing at Barua-Sagar (Dist. Jhansi). A *nirandhāra-prāsāda* surmounted by a lofty curvilinear *śikhara*, it is one of the few surviving monuments representative of Gurjara-Pratihāra style in our area. The placing of *aṣṭa-dikpālas* on the *jaṅghā* of the temple commenced during the period mentioned already, and we see them here occupying their allotted positions. The richly sculptured *jaṅghā* also becomes a prominent feature of central Indian temple style from here onwards. Facing west the temple is *pañcaratha* in plan as well as elevation. A high *adhiṣṭhāna* and a horizontal frieze of *kirtimukhas* running right round the structure marks it out as the precursor of developed Khajuraho temples (fig. 16). The five-*Śākhā* door-way of the sanctum is richly carved. Figures of the river-goddesses, whom we meet for the first time, occupy their respective positions on the door-jambs riding their mounts. On the lintel, in addition to the orthodox Brāhmaṇical triad, Navagrahas and Sapta-mātṛkās (preceded by Vīrabhadra and followed by Gaṇeśa) are also present (fig. 42). Another interesting feature meriting mention is that *aṣṭa-dikpālas* bearing their respective *ayudhas* and riding their respective mounts also find place above the lintel. The temple has been dated to the ninth century A. D.[90]

The socalled Brahmā temple of Khajuraho was originally a Vaiṣṇava shrine, which can be verified from the figure of Viṣṇu occupying the *lalāṭabimba* on the door-lintel.

With Viṣṇu temple of Bhenswaha (Dist. Sagar) we will deal in detail since it was discovered in course of explorations undertaken for the present work. Bearing a deserted and dilapidated appearance and belonging to a village that now exists merely in name, the temple stands right on the bank of the Naren river. Consisting of a fragmentary *ardhamaṇḍapa*, an empty *garbha-gṛha* and a crumbling *sikhara*, the temple seems to have stood on a *jagati*, of which only few traces can be made out. As for the *maṇḍapa*, *mahāmaṇḍapa* and *antarāla*, they can be postulated from the space intervening between the *ardhamaṇḍapa* and *garbhagṛha*, now overgrown with thorny bushes and wild vegetation (fig. 35). The Vaiṣṇava dedication of the temple is clear from figure of Garuda occupying the *lalāṭabimba* on the lintel of *ardhamaṇḍapa*. Possibly a *sikhara* with pyramidal shape once crowned this portico. The gateway measures 2 mrs. high and 1 cms. wide. The sanctum interior is severely plain save for some flower medallions on pilasters and geometrical patterns in the upper section. The sanctum is 4 mrs. 65 cms. by 3mrs. None of the outer walls is completely preserved. Still one can make out that shallow pilastered niches had been executed on the *adhiṣṭhāna* as well as *jāṅghā*. Each niche was canopied by a miniature tower. *Áṣṭa-dikpālas* were also represented in their allotted corners.

The only notable sculpture surviving now is that of *Govardhandhāri* Kṛṣṇa inside a niche. The icon is important because panels representing scenes from *kṛṣṇa-līlā* found elsewhere in Bundelkhand do not include this feat of Kṛṣṇa (fig. 36). Even Deogarh and Khajuraho relics which have yielded numerous episodes do not offer us this. The *śikhara*, now shorn of all its majesty, rises in *pancaratha* plan and contains a few *Karaṇa-āmaalkas.* Dating the temple was a problem since no epigraphic record has come to our notice. Nor can it be definitely associated with any royal dynasty. Tentatively, it could be fixed round about mid-tenth century A.D. when fully-developed central Indian temple architecture shaped up elsewhere in our area.

Among Candella Vaiṣṇava shrines, the Lakṣamana temple of Khajuraho has already been referred to above. Two more stand there known as the Jāvāri and the Caturbhuja. Even the socalled Devī Jagadambī temple is also regarded as having originally been Vaisuava in affiliation.

At Chandpur (Dist. Lalitpur) the ruins now known as Chhoti Belmari and Bali Belmari were consecrated to the worship of Viṣṇu who occupies the *lalāta-bimba* of the door-lintels. The sanctums are all empty. In size the temples are modest consisting invariably of a sanctum crowned by a small *śikhara* and having a shallow *maṇḍapa* in front. This indicates their making by those sections of society who had limited resources. Of the two Brahmanical temples standing side by side at Madanpur, one was definitely dedicated to Viṣṇu. The remains of Doni (Dist. Damoh) also speak of some Visnu temples having been there. We have here a *caitya-gavaksa* containing representation of *Yogāsana* Viṣṇu. Some more Visnu temples must have dotted the area since a number of door lintels with Visuu in *lalāṭabimba* we get from Mohendrā (Dist. Panna) Mahūṭā (Dist. Sagar), Nohaṭā, Banavānsā, Hindoriā (Dist. Damoh), Burogaon (Dist. Jhansi) and museums of Damoh, Jhansi and Sagar.

Temples consecrated to incarnatory form we do have but very few. At Chandpur and Dudhahi (Dist. Lalitpur) Varāha temples were constructed. Perhaps in plan they were merely four-pillared canopy like one surviving at Khajuraho. They normally accommodated Bhūvarāha form of the deity. *Vāmānāvatara* was also important enongh to have a temple dedicated to it. We can also postulate some more Vāmana temples on the basis of giant Vāmana icons in Papat Museum, Knudesvara (Dist. Tikamgarh) and Banda Museum. In State Museum collection as well as Palace Museum collection of Jhansi we have numerous Vāmana icon in whlch the Lord is represented as holding an umbrella for which we do not have any textual injunction. Trivedi refers to a four-armed icon found at Pathari village in Dist. Jhansi which is remarkable for showing a dagger attached to the girdle of the god.[90]A He postulates the existence of a Vāmana temple at Siron on the the basis of numerous icons found there. A Nṛsimha temple of the period we do not have but Rāmāṣraya Awasthi has postulated existence of one the basis a sixty-four-armed image of the god from Khajuraho.[91] It is strange that we have so many scenes of *Kṛṣṇa-līlā* but no shrine dedicated to him.

The *Prabodhacandrodaya* repeats the well-known Vaisnava assurance that Visnu incarnated himself for the welfare of all the creatures coming down to earth many a time.[92] The play also reveals popularity of Nṛsiṁha, Varāha Vāmana, Paraśurāma and Kṛṣṇāvatāra of Visnu.[93] We are yet to chance upon temples dedicated to the last two.

Turning to Vaisnava sculpture of the period we should first take up *Govardhandhārī* Kṛsna from Bhenswaha mentioned above. Placed within a deep niche, it measures 51.62 cms. in height. The ease and grace with which the Lord worked the wonder have been perfectly rendered. So symmetrical are his physical proportions and such realistic the depiction of the feat that the icon alone is enough to attest the genius and accomplishment of the Bhenswaha artist. Standing in *dvibhaṅga* posture, the god holds aloft the mountain Govardhana by his right hand, resting the other gracefully on the left thigh. Behind him are distinctly shown three tiny figures of cows. Some heads of animals high on the mountain can also be made out. The tale is beautifully captured here.

An exellent icon of Nṛsiṃha on display in Dhubela State Museum deserves notice (fig. 54). The physical dimensions of the deity in this broken but beautiful icon far surpass those of the demons who with their boyish figures and curly hair are far from ferocious and, to that extent, the depection is not true to the tale. The four-armed god has been shown in the central act of the myth firmly pressing down the demon with one of his front hands and ripping open the belly with the other. With left leg slightly raised, the god stands erect in all his might and majesty and solely occupied with his act of grace. The lion-face has found realistic rendering with prominent moustaches and round protruding eyes. He is endowed with usual ornaments which together with artistic hair-dressing add to his charm. Of his upper hands the right is broken and the left seems to be holding a flower. Beyond doubt, the panel is remarkable piece of the plastic art.

A square pillar fragment measuring 15 cms. in height and lying in the courtyard of Pārvati temple, Nachna (Dist. Panna), also deserves mention as well as illustration (fig. 53). It represents four *avatāras* of Viṣṇu. Three of them—Varāha, Nṛsiṃha and Trivikrama—are easily identifiable. The fourth is badly damaged. Varāha and Trivikrama have been shown in the central act of the myths associated with them. Free icons of Balarāma and Paraṣurāma we do not have, but their accommodation on the outer facades of the sun temple at Markhera (Dist. Tikamgarh) is significant.

Vaiṣṇava sculpture of Khajuraho does not need any description here since a number of independent monographs on the subject by competent authorities are already published and easily available. Only a brief notice is warranted. A bewildering variety we get. Ramaśrya Awasthy has divided all the *sthānaka-mūrtis* of Viṣṇu into two broad categories—ordinary and extraordinary or rare. We are well familiar with the former. The latter are larger of the two and contain more figures in the *prabhāvalī*. Standing for the *para* aspect of Viṣṇu, they should be taken to be *dhruvaberas* in the true sense of the term. Some of these are accommodated in the sanctums of shrines whereas the others occupy *bhadra* niches outside, a few are on display in the local museum. All of them represent the concept of *Bhogasthānakamūrtis* as described in the *Vaikhānasāgama* though complete obedience to injunctions has never been rendered.[94]

The chief image of the Caturbhuja temple is unique for which no text can be quoted and no likeness can be cited. Here Visnu is without *Vaijayantimālā* and usual emblems. He is adorned with a *jaṭā-mukuṭa* and is accompanied by the navagrahas represented on the *makara-toraṇa* above (fig. 44). At Rāhilyā, 3 kms. away from Mahoda inside a one-room shrine of modern make is preserved a beautiful but partly mutilated icon of Visnu Standing *samabhanga,* the Lord is heavily but tastefully ornamented. The sharpness and precision of carving are simply marvelous of his our arms only upper ones survive in which he is holding a *cakra* and a *gadā* three attendents are shown below on each side. Among other icons Vaikuṇṭha has already been described.[24] Almost alike is Ananta image of the god. The image of *Maunavratin* Viṣṇu is classed under *Yogasthānakamūrtis.* The central image of the Jāvāri temple is also rare one. Viṣvarūpa and Hayagrīva forms of the god also found manifestation in the art of Khajuraho. Gangā has not been seen as consort of Viṣṇu in ancient art though in one Khajuraho record she has been so conceived.[95] It is interesting that Khajuraho witnessed variety of Viṣṇu inconography translated into stone but this myth we are yet to come upon. In the collection of Jhansi archaeologlcal museum we have this rare representation. Gaṇgā is shown beside the lord riding her mount (fig. 43). Erecting pillars in honour of Viṣṇu was a well-known practice of the preceding period. At Paṭhāri we do have Garuḍa-crested pillar with dedicatory inscreption by a Rasṭrakuta king.[06]

In comparison with numerous *parivāra*-deities of Śiva getting independent depiction, Viṣṇu has only one. Laksmī in Bundelkhand art, if represented indepedently, is always Gajalakṣmī. In the collection of P.R.O. office, Datia, we have an icon of the goddess. Another is on display at Mahatma Gandhi Hindi Museum, Kalpi (Dist. Jalaun). She also figures on the *jaṇghā* of chhoti Belmari temple at Chandpur. In Candella records she is mentioned with three names **1.** Laksmī **2.** Payodhiputrī 3. Kamalā.[97] Since she had come to be conceived as the presiding deity of wealth and fortune, she was no longer a subsidiary deity of Vaiṣṇavism. No wonder, she found place on the coin of Candella kings.[98] Of Sarasvati, we have not heard as yet. From Dudhahi-Chandpur we do have some of her icons now included in the Palace Museum collection, Jhansi.

The roots of the Tantrism have heen traced to the prehistoric past and contribution of non-Aryan aboriginals has come to be recognised.[99] We have already shown that substantial segment of Bundelkhand society through the ages consisted of the socalled Pulindas Śabaras and allied people. When almost every sect was effected by Tantrism, the cult of the Mother-goddess, which by now had developed into independent sect of higher Hinduism, was bound to come under its shadow. The central foundation of Śāktism is the philosophical theory that no god as such but god in associattion with his power (Sakti) is responsible for the creation, pre servation and destruction of the universe.[100] Elaborating concept of Durgā an authority remarks, "The ten arms may represent the combined ten hands of the four-handed Brahmā, the four-handed Viṣṇu and the two-handed Śiva, seeing that Durgā was considered to be Mahākalī, Mahālakṣmī and Mahāsarasvatī in one."[101] The Mārkaṇḍeya Purāṇa is taken to be the locus classius for the exploits of the goddess. Its Devi Mahātmya chapter relates Mahiṣamardinī episode in addition to some other accounts of Śakti's achievements as also the promise of her periodic appearance as and when the demons disturb the world order.

Earliest among Mahisamardini temples is one surviving at Khamera in Datia dist. Made entirely of granite, it consists of only sanctum surmounted by an elemental *sikhara.* A little way off, the figure of Mahiṣamardini is enshrined within a new-brand temple. From Bhenswaha also we have an eighteen-armed icon of the goddess.

The Tantric influence on Saktism could be seen in the birth of Yogini centres. The worship of Yoginīs in the form of a regular cult seems to have come into existence during 8th-10th centuries A.D. Founded by Matsyendranatha the cult was known as Yoginī Kaul. The alliance and almost assimilation of Śaktism with Śaivism in this cult may be noted since the sixty four Yoginis are so many angles representing the equal number of manifestations of Sakti embracing Siva.[101]A The central Shrines of Yogini temples usually enshrined images of Śiva, Pārvati and Ganesa. At Khajuraho the earliest to appear was the Causaṭha Yoginī temple. Built fully of granite stone and raised on a lofty *jagati,* it is quadrangular in shape consisting of sixty-seven peripheral shrines. K. D. Bajpai came upon an 8th century Yogiuī center near village Lokhri in Banda district. In all 29 Yoginī images were found, 19 being identified on the basis of their iconography as given below :—

(1).	Vaisnavi	: riding Garuda
(2).	Vārāhi	: (3). Vasudhārā ;
(4).	Aindri	: holding a coconut and vajra.
(5).	Kankāli	: four-armed, holding fire, *khappar*, and triśūla, whereas the fourth is held near lips. Wearing a beautiful crown *kuṇḍalas*, necklace and a loose girdle her bony structure has been remarkably rendered. Her

legs are balanced on her skeletal *vāhana*. With protruding eyes, gāping mouth, sunken belly and ribbed frame her kaṇkāli from has been rightly rendered (fig. 2) bearing a close likeness to Cāmuṇḍā.

(6). Nārasiṃhi : riding lion, holding Prahalāda, Śūla, mirror and *kamaṇḍalu*.

(7). Vaināyaki : riding elephant, holding coconut and vajra

(8). Yāmi : riding buffalo, holding *khappar* and *vyālaśūla*, the the goddess wears necklace armlets, bracelet and anklets (fig. 1).

(9). Āgneyi : riding meṣa, holding rosary.

(10). Kaumāri : riding peacock as well as feeding it with a fruit held in the right hand. Sitting with left leg astride her *vāhana* and holding a weapon which is now broken, the goddess has deen endowed with animal head by the artist in confirmity with some other members of her order found at the place (Sketch No. 3).

(11). Meṣamukhi : Two-armed holding a child by left and a *khappara* in the right, she is seated *ardha-paryaṇkāsana* on a *kaṇkāla*. The mother as well as the child look upwards. Her bulging fleshy body is in curious contrast to the bony structure of her *vāhana* (fig. 4)

(12). Hayagrīvī : riding vidāla, holing *daṇḍa* in both hands

(13). Śaśi : riding hare holding *Yajnapaṭṭa* and *Kamaṇḍalu* in right hands and a *mālā* in left

(14). Māhesvari : riding bull, holding Kārttikeya and fruit in front hands and *śūla* and *darpaṇa* in back hands.

(15). Hariṇa-sṛṇgā : riding deer, holding *vijapūraka* and śūla in right & left hand respectively.

(16), Vārāhi : fonr-armed, riding a boar, holding *ćakra* and *padma* in back hands and *gadā śaṇkha* in front hands.

(17). Nāgi : riding elephant, holding vajra and fruit in left aud right hands respectively. She is seated *ardha-paryankāsana* wearing a tiny flower-like crown and beaded necklace-type ornament around her head. She is endowed with large beautiful ears hanging from which one *saṇkha* may also be noticed on each side. The use of conch in this fashion is rare

in Indian iconography (fig. 3). Among other ornaments bracelets, armlets, anklets, girdle and a neklece are noteworthy.

18. Ulūkī : four armed, riding on owl, holding *āmraphala* and *sula* in upper and left hands respectively and a cup in lower right.

19. Rurādai[102]

A temple with a definite dedication to Pārvatī or Mahisamardinī we cannot point out but the existence of some such shrines can be postulated on the basis of large-size representations of the goddess, available in museums at Khajuraho, Damoh and Jhansi. In Palace Museum collection at Jhansi we have two remarkable types of her iconography. In one, she holds *liṅga* and Gaṇeśa in two of her hands and in the other, Skanda appropriates the place of Gaṇeśa. Besides, Kālañjara stone inscription records the erection of temples in honour of Kamalā and Kāli.[103] It seems that part of the force of Śaktism was absorbed by Śaivism. This should be evident from the names with which the goddess finds mention in contemporary records :—

1. Umā[104] 2. Ślocayasutā[105] 3. Girijā[106] 4. Pārvati[107] 5. Bhavāni[108]. Considered practically the consort of Śiva, the Devi with many of her devotees merged into Śaivism. One of the subsidiary shrines attached to Viśvanātha temple, Khajuraho, was dedicated to her. The colossal *Sahasralinga* of Chandpur (Dist. Lalitpur) contains her icon among the four deities represented on it. The Smārtas did a lot in bringing together Śiva and Śakti. The special *liṅgas* worshipped by them have Pārvati in a corner of the *gaurīpaṭṭa.*

The gigantic rock-cut representations of *Aṣṭa-śaktis* outside the Tarhaoni gate of Ajaygadh are also noteworthy. Of these seven, six are seated and one stands. Executed roughly, each of them is accommodated within a separate frame. Among the inscribed names below, Śrī Caṇḍi, Śrī Cāmuṇḍā, and Śrī Kālikā are clear.[109]

The sun cult came into being quite early in Bundelkhand as we have seen in chapter IV. However, no trace of it survived from the Classical Age. In the period under review, again we find it independently flourishing. We have beautiful temple, wholly intact, dedicated to Sūrya at Markhera (Distt. Tikamgarh).

Standing on a low *jagatī* and consisting of a *garbha-gṛha* with a surmounting *śikhara* and possessing an *antarāla* as well as a *maṇḍapa*, the temple is *pañcaratha* in plan as well as elevation, the *rathas* being projected even beyond the *grīvā.* Carved with caityawindow design all over, the *śikhara* is crowned by an *āmalaka*, the other members having fallen now. The *jaṅghā* contain numerous niches crowned by long *udgamas.* The *bhadra* niches accommodate icon of the sun-god in variety of poses. The *antrāla* niches contain Durga and Gajalakṣmi in southern and northern facades respectively. Figures of *aṣṭa-dikpālas* occupy their respective corners. The *pañca-śākhā* doorway to the sanctum has river-goddesses riding their respective *vāhanas* on the door jambs. A four-armed icon of Sūrya occupies the *lalātabimba* on the *uttaraṅga*. Riding a chariot drawn by seven horses, he is accompanied by Uṣā-Pratyuṣā and Aruṇa. Figures of four horse-riders that also appear on the *Uttaraṅga* seem to stand for his four sons. Lastly, the navagarhas and Saptamātṛkas also find place in the composition.

The sanctum enshrines large and beautiful icon of Sūrya. The god stands *samapādasthanaka* on a *tri-ratha* pedestal. He is appropriately attired in *udīcyaveṣa*, also wearing boots. Adorned with *Kirīta*, *kuṇḍalas*, *hāra*, *yajñopavīta* and *mekhlā* he is accompanied by Daṇḍa-Piṅgala, Ūṣā-Pratyūṣā and Rajani-Nikṣubha. Another Sun-temple of the Pratihara period also survives in Tikamgarh Distt. at village Umarai.

Among all the Brāhmaṇic gods, Sūrya is one who never attained supremacy but at the same time, never lost popularity. In *Prabodhacandrodaya*, the saura sect has been classed with Śaiva and Vaiṣṇva sects. As a matter of fact, just as Saktism came to be closely allied to Śaivism. Similary Sūrya-cult was allied to Vaiṣṇavism. Independent worship and temples we do come across in both the cases but the tendency to merge also seems to have been at work. We have mentioned above how Devi was considered practically a consort of Siva, likewise taking Sūrya as an aspect of Viṣṇu goes back to very early times. In Khajuraho Stone Inscription Viṣṇu and Sūrya have been jointly invoked.[110] The Bhailsvāmideva of Siyadoni record could as well be Viṣṇu as Sūrya.[111] Most convincing evidence of the alliance between Viṣṇu and Sūrya is accommodation of Sūrya in place of Viṣṇu while representing Brāhmaṇical triad in the upper section of *Prabhāvalī* of numerous Viṣṇu icons. The Citragupta temple of Khajuraho which is a Saura shrine has numerous Viṣṇu icons on its *jaṅghā* and Caturbhuja temple, which is a Vaiṣṇava shrine at the same place, has those of Sūrya.

The earliest Sun-temple of Candella period stands in dilapidated condition at Rāhilya (Distt. Hamirpur). Rāhila or Rāhilyavarman, the great-grand father of Dhaṅga, is credited with having raised it.[112] Built entirely of granite, it consists of a *garbha-gṛha*, an *antarāla* and a *maṇḍapa*. The sanctum and the *śikhara* are *saptaratha* in plan and elevation. The Citragupta temple, Khajuraho is a *niraṅdhāra prasāda* of finer sandstone. At Rehli in Sagar District exists a ruined Sun-temple of the period under review.

Of Sun-icons we have two varieties. Either he is represented with his full retinue and *parivara* or he appears alone riding his seven-horsed chariot. Of the former type we have very well-preserved icon from Rehli and of the latter we can cite rock-cut figures in Rājaghāṭī and Nāharghāṭi of Deogarh (Distt. Lalitpur).

The Rehli icoṇ (fig. 55) is the central image of Sun-temple struggling hard to survive. Woefully weather-worn, the panel is so badly blackened that the Lord appears to be literally emerging from darkness to brighten the world. Interestingly, the faces of most of the figures in the panel are fairer than their bodies creating an impression of light falling first on their faces. Standing *samabhaṅga* and crowned by a beautiful *kirīta* he is endowed with lotuses in both of his hands. Surrounding his head is a large oblong *śirascakra* near which Uṣā and Pratūṣā bearing bow and arrow have been accommodated. Normally they are represented in the middle of the image, so this constitutes a noteworthy feature of this icon. Devi Mahāśvetā stands in front with right hand in *abhaya-mudrā* and left holding a water-vessel. Below her Aruṇa is seen driving seven-horsed chariot. Near the lotus foot-stool of the Lord one male figure seated *sukhāsna* on each side could be taken for his sons. Among standing figures flanking him Daṇḍa and Piṅgala can be recognised on the basis of emblems they bear. Barring a lady attendent on each side all other figures in the lower section are devotees. At the top in the centre a *padmāsana* deity flanked by garland-bearing denizens can be made out. The whole of this huge panel is carved every inch and being overcrowded seems to be bursting with people presented on it. Another icon of this type we have from Rahilya in Distt. Hamirpur. A rare icon of Sūrya shown three-headed, is on display in the Palace Museum, Jhansi. The multi-armed god is accompanied by Daṇḍa and Piṅgala. Devi Mahāśveta is also represented between his legs. The Jarāya Mātā temple, Baruasagar, contains a beautiful icon of Sūrya in its back wall in which the god is seen riding his seven-horsed chariot. Very rarely he is depicted in one-horsed chariot for which only *Agni Purāna* offers injunctions. In Palace Museum, Jhansi, this rare example is included. Normally the Sun-cult is believed to be free from Tantric influence but in the same collection we have an icon of Piṅgala with his consort. Among the *parivāra* deities of Sūrya only Revanta finds independent depiction in one of the base-reliefs of the Lakṣmana temple, Khajuraho.

Gaṇeśa is the fifth among great deities around whom an independent cult developed towards the close of our period. Prior to that he continued as one of the *parivāra* deities of Śiva if we are to go by sculptural and architectural evidence. Inside Caturmukha-Mahādeva temple, an icon of god is lying, though it is difficult to say whether it belonged to the temple or not. Seated rājalilāsana and having four-arms, he holds *pāṣa* and *modakas* two of them, the other two being mutilated. Similar icons we have at Tejgarh and Raneh (Distt. Damoh).

Even after advent of Candellas, we do not get epigraphic or literary evidence showing separate sect of the Ganapatyas. But the fact is well-established by art-relics and religious ruins. A Kālanjara rock inscription contains invocation to Gaṇeśa.[113] Another record from the same site speaks of the setting up of a Vinyaka statue by Gaṇapati, the minister of Vīravarman.[114] In Siyadoni inscription Gaṇeśa is invoked with words "Om Om Namo Gaṇapataye." The second part of the inscription preserves two verses invoking the blessings of Gaṇeśa.[115]

By far the most convincing proof of Gaṇeśa's becoming a super-god is the Sahasraliṅgeśvara shrine of Chandpur (Distt. Lalitpur). He figures here on the chief *liṅga* as the fifth principal deity alongwith Viṣṇu, Sūrya, Śakti, the liṅga itself symolising Śiva. Likewise, a number of *Smārta-liṅgas* lying in the courtyard of the temple contain his miniature representation in one corner of the *Gaurīpaṭṭa*, the other three being occupied again by Viṣṇu, Sūrya and Śakti.

Some temples were definitely dedicated to the god but none has survived. Cunningham located a Gaṇapati temple standing on a lower level of the rocky ridge facing the Causaṭha-yoginī temple of Khajuraho.[116] A numper of icons depicting Gaṇeśa have come to light. Commonest among them are four-armed *Sthānaka-mūrtis* that show the god carrying lotus, *paraśu*, *modaka* and *svadanta* or sugar-cane-piece. His seated posture is generally *mahārājalīlāsana*. *Nṛtta-mudrā* is also common. Sometimes he is accompanied by his consort. We would describe only a rare but giant-image available to us from Dudhahi (Distt. Lalitpur). The figure of the deity is rendered as per usual iconographic injunctions. The uniqueness of the icon appears in the upper section of the *prabhāvali*. Accommodated at the top is a figure of Ardhanārīśvara, riding Nandi and holding a watervessel in the left hand. The right one is varada. *Jaṭāmukuṭa* adorns the head. Flanking the figure of Ardhanārīśvara is a divine couple on each side seated *lalitāsana*. The goddess to right has a flower and that on the left has a club (?). As the pairs possess no other weapons or symbols, their identity remains uncertain. Possibly they stand for other members of the Brāhmaṇical triad, Śiva being already present in his Ardhanārīśvara form. Slightly below on each side is shown one goddess seated *lalitāsana* and holding *vīnā*, which is characteristic musical instrument of Sarasvatī. The lower section of this large but beautiful panel is buried in the earth and the portion visible measures 1 mr. 42 cms. in height and 1 mr. in breadth. The survival of this unique icon at Dudhahi demonstrates the hold of Ganapātyas over here who must have financed the dedication of a temple to their dear god, which is now missing in the mist of time.

Almost every sect wanted to see its god through a magnifying glass. The best way to accomplish this was either to execute the icon life-size and hill size or to endow the deity with multiple arms. Sixty-four armed Cāmuṇḍā icon we have described earlier. An identical image of Nṛsiṃha from Khajuraho has been listed. Sixteen and eighteen armed Gaṇeśa we also have : the former is on display in the collection of Jhānsi museum and the latter is enshrined within a small unpretentous temple of a village near Banpur (Distt. Tikamgarh). The Ganapātyas seem to have built another strong-hold at Nohatā in Damoh District. About half-a-dozen massive icons of the god are lying scattered in the lanes and by-lanes of village. Quite likely a temple or two must have stood here in times past.

Of the members of the orthodox Brāhmaṇic triad, Brāhmā is never known to have enjoyed an independent cult of his own. One wonders how he maintained his position on terms of equality with such super-gods as Viṣṇu and Śiva and found place not only on *uttaraṅga* of the temple but *prabhāvāli* of icons as well. Perhaps, long ago he was taken as creator in the Trinity and could not be cast aside once the concept caught popular imagination. Viṣṇu and Śiva grew into super-gods in course of time with variety of factor and Brāhmā continued original humble self. But we do have a solitary shrine of the god surviving from the period under review at Dudhahi. Locally known as 'chhoti suraṅga'. Cunningham came upon it in course of his tours. The main icon was missing but three-headed bearded figure of Brāhmā riding goose and occupying the *lalāṭabimba* settled the question.[117] Reinforcing the identification was found a pilgrim's record paying homage to the *caturmukha* and his consort Sāvitrī.

Another minor god to make meteoric rise during the period is Hanumāna, manifestly a folk-deity. Nothing more illustrates it better than Candella coinage on which he finds accommodation.[118] Equally significant is the fact that the earliest dated inscription from Khajuraho comes from the pedestal of a Hanumāna image.[119] It belongs to the year A.D. 922 and invokes the deity under the name *Pavanātmaja*. Interestingly, the solitary shrine we can ascribe to him also stood at Dudhahi like that of Brahmā. It was located in the group of ruins now known as 'Baniya Ki Barat'. Save for some heaps of sculptures and architectural members, nothing survives to tell us of its existence. Amid them continues to stand the huge but headless icon of the god evoking pity and remorse in the onlookers and silently bearing witness to the fact that here stood his temple once upon a time. Holding left hand near heart, the god is heavily ornamented with *vanamāla*, necklace, girdle, bracelets, armlets and anklets, all beautifully carved (fig. 23).

A couple of Hanumāna icons in the State Museum, Dhubela (Distt. Chhatarpur) are also worthy of description as well as illustration. One of these resembles the Dudhahi image in some respects. (fig. 56) Here, the left leg of the monkey-god is raised upto knee trampling a demon underneath. The god is endowed with usual ornaments and has a dagger hanging from the girdle. His right hand which is held above the head is mutilated whereas the right one is shown *śucihasta* near the heart. Artistically, the icon is much inferior to the one standing at Dudhahi. Another image in the same collection represents the myth of lifting and carrying the hill with Sanjivani herb (fig. 57). The two-armed god stands with slight bend in his leg which is more pronounced in the right one. He wears a lower garment of which the central fold is clearly visible. Apart from usual ornaments, he is endowed with a long garland. Bearing his characteristic weapon mace in the right hand and holding the hill near héad, the god has his hair tied in a top knot. Stylistically, the icon appears to be very late one.

Of folk cults our sources speak very little since they invariably come to us from the royalty and the nobility and a long interaction found majority of folk gods subordinated to the super ones. Snake was one such divinity figuring in the mythology of many high cults but retaining all along an independent place in the folk-mind. Art-relics of our area belonging to the period under review show that like Hanumāna, a special place was carved out by the Nāga also in the higher sections of Hindu society. We come across snak-icons in both the forms—theriomorphic as well as anthropomorphic. Particularly in Damoh District we have numerous representations of the popular deity. One might argue that they constituted the sculptural decoration of Brāhmaṇical temples. That is fairly probable but the massive character of the icons, such as we get from Mohendra (Distt. Panna), Papat Museum, Kundeshwar (Distt. Tikamgarh) and Damoh Museum shows that shrines of elementary design must have been raised to consecrate them. In fact, at Kundeshwar we have an image of Manasā Devī in well state of preservation which must have served as central image in one of such shrines.

If we go strictly by the frontiers laid down for the present work, Buddhism never enjoyed the kind of ascendansy it have had elsewhere in the country for a while. At the same time, it never lost the limited ground it managed to aquire. Royalty did encourage it but nor did it discourage and isolated pockets in far-flung sectors continued to hold the law of the Buddha. Outside contact it must have maintained which certainly modified its character bringing it in tune with Buddhism of north India. A couple of records and references concerning the sect we do have but they speak absolutely nothing about structural or doctrinal changes within. Between them, Śaivism and Vaiṣṇavism shared the religious affiliation of the labouring masses and lordly classes leaving a little ground to Jainism in middle section of the mercantile society. The appeal of Buddhism, therefore, was bound to be confined to the descendants of few faithfuls found generations earlier. With minor variations, naturally marking the system for a period so long, the history of Buddhism could be summarised in one word—status quo.

Buddhist establishment at Gopeśvara hills in Datia District continued to maintain its position. The collection of art-relics housed in P.R.O. Office at Datia includes a broken slab with Buddhist theme. A finely executed Cakra is followed by a couchant deer, a lady in *añjali-mudrā* and a lion. Possibly it is a surviving fragment of Buddha icon in *dharmacakra-mudrā*. Unfortunately the find-place of the piece could not be ascertained. An icon of Tārā was discovered from Radhuapura, another establishment in the same district.

At Khajuraho, Cunningham, came upon a massive Buddha image amid the ruins of Ghaṇṭai temple which led him to believe in its Buddist dedication. But now we know that Ghaṇṭai is a Jaina Shrine. The icon showed the god in *bhūmisparśa-mudrā* and is inscribed with the usual formula "Ye dhammā hetu prabhavā.. ......" in characters of 9th century A.D. which renders the image as of the earliest from Khajuraho. The truth of Hiuen Tsiāṅg's noting Buddhist monasteries here cannot be authenticated though Cunningham was inclined to locate them in the northern group of ruins.[120]

Among an overwhelming number of Jina-icons at Deogarh, Klaus Bruhn found that of the Buddha indicating a foot-hold of the faith on the hill. It is now fixed into a wall. The face, the lower arms and the *parikara* are badly damaged.[121] The missing parts probably looked like the corresponding parts of the Buddha from Sarnath.

In *Prabodhacandrodaya* the Buddhists are named as Saugatas.[122] We get a clear reference that its followers had fled to Bengal, Orissa, Magadha and Sindh. We know that under the influence of Tantrism, sects such as Mantrayāna and Vajrayāna were born with addiction to wine and woman.[123] The bhiksu of the drama appears to have hailed from them being given to wordly joys. With Saffron cloak and shaven head, the Buddhist monks would speak high of their creed simply because it permitted greater scope for sexual licence than other sects.[124] The *upasakā* were not to mind if the monks committed adultery with their women. The remark of Bhiksu on seeing a Jaina monk over intoxicated is self-revealing—"This *tapasvin* has become mad because inspite of his being unaccustomed to drinking he has drunk much wine." Contact with the courtesans is clealy confessed in another dialogue. The monks sought admission to the order for the freedom it offered. They were ready to switch over to any other sect if it allowed greater scope for satisfying sexual desires. Bhikṣu is shown talking high of his creed till embraced by the kāpālikī. The fair touch transfers his praise to *Soma-Siddhānta* and he desires to become disciple of the Kāpālikā.[126]

This picture of Buddhism has been deliberately overdone since the specific and stated aim of the dramatist was to glorify Vaiṣṇavism. The evidence of Śri-kṛṣṇa Miśra, therefore, should not be taken at its face value. A historian cannot be protagonist of any idea and he has to eliminate the subjective element from his sources holding up the minor to plain and dry facts devoid of all colouring. But we are handicapped here from the fact that his is the only contemporary testimony on the subject and we have no other angle to view Buddhism from. Conceding, therefore, that some of the evils attributed by the playwright to Buddhist monastic order crept in under the impact of Tantrism, we might reject the rest. It is possible that a monk or two with love of luxury and laxity of character may have entered the order but to hold that the whole order abounded in slaves of senses would be unfair.

The law of the Buddha had a hold in Hamirpur Distt. We have inscriptional as well as sculptural material in evidence of it. While making over a village to certain Vedic scholars king Paramardideva made exception of five *halas* of land belonging to a Buddhist shrine.[127] A Mahoba mound yielded on digging several beautiful Buddhist sculptures. One of them ranks as masterpiece of Indian art. Mahoba was the seat of Candella government and we have no knowledge if any Candella monarch was Buddhist in his religious affiliation. Royal tolerance in religious matters is as much reflected in the find as the potential to survive without royal shelter on the part of Buddhism. The find includes two icons of Bodhisattva and an icon each of Buddha and Tārā and an inscribed pedestal. On grounds of palaeography the material is assignable to 11th-12th centuries A.D.[128] Citanaka and Satana, figuring in the pedestal records of the images were donors as well as carvers.

The icon of the Simhanada Lakeśvara is now in the collection of Lucknow Archaeological Museum. Seated in *rājalīlāsana* and clad in a lower as well as upper garment, the deity is shown holding a lotus flower in left hand and riding a lion. Adorned with a beautiful headdress, a scroll ornament and a crest-jewel, he wears a garland. With earlobes elongated and eyes extended at the corners, the face radiates sublime charm and spiritual grace. A lotus-shaped halo is carved around the head. Behind right hand stands a trident entwined with a cobra. On either side stands a pilaster with a miniature shrine in front accommodating an attendant in *namaskāra-mudrā*. The icon is indeed a matchless woık of art dissolving, as it does, the hardness of stone into the holiness of life.

Equally artistic is the icon of Padmapāṇi. Seated *rājalīlāsana* on a lotus, the god holds lotus with his left hand whereas with right he makes a mystic sign resting elbow on the knee. A third lotus rises on the right. Endowed with usual ornaments, the deity has a fine oval-shaped halo behind head. The face glows with devine grace and the whole composition is very close to life.

The images of Tārā and Buddha are no less remarkable and together, the four panels constitute the best specimens of Buddhist art of the period offering a vivid contrast to the lifeless productions of the contemporary Magadha school. Worthy of note is the representation of five *dhyāni* Buddhas in the upper section of Tārā's statue, clearly reflecting Tantric influence. Jainism also offers parallels to this panel which we would shortly survey.

From the district of Damoh no evidence of Buddhism was known till now. However, at Bāsā Tārkhedā, a Buddha image was noticed a few years ago which could be assigned to the period under review on the basis of palaeography of the pedestal record. The inscription is usual Buddhist formula "Ye dhammā hetu prabhavā......"[129]. An identical image with identical inscription is included in the collection of Banda museum, though its find-place is uncertain. Together, the two statues prove pockets of Buddhism surviving in Damoh and Banda districts during the early-medieval period.

The place and prestige of Deogarh in the history of Jainism is comparable to Khajuraho in the history of Śaivism and Vaiṣṇavism. Such was its sway that it enjoyed virtual monopoly of spiritual expression there, permitting no other cult to enter and acquire influence. In the classical age, Vaiṣṇavism did have considerable ground but the early-medieval saw the exclusive hold of Jainism on the sacred hill beside the Betwa. In respect of sculptural architectural and inscriptional wealth, no other Jaina site is as rich as Deogarh. Klaus Bruhn classified the Jaina remains of Deogarh into six periods all of which fall in the period covered by this chapter. His basis of classification is inscriptional evidence and architectural type[130]. To the post-Gupta period he assigned several architectural fragments lying to the west of temple No. 20. The earliest of the Jina-icons he dated to the 7th-8th centuries A.D. assuming thereby the existence of a temple at the place. Around the date of Bhoja's record have been placed temples No. 12 (Vimāna with porch), 15, 3, 13, 16, 17, 18, 20 and majority of the small shrines numbering 12A, B, D, H, 22, 24A and 27. The proliferation of these small unpretentious temple structures reflects the economic background against which they sprang up. They appear to have been financed by a middle-class which was not wealthy enough to raise temples of Khajuraho type but at the same time had some surplus capital for the expression of their fervour.

Worthy of study and description among the early temples are Nos. 12 and 15. The former (fig. 29) enshrines an image of Śāntīnātha known as 'larger Śāntī' (image No. 1), placed against the backwall of the sanctum. The fact of his being Śāntīnātha is not clear from the *lāñchana* which is missing here but by five records mentioning his name and appearing elsewhere. Of utmost importance among these is the pillar inscription of Bhoja Pratihāra coming from the year A.D. 862. We are told that the pillar was caused to be made and set up near the temple of Jaina Arhat Śānti by Deva, a disciple of acarya Kamaladeva [131] Another record datable to the year 994 A.D. shows that the whole place was known after Śāntī as *Śrī-Śāntināthatīrtha.*[132] We also have the gazelle symbol below the middle Jina of the lower *tri-tīrthikā*, placed on the lintel of the inner door-frame and pointing to dedication of the temple to Śāntīnātha. The icon of Śāntīnātha in the sanctum is flanked on one side by the *caurī*-bearing Indra and on the other by Ambikā Yakṣī.

Temple No. 15 is the only temple at Deogarh with three cellas and an enclosed porch. The cellas do not extend to any depth, since in each case, a niche was hollowed out of the corresponding part of the outer wall (Fig. 30). The similarity with the famous Gupta temple of Deogarh is obvious, whose influence on the plan and design in this case may not be altogether ruled out. A pavilion rises over the flat roof of the temple. In each of the niches, three Jina images stand reminiscent of a *tri-tīrthkā*. B.C. Jain regards the temple as of *Śodaṣabhadra* variety recognising in it full execution of scriptural injunctions.[133] He takes it to be the earliest among Jaina shrines at the place. Interestingly, the river-goddesses riding their respective mounts also make their appearance here on the door-jambs.

At chhoti Badoni (Distt. Datia), ruins of a granite Jaina temple lie scattered. Locally the shrine is known as Buddha-mandira, since a Jina-icon and Buddha-icon strike same to popular imagination. The huge panel representing Neminātha is still lying amid the ruins. The *padmāsana* god is flanked by a cauri-bearer and a *kāyotsarga* Jina on each side. In top corners are flying Vidyādharas. Yakṣī Ambikā, seated *lalitāsana* and holding a child is also in upper section whereas normally she is assigned a place below the deity. In Hamirpur district, the Makarbai temple is also Jaina in affiliation. Like temple No. 15 of Deogarh, it also has three cellas round a common *maṇḍapa*. Cunningham felt that one of the sanctums was dedicated to Śiva[134] but Daya Ram Sahani disagreed on the ground that "none of the images worshipped in the temple have come down to us."[135] The lintels in each case had navagrahas and Jaina figures sculptured on them. U.P. Shah also held it to be a Jaina temple.[136]

The Jaina temples of Khajuraho belong to a different category, not only in terms of plan and elevation or design and decoration but also in terms of financial back-ground and support. The class that funded their making commanded much more influence and wealth than the countless devotees of Deogarh records. We have already seen how by a single brief inscription no less than seven gardens were made over by a merchant for the maintenance of a Khajuraho Jaina temple. The donor was held in high regard by Dhanga Candella himself, and so also his Mahārāja-guru, Vāsavacandra, figuring in the record.[137]

It appears, the same guild of temple-makers functioned for all the cults. Not unoften we have Brāhmanical gods on the *jaṅghā* of Jaina temples. Far from showing their subordination to the Jina, the idea was merely to use them as decorative motifs because, in the first place the artist was ignorant of Jaina themes to be used for such a purpose, and in the second, he had no training and experience of representing the Jaina myths which were yet to percolate down to popular level. Prolific though the production of Jaina sculpture is during the period under review, surprisingly not a single myth translated in stone has been handed down to us. The Jaina literature abounds in hundreds of episodes associated with *Tīrthaṅkaras*, yet in the art of Bundelkhand we have not chanced upon panels presenting one of them. The wide and vertical canvass of the Pārśvan-tha temple at Khajuraho offered ideal opportunity to the artist to express his genius, but we are sadly disappointed finding repetition of Brāhmanic iconography. As a matter of fact, save for the Jina icon within the cella and on the lintel, a Jaina temple of Khajuraho is hardly distinguishable from its Brāhmaṇical counterpart a few yards away. The causes of this barrenness in Jaina art are not far to seek. The artist of Bundelkhand was well-versed in Brāhmaṇical themes and had a long training and tradition of representing them. We have already referred to sculptural rendering of numerous episodes from the epics found from Deogarh Gupta temple complex. Temple-rearing commenced quite early in orthodox faiths whereas very few Jaina temples can be dated to pre-Candella time in Bundelkhand. The sculptors must invariably have been Brāhmaṇical in religious affiliation and training and so could easily and expertly handle orthodox mythology, whereas Jaina canon was confined to a few faithfuls and Jain mythology was yet to shape up for clarity with conciseness in artistic expression on a lithic medium. An independent Jaina school of art could not develop owing to variety of factors like restricted employment-potential, exclusive character of the sect and prohibitive nature of the doctrinal appeal. It so happened that by the advent of the Candellas, the artist had fully mastered orthodox myths but for Jaina themes he was yet to make a beginning.

Deogarh Jaina temples are a class by themselves. Sankalia has fixed them within a long period extending over a thousand years—A.D. 800-1800.[138] Only temple No. 28 conforms to the concept of North Indian temple with a sanctum surmounted by a *Śikhara*. All others are merely flat-roofed rectangular rooms without windows and could be termed hall-temples. Some are provided with a porch. The development of the architecture comes to a standstill in the later half of the 11th century A.D. and that of sculpture in the correspoding part of the next.

IV group of Bruhn's classification, referred to earlier, includes those hall-temples where the walls consist of slabs. To this group belong temple Nos. 2, 3, 11 and 19. The images inside the first are dated[139] in the years V. S. 1023, 1051 and 1052. The records inside temple No. 11 have the dates V. S. 1105 and 1129. The temples are reminiscent of monastic architecture at Ranod, Kadbaya and Surwaya in the adjoining region. In the next group temple Nos. 21, 24 to 28, 30 and 31 have been included. No. 5 and several Mānastambhas also belong to V period. The last group has some repair measures and rebuilding work under it.

Jainsim had the strongest sway in the district of Lalitpur. Deogarh we have duly covered. A few more we may now cover. Dudhahi antiquities speak of about 4 temples having been raised there. Two of them had Ādinātha and Śāntīnātha as presiding deities. For a change in otherwise monotonous scroll of Jaina art, we have here on an architrave sixteen auspicious symbols. Equally refreshing is the theme of a Jina figure being bathed by devotees coming on crocodile, camel and elephant. Possibly it stands for ceremonial *Snāna* of the Lord by Indra and other gods. The largest temple of Dudhahi is also of Jaina affiliation. It consists of two rooms each of which opens into a pillared hall. The two halls are connected by a narrow passage running along each side of the two central rooms. In front of each hall there is a large pillared porch and a smaller one in the middle of each of the side passages. This plan imparts a perfect symmetry to the building seldom found elsewhere.[140] All other Jaina temples of Dudhahi are planned after north Indian pattern. Of the two Chandpur Jaina temples very little survives. Their dedication seems to have been to Śāntīnātha and Ādinātha.

Madanpur Jaina temples mostly belong to the time of Madanavarman.[141] One, earlier than him, has a record dated in V.S. 1112. In all, about 10 Jaina shrines stood at the site. At Banpur the only shrine worth noting is Sahasrakūṭa Jinālaya, a beautiful monument though modest in size. In plan it consists of a sanctum and canopied porticoes on all sides. Few Jaina temples are as ornate as this one. Surprisingly, save for the dikpāla figures, all the deities used for ornamenting the facades have been taken from the Jaina Pantheon. River-goddesses stand on the western doorway and navagrahas sit on the lintel of northern gate. Pārśvanātha occupies the *lalāṭabimba* of the southern and western door lintel. The *Śikhara* is tall and curvilinear with an arrangement of 11 *Karṇa-āmalaka* and is crowned by a large *āmalaka*, a *candrikā*, a smaller *āmalaka* and a *vijapūraka*. The Pārśvanātha temple of Khajuraho has been regarded as a close successor of the Lakṣamaṇa temple. The inscriptions place both in proximity of time, the date recorded being V.S. 1011. Ādinātha was the original presiding god[112] and the present image of Pārśvanātha is believed to have been installed about A.D. 1860 The Ghaṇṭai Temple of Khajuraho has been assigned to the end of the tenth century A.D. Essentially of the same design as the Pārśvanātha temple, but grander in conception, larger in dimensions and finer in execution, all that has survived of this beautiful shrine is an *ardhamaṇḍapa* and a *mahāmaṇḍapa*. The sixteen auspicious dreams of the Jina-mother have found place on the architrave. The Ādinātha temple is a *nirandhāra-prāsāda*. The enshrined icon is a modern substitute.

Coming now to Jaina sculpture Deogarh, again, tops the list with most prolific production. An interesting fact here is that vast majority of icons, fixed or unfixed have no connection with architecture. They were individually donated and gradually fixed in existing temples. In fact, temple Nos. 4, 8, 13 and 14 look so gaudy that a relationship between the images and the building i,e, between a nucleus of the images and the original structure, is altogether ruled out. To put it in plain terms, the temples look more of a museum than places of worship.

A post-gupta Jina (image No. 9) has been held to be the earliest Jaina icon of Deogarh. Of uncommon char and incomparable excellence are two Jina icons (image Nos. 13, 14) for which the Deogarh artist handsomely deserves our highest appreciation. Their identity cannot be established since *lāñchana* is not available. One of these remarkable icons is the presiding deity of temple No. 15. *Dharmacakra* flanked by a lion on each side is appropriately carved on the pedestal. *Trichatra* canopying the deity has also been provided. Cauri-bearers and Vidyādaras find place in the *parikara*. A rare and notable feature of this image consists in the presence of a miniature Jina seated *padmāsana* on *viśva-padma* and accommodated in the second *parikara* at the top. Indeed, nowhere do we come across a representation showing miniature Jina above a Jina or a miniature Buddha above a Buddha. With ethareal grace and indescribable calm characterising deity's face, no wonder, the discerning visitor is struck by his similarity with the world famous Sarnath Buddha.

A panel presenting *Tīrthaṅkara*-mother is also worth noting. It is placed in temple No. 4. Normally we do not get her representation. She is shown in *Śayana-mudrā*. We can not be sure that she stands for any particular *Tīrthaṅkara*'s mother, since she is accompanied by miniature figure of all 24 Jinas. Independent depiction of *ācāryas* and *upādhyāyas* is not known elsewhere. At Deogarh we have their life-like representation in image No. 82 placed in temple No. 4. Sitting in the centre of the compositon is an *ācārya* holding a *mukha-paṭṭika* in one hand and resting the other on his knee. Figures of *Upādhāyas* and *Sādhus* flank him on each side. In Jaina pantheon, *Tīrthaṅkara* occupies the highest position followed by *Siddha, Ācārya, Upādhyāyas* and *sādhu.* But these last four are rarely offered worship on regular basis and are never put on par with the *Arihanta* i e. *Tīrthaṅkara.* But at Deogarh, it seems that the *ācāryas* and *Upādhāyays* rose into such prominence that this hierarchical and age-old theory was set aside as would be evident from a panel in which an *ācārya* flanked by an *Upādhyāya*, all three in *padmāsana*, has further been flanked by a *Tīrthaṅkara* in *kāyotsarga mudrā.* An attendent bearing *cauri* stands on either side whereas in the upper section three miniature *padmāsana Tīrthaṅkaras* and two garland-bearing *vidyādharas* have also been accommodated. The lower section of this weather-worn huge panel shows lions flanking *Dharma-cakra* below the *Tīrthaṅkaras* and the three wooden stands among *Sādhus, śrāvakas* and *śrāvikās* below the *ācārya* and *Upādhyāyas.*

An icon of Jina Mallinātha is lying in a bylane of Mohendra (Distt. Panna), trampled upon by the villagers everyday. It could have been the pride of any museum but such· is the cruetly of time callousness of man that far from getting reverence or admiration, it is subjected to indignity all the while by the ignorant villagers and unlettered urchins. This massive but magnificent icon measures 1 mr. 54 cms. in height and 1mr. in breadth. The lower portion of the image is sunk into the ground.

Jñāna-śilā of Deogarh is an epigraphical curiosity. It is a rare record with no example from elsewhere. The inscription has letters party invented and derived from existing alphabets. The first seven lines contain different alphabetical orders including the Dravidian[143]. Below it is mentioned that the slab was a *Jñānaśilā* having 18 different languages as well as scripts. The jaina tradition credits the first *Tīrthaṅkara* with having invented the 18 alphabets.

Among the *Tīrthaṅkaras,* Ādinātha, Śāntnātha, Neminātha and Pārśvanātha stand out as popular ones to whom the temples were generally dedicated and of whom we possess the largest number of representations. Of *Dvi-mūrtikās* and *Tri-tīrthikās* we have not heard till now. During Candella times, icons illustrating them came into worship. Image Nos. 256, 257 and 642 at Deogarh stand for the former and show two figures of Pārśvanātha in *Kāyotsarga-mudrā* standing side by side : of the latter we have a representation from Banpur in which Śānti-nātha is shown flanked Arahanātha and Kunthunātha In the collection of Jhansi Museum, panel No. 272 depicting five Jina figures with Pārśvanātha in centre may be held as *Pañcatīrthaṅkara.* Sahu Jain museum, located below Deogarh hill-fort, houses some icons of Bahubali and Bharata Cakravati. The former is usually *kāyotsarga* with creepers climbing his body and scorpions and lizards moving up and down to bring home his condition of complete withdrawal from the contact world. The latter is also renderd *kayotsarga* but to highlight his *cakravarti* status kalaśas representing *nava-nidhis* have also been depicted beside him.

Offering of worship to the foot-impressions of the *Tīrthaṅkaras* also developed during the period. Temple No. 6 of Deogarh has also a slab with representation of 24 pairs of foot-impressions standing for the 24 Jinas. In tune with Vaiṣṇava practice of raising *dhvaja-stambha* to Viṣṇu, we have at Deogarh a good many *mānastambhas* facing the temples or standing free. In addition to those of Deogarh, we also have one from Mahoba (Distt. Hamirpur), one from Mohendra (Distt. Panna) and two from Madanpur (Distt. Lalitpur). Extremely ornate and of moderate height, the crowning member of the pillar normally has four Jinas in four faces.

Certain iconographic peculiarities of the Jaina sculpture may also be noted. An Ādinātha image of Deogarh (No. 292) has been shown wearing a necklace. Yakṣa Dharaṇedra is depicted holding umbrella over Pārśvanātha in another icon placed in temple No. 14. Navagrahas getting place on the *uttaraṅga* of the doorway or architrave of a *maṇḍapa* we are well familiar with. At Deogarh we see them finding representation in an icon (No. 462) of Ādinātha. Four appear to his right led by Sūrya and five to his left. The injunctions with regard to the placingof *lāñchana* has often been violated. Of seven colossal Jina icons (Nos. 15 to 21) arranged in the *pradakṣiṇā patha* of temple No. 12, none has the *lāñchana* carved below. Icons of Pārśvanātha and Supārśvanātha we meet not only with the usual snake canopy but with seat of Snake-coil as well. The *Jaṭāmukuṭa* of Śiva has sometimes been copied with a knot at the top and some hairs reach upto knees. Needing particular note in this regard are some rock-cut Jaina sculptures at Mahoba. Inside a cave behind Bai Caṇḍikā temple of the town, we come upon carving of a *kāyotsarga* Pārśvanātha flanked, as usual, by a *cauri*-bearer on either side with a *dharmacakra* below flanked by lions. What strikes us here is the canopy of nine snake-hoods over his head and the depiction of *pañcachatra* above instead of the usual *tri-chatra*. As though this was not enough to emphasize the depth of devotion to and power of pārśvanātha, three more representations of the deity in *padmāsana* have been carved on either side, endowing them as well with a canopy of nine-hoods. We cannot be sure about the symbolic significance of the composition but if number is any indication, then it stands for *Sapta-mūrtikā*. We possess very few independent representations of Yakṣī padmāvatī. One of them is here. Endowed with a snake-canopy of seven hoods, the goddess is shown four-armed. Her front right hand is in *varada-mudrā* and back right holds a *dhvaja*; back and front left carry *pāśa* and *kamaṇḍalu* respectively. Interestingly, the figure of presiding god is of puny proportions in comparison with her: perhaps an instance of long interaction of Jainism with Śaktism and Tantrism.

At Deogarh the phenomenon is clear and Sankalia suspects Tantric influence on Jainism basing his view on Yakṣa-Yakṣī iconography.[144] The *Śikhara* niches girdling the wall of temple No. 12 in between the plinth and the entablature accommodate 24 Yakṣīs. The actual number of niches is 26, but only 24 are open to view. Each of the Yakṣī icon is inscribed with the names of a Jina and that of the goddess. Names of the Yakṣīs agree but sporadically with the known names from the Jaina Pantheon. The sequence is also faulty. Sankalia felt that the iconography of the Yakṣīs was at a formative stage when this scroll running round the *Śikhara* came to be composed. But disregard or ignorance of injunctions in Yakṣī iconography of Deogarh can be noted from free icons as well. We have icons of the same Yakṣī with two, four, ten and twenty arms. In this regard Śāktism seems to have affected Jainism. Icons of Padmāvatī never show her third eye. She is depicted holding a child contrary to injunctions. Sometimes a Yakṣī theoretically associated with one *Tīrthaṅkara* is shown accompanying another. An Ādinātha image (No. 106 in temple *No.* 4) is carved with figures of Cakreśvarī as well as Ambikā. Plenty of evidence we have attesting the elevation of Yakṣīs in Jaina worship during the period. The spectacular rise of Cāmundā in Śaiva Pantheon, being held in special regrad at Mahoba has already been referred to. Likewise Ambikā and Cakreśvari acquire prominence in Jainism at Deogarh. We meet with numerous larger than life, multi-armed and heavily ornamented figures of these goddesses. At times their physical dimensions are twenty times bigger than those of the Jina surmounting them. In the collection of Sahu jain Museum of Deogarh we have these massive icons. This reflects the reverence to the Jina being relegated to the background in preference for the *Śasana-devatā*.[145] Among Vidyādevīs, Sarasvatī had some importance and has been accommodated on the door-lintels of some Deogarh and Khajuraho temples.

We may also note representation of *Caturviṃśati Paṭṭas* and *Pratimāsarvatobhadrikās* in Jaina art of the period. Image No.12 of Deogarh is a beautiful example of the former and of the latter a fragmentary survival in the garden of S.D M.'s Bungalow at Mahoba is noteworthy. Made of sand-stone and standing on a *Sapata-ratha* pedestal, it has a miniature Śikhara crowning it. Each of the four Jinas is shown *Kāyotsarga* and canopied by a *pañca-chatra* which is typical of Mahoba Jaina iconography. Their *lāñchana* and *srīvatsa* symbols are missing. The sculpture gives an idea of a *mānastambha* in ministure. Among the art-relics lying in the courtyard of Banpur *Sahasrakūta caityālaya* a rare representation of *tri-caubisī* is available. We do not have any from Deogarh art. Ādinātha is the presiding deity in the panel and seated *padmāsana*, he is flanked on each side, not only by *kāyotsarga* figures of pārśvanātha and Supārśvanātha, but a full *caubīsī* as well.

In *Prabodhacandrodaya* of Srikriṣṇa Miśra, Jainism is represented by Digambara sect only. As the dramatist aimed at playing down all other sects save his own, the picture of Jainism emerging is an ugly one. Such was the dirtiness of Jaina monks, we are told, that some people mistook them for creatures of hell (Nāraki) while others thought them to be rākṣasas and piśācas.[146] Neither did they clean themselves nor donned any dress. They carried peacock's tails and got their hair uprooted. kṣapaṇaka, the Jaina monk, drinks wine on persuasion though he himself admits prohibition for his order.[147] He is shown telling the laity to welcome monks by serving delicious food and allowing entertainment by their ladies.[148] The sweet embrace of Kāpālikī is enough for him to give up his faith and switch over to Śaivism. He becomes interested not in *nirvāna* but *Siddhis* which would enable him to kidnap women. Dancing merrily with the Kāpālikī, he addresses the Kāpālika as Ācārya and *Kulācārya.*[149] After painting this picture of degradation and degeneration characterising all sects other than that of Viṣṇu, the dramatist claims that Jainism as well as Buddhism lost their hold on the people at the rise of Viveka. That the playwright was badly prejudiced and strongly motivated we have already mentioned. His testimony cannot be accepted at its face-value. The long survey of Jaina architecture and sculpture we have done, which is by no means exhaustive or completed, shows the spread and sweep of the sect manifesting at a number of new sites. In fact the hold of jainism was never as strong as now and hardly any archaeological site with Brāhmanic remains is devoid of Jaina relics. Of moral laxity stray instances cannot be totally ruled out but to believe that the whole order of Jaina monks had sunk low would be contrary to canons of sound historical research. Confirmatory evidence from other quarters is called for to support the references in the *Prabodhacandrodaya*. The sculptural representation of the Jaina *Ācāryas* and *Upādhyāyas* from Deogarh radiate restraint and renunciation from their faces and must be taken as modelled on contemporary monks.[150]

Jaina epigraphy from Deogarh is no less rich than iconography though monotony in both the cases mars much of their value for historical investigation. Upwards of 400 records have been recovered from the vast temple complex, a good many being pedestal inscriptions. More than half of them date from the middle of the 12th century A.D. We learn that upto four persons were involved in the setting up of an image or a *mānastambha*: the donor who gave the order for the piece to be prepared; the person for whose spiritual welfare the donation was meant (either a relative or the donor himself); the monk who consecrated the image and finally the artist or craftsman responsible for executing the wish To these may be added living or deceased relatives of the donor.[151] An important feature of the Jaina religious order was institution of spiritual titles. Some of them find mention in Deogarh records. Among these *bhaṭṭāraka* is of especially significance since in elevation of Yakṣī worship and introduction of profuse ornamentation in Jaina art the role of *bhaṭṭārakas* appears to be decisive. Many of them are mentioned in later records showing the high status they enjoyed. It is noteworthy in this regard that like *ācāryas*, who figure in later inscriptions, the *bhaṭṭārakas* frequently had no contact with Deogarh. Yaśahkīrti, Ratnakīrti and Vijaykīrti are exceptions to this observation. *Maṭhapati* is another spiritual title of which the documents make mention. One of the *maṭhapatis*, Rajyapāla figures in more than one. Likewise, we have some more names appearing again and again. Among these Mādhavadeva of the Double snake group, Gunanandin of Gunanandin group and Tribhuvanakirti and Vīracandra of the Larger group need particular notice.[152]

We have already referred to Deogarh record of Bhoja's time. It describes that the pillar was set up by Śrīdeva, the disciple of Kamaladeva. It is interesting to note that their names recur on a pillar fragment below the small size representation of a monk and an *ācārya* respectively. The *ācāryā* is rendered in the preaching attitude characteristic of this iconographic type whereas the monk sits to the left with folded hands. The pillar is definitely of much later times than V.S. 919, the date of Bhoja's record. But their identity is established beyond doubt. The representations speak volumes for their prestige and popularity at Deogarh or else they would not have been remembered after such a long span of time.

The division of the monastic orders is also very well reflected. Teachers belonged to various *Saṅghas* and *gacchas* and accordingly the name-suffixes were adopted. Mulasaṅgha, Senasaṅgha, Devasaṅgha and Siṃhasaṅgha are recorded as also the Sarasvati gaccha.[153] Outside Deogarh only Khajuraho Jaina inscriptions need our notice. One incised on the left door-jamb of the Pārśvanātha the temple and dated in V.S. 1011 records a gift of no less than seven gardens to the temple by one pāhilla of grahapati famliy.[154] The family figures in the Darbar Śāntinātha image inscription also in which two members are mentioned as hereditory ministers of Kirtivarman Candella.[155] Pāhilla was also held in high regard by King Dhaṅga. In any case the very gift shows that Khajuraho Jain temples sprang up against a different economic background than those of Deogarh. Our view gets strength from the fact of another grahapati family mentioned in the records. A one line inscription gives us the name of *Sreṣthin* Pāṇidhara. In the next he figures with his sons *Sreṣthin*, Trivikrama, Ālhana and Lakṣmidhara.[156] We meet Pāhilla again as son of *Sreṣthi* Dedu and father of Salhe, Mahagana, Mahicandra, Śirīcandra, Jinacandra, Udayacandra and others bowing down to Sambhavanātha. Together the two grahapati families bearing the professional title *Śreṣthin* show that financial support to Khajuraho shrines came from devotees with vast wealth.

The picture of inter-sect relations as painted by the *Prabodhacandrodaya* is very dark and unhappy. The very plot of the play is based on inimical feelings between two brothers Viveka and Mahāmoha. The former has the support of Upaniṣada and Gītā whereas the latter has the backing of kāpālika, Bhikṣu and kṣapaṇaka[157]. In the III Act we witness a discussion in which passions rise so high that kāpālika attempts to kill kṣapaṇaka.[158] But Srīkṛṣan Miśra was not holding mirror to religious reality of the time. He aimed at elevating Vaiṣṇavism downgrading others. Highlighting merits of his sect and demerits of all others he fulfilled his aim, but, for this very reason, his picture is not acceptable to us. In fact, unconsciously though, the dramatist himself hints at cordiality characterising inter-sect relationship. At one place Śraddhā notices the unity of different *āgamas* and holds that all the different *śāstras* speak of one Supreme God in different ways.[159] Elsewhere Viṣṇu is said to be beloved of Śiva.[160] Finally, and of course, surprisingly, the dramatist who was manifestly a protagonist of Vaiṣṇavism offers his prayers to Candradhamauli.[161]

Inscriptions are far more vocal and reliable on the subject. Catholicity of rulers in religious matters we have already covered. Yaśovarman raised a wonderful temple to install a wonderful icon of Vaikuṇtha whereas his son Dhaṅga did so for consecrating not one but two Śiva-Liṅgas. Jaina monk Vāsavacandra was his

Mahārājagurū. From *Bāppa Bhatti Carita* of Candraprabhāsuri we note that Nāgāvaloka (nagabhaṭṭa Pratihāra) gave up his life after worshipping *Pañcaparameṣṭhi*.[162] From Dahi Copper Plate we learn that Trailokyavarman paid worship to Mahādeva, Sūrya, and Bhavāni. Neither it is possible nor it is necessary to enumerate, describe and illustrate all the syncretic icons of Bundelkhand which are mostly the product of the period under review. Khajuraho alone supplies us with dozens of them. We take up here a beautiful icon of Harihara fully preserved inside a *janghā* niche of a Rehli temple. Standing *tribhaṅga* the four-armed syncretic god is endowed with usual ornaments, his crown being half-*jaṭā* and half *kiriṭa* as per iconographic requirements. Of his front hands, right one is broken and the left one holds Viṣṇu's emblem *śaṅkha*. His back right hand bears a *triśulā* and back left carries a *cakra*. To his right stands Śiva's *vahana* Nandi looking up to the master whereas cakra-puruṣa of Viṣṇu is accommodated to the left. Slightly damaged, the icon testifies to the artistic excellence of Bundelkhand artist.

The fact that *Smārta* cult flourished during the period is enough to show the happy state of inter-sect relationship. Dissension and tension emanating from social and economic causes and poisoning the religious life may not be altogether ruled out but our sourses do not reflect them. As a matter of fact, we have a massive panel in the Palace Museum, Jhansi, showing multiple representations of many Brāhmaṇical deities, high as well as humble, standing side by s:de and it would be most appropriate to end our narrative on this happy note. Measuring 117 cms. in breadth and 68 cms. in height, it is divided into several horizontal bands intervened by pilastered niches. The top section contains fourteen miniature *liṅgas*. The band immediately below shows fourteen figures of male and female. This band is intervened in the middle by a pilastered niche accommodating seated male figure in *kukkutāsana*. The third band from top shows twelve figures of Viṣṇu but it is also intervened by a pilastered niche containiug a lady with water vessel in one of her hands. The fourth band contain figures of Gaṇeśa and seven figures of Sūrya. The last and lowest band accommodates figures of navagrahas with Gaṇeśa being also intervened by a pilaster containing a pair of male and female devotees shown in *añjali-mudrā*. The panel is in well state of preservation. (Fig. 47)

REFERENCES

1. Weber, Max : *The Religion of India.* The Free Press, Glencoe, Illinois, 1960, p. 16.
2. E.I., I, p. 131
3. Ibid., p. 134
4. Ibid., p. 203
5. Ibid., p. 13
6. E.I., XXX, No. 17 v. 7
7. E.I., I, p. 205
8. Ibid., p. 131
9. Ibid., p. 212
10. E.I., XIX, No. 2
11. E.I., XX, No. 14—A,B and D
12. E.I., IV, No. 20. We have a literary corroboration of this generosity of Paramardideva in granting land. Uatsaraja, his minister dramatist, makes his Sutradhāra of the play—*Tripuradaha*—speak the following verse in praise of the sovereign :

    अज्ञाता दानपरम्पराभिर्विवेदमायावि कक्षचिद्दुर्वी ।
    बिभर्ति तत्पूर्वमिव प्रहंर्ष मुहुःप्रदानैः परमर्द्दिराजः ।।

    R.S., p. 75.
13. *Apastamba Dharma Sutra,* II, 7, 16, 1 *Saha deva-manusya asmil—loke pura babhuvuh* ABORI, X, p. 245 ff.
14. E.I., I., p. 139
15. Ibid., p. 152
16. Ibid., p. 338
17. Ibid., No. 20
18. Temples figuring in Siyadoni stone inscription are a class by themselves and will be separately treated.
19. Yadava, B.N.S.: *Society and Culture in Northern India,* Central Book Depot, First Edition, Allahabad, 1973, p. 21
20. E.I., XXXIII, No. 22
21. E.I. XXVIII, No. 19
22. E.I., I, No, 20
23. E.I., 1, p. 152
24. E.I., I, p. 206
25. E.I., XXVII, No. 29
26. Weber, Max : Op. cit., p. 22
27. Pande, R.B. : *Historical and Literary Inscriptions.* p. 167 ff.
28. E.I., XX, No. 14.
29. Names from 1 to 12 figure in Khajuraho Stone Inscription of Yaśovarman and Dhaṇga, Khajuraho Stone Inscription of Dhangadeva, Khajuraho Stone Inscription of Kokkālla, and Bateśvara Stone Inscription of Paramardideva, Ajayagadh Rock Inscription of Viravarman and Ajaygadh Rock Inscription of Bhojavarman. All these records have been edited in *Epigraphia Indica,* Volume I ; No. 13 is from Charkhari plate of Deravarman (E.I.. XX, No. 4) ; No. 14 figures in Kalanjara stone Inscription of Paramardideva (ASR, XXI, p. 37) ; No. 15 in Ajaygarh Rock Inscription of Paramardideva, (ASR, XXI, p. 51); No. 16 to 19 in Madanpur Temple Pillar Inscription (A.S.R., X, p. 100) ; Nos. 20 to 22 in Mdhoba Plates of Paramardideva (E.1.,

XVI pp.9-15); Nos. 23 to 25 (E.I., I, No. 19); No. 26 and 27 (A.S.R., XXI, pp. 37-38) No. 28 (SA., XVIII, pp. 237-39); No. 29 (E.I., I, No. 25); No. 30 (A.S.R., II. p. 436).

30 Names from Nos. 1 to 4 are from Khajuraho stone inscription (E.I., I, No. 19); No. 5 from Gwalior stone inscription (E.I., I, No. 20) ; Nos. 6 to 12 are from Siyadoni record (E.I., I, No. 21) ; Nos. 13 to 15 are from Mau stone inscription of Madanavarman (E. I., I, No: 25) ; Nos. 16 and 17 from Batesvara stone inscription of Paramardideva (E.I., I, p. 207 ff) ; Nos. 18 and 19 from Mahoba stone inscription (E.I., I, No. 27). It is interesting to note however, that kalanjara which for long was monopoly of Śiva worshipped under the name Nilakaṇtha recommodated Viṣṇu also under the name Cakrasvami though for this we have a solitary reference from a drama of Vatsaraja staged in honour of the deity:

ग्रहं हि कालञ्जरे चक्रस्वामि यात्रा समागमे विदग्ध सामाजिकेरादिष्टयेऽस्मि। यदद्द चन्द्रोदये देवस्य चक्रस्वामिनः पुरत्रो रूक्मिणी हरणा हृवयः कवि वत्सराज विरचित ईहामृगोऽभिनेय।

R.S., p. 37

31. E.I., IV, No. 29
32. I.N.S., p. 156
33. A.S.R., XIII, p. 99
34. J.M.P.I.P., No. 1, 1959, p. 70
35. C.A., p. 518
36. Deva, Shrikrishna : Op. cit., p. 52
37. *Aspects of Indian History and Archaeology*, p. 127
38. E.I., XXV, No. 28
39. E I., I, p. 150
40. Ibid., p. 138
41. E.I., XXVII, No. 29
42. I.A.A.R,, 1963-64, p. 87
43. C.I.I., III (Revised), p. 239
44. I.A.A.R.. 1962-63, p. 78
45. Ibid., p. 50
46, Awasthi, R. : "Two Sadāsiva Images from Khajuraho" *Journal of Indian History*, Vol. L III (Aug. 1975), pt. II pp. 211-13

46A. B.P., pp. 49-50

47. A.S.R., XXI, p. 34
48. Pande, R.B. : *Historical and Literary Inscriptions*, p. 168
49. E.I., XXXI, p. 163
50, Yadava, B.N.S, : Op. cit., p. 355
51. Ibid.
52. P.C., III, p. 111
53. Ibid., p. 125
54. Ibid., p. 122
55, Ibid.. p. 116-117
56. Ibid., p. 112
57. Kanwarlal : *Immortal Khajuraho*, Asia Press, Delhi, 1965 p. 132
58. Ibid,. p. 141
59. B.S. 74.20 ग्राब्रह्मकीटान्तमिदं निबद्धं पु स्त्रीप्रयोगेण जगत् समस्तम्।

    ब्रीडात्र का यत्र चतुर्मुखावमीशोऽपि लोमाद गमितो युवत्याः ॥

    From Vatsaraja, the dramatist minister of king Paramardideva we have a contemporary reference to Śiva delighting sexual pleasure and this fact finding free expression in a drama staged publicly :

    R.S., p. 118

भूयिष्ठा: परिरम्भकेलिषु भुजा: सोत्कण्ठमालोकने
नेत्राणि प्रचुराणि चुम्बनविधौ भूयांसि वक्त्राणि ते ।
इत्थं भूरिवधूविलास घटना सज्जस्य काऽहं तव
प्रोक्त: क्रोधविरुद्धयेति शिवया स्मेरो हर: पातु व: ।।

60. Vidya Prakash : *Khajuraho* Taraporevala sons & co., Bombay, 1967, p. 186
61. Vide Kanwarlal : Op. cit., p. 136
62. B.S. 55.15 शेषं मङ्गल्यविहगै: श्रीवृक्षै: स्वस्तिक छटै: ।
मिथुनै: पत्रवल्लीभि: प्रमथैश्चोपशोभयेत् ।।
63. Mehta, R.J. : *Konarak*, D.B. Taraporevala Sons & Co., Bombay, p. 30 ; also Leeson, Francis : *Kama-Shilpa—A Study of Indian Sculptures Depicting Love in Action*, D.B. Taraporevala & Co., Bombay, 1962, p. 31 & 34. Most of the interpretations have been taken from these books only.
64 उपाध्याय, भगवत शरण । "भारतीय मंदिरों पर यौनचित्रण", नई दुनिया, 18 अप्रैल, 1974, इन्दौर. पृ. 4
65. A.S.R., XXI, p. 56
66. Deasi, D. : *Erotic Sculpture of India*, Tata Mcgraw Hill, New Delhi, 1975, pp. 138-39
67. Ibid. pp. 143-44
68. *Aspects of Indian History and Archaeology*, p. 128
69. Leeson, Francis : Op. cit., p. 31
70. Desai, D. : Op. cit. p. 135
71. Vidya Prakash : Op. cit., p. 187 ; See also Upadhyaya, Vasudeva : *The Socio Religious Condition of Northern India*, Chowkhamba, Varanasi 1964, p. 82. Three possible causes have been suggested by him for accommodation of obscene figures on temple walls :

    1. Influence of Tantra on the temple structure.
    2. Firm hold of *Mithuna* movement in the society.
    3. It reminds the worshippers that elemental observations of the world which they represent may be done outside and the inside is pure and holy.

    These have more or less been covered in our analysis.
72. Pande, R.B. : *Historical and Literary Inscriptions*, p. 166
73. E.I.,I, No. 20
74. E.I., XVIII, p. 109
75. Puri, B.N. : *The History of the Gurjara-Pratiharas, Bombay* 1957, p.153 *ff.*
76. E.I., I, No. 20 p. 161: "One can feel legitimately proud about this religious catholicity since it is so much lacking today even among Hindu sects. Max Weber in his book *The Religion of India* (p.21) has recorded how the Brāhmaṇas of some Vaiṣṇava and Śaiva sects would not even utter the names of each other's gods.
77. E.I., I., p. 168
78. Ibid., 213
79. E.I., XXVIII, No. 19
80. E.I., I, p. 130
81. Ibid.
82. A.S.R., X, 103
83. E.I., I, No. 27, v. 26
84. Ibid., No. 25.(I)
85. Ibid., No. 38, v. 7
86. Ibid., v. 9
87. A.S.R., XXI, p. 39

88. E.I., XX, No. 14
89. P.C., I1, p. 72
90. Deva, Shrikrishna : Op. cit., p. 44
90A. B.P., pp. 47-48
91. अवस्थी, रामाश्रय : खजुराहो की देव प्रतिमाएं, आग्रा, 1967, पृ. 103
92. P.C., I, p. 11
93. Ibid., pp. 4-5
94. अवस्थी, रामाश्रय : वही, पृ. 66 S. D. Trivedi has referred to a rare icon of fourteen-armed viṣṇu from Kalanjara but has not-included it in his illustration plates. (B.P., P.46)
95. E.I., I, p. 130. Here falling of the hoiy Gaṅgā waters at the feet of Hari is an allusion to the myth.
96. E.I., IX. No. 34
97. First name is in Mahoba Stone Inscription (E.I., I, No. 27) ; Second in Batesvara Stone Inscription (E.I., I, No. 25 (1)) ; and third in Kālañjara Stone Inscription (A.S.R. XXI, p. 39).
98. Roy, P.C. : *The Coinage of Northern India,* Abhinava Publication, First Edition, 1980 p. 50 ff.
99. Yadava, B.N.S. : Op. cit., p. 360
100. A.I.K. p. 336
101. Ibid. p. 338
101A. Sharma R.K, : The Temple of Causatha Yogini at Bheraghat Agam Kala, Delhi, 1978, p. 30 ff.
102. I am indebted for the names and photograph to the Department of Ancient Indian History, Culture and Archaeology, University of Saugar. The names of the Sixty-four yoginis are given in the *Kalika-Purana*, the *Brhannaradiya*, the *Durgapujapaddhati*, *Pithori-vrata-katha* and *Yogini-Cakra Pujana.* But only six names out of sixty-two preserved in Beraghat records, tally with those of *Kalika-Purana* and five with *Durga-puja Paddhati*, the iist avaiiable from shahdol images varies totally from Bheraghat as well as Puranic and other texts named above. It is very difficult to say which list is reliable and factual. It appears that new names were invented from time to time according to local tastes and traditions and additions and alterations were made in the original list. See-Sharma R.K.: op.cit., P.31ff:
103. A.S.R., p. 40
104. E.I., I, No. 21
105. Ibid., No. 38
106. Ibid.
107. A.S.R., XXI, p. 53
108. A.S.R., X. p. 100
109. A.S.R.. XXI, p. 47
110. E.I., I, No. 19
111. Ibid., No. 21
112. A.S.R., II, p. 441
112A. B.P., p. 51
113. A.S.R., XXI, p. 54
114. Ibid., p. 52
115. E.I., I, No. 21
116. A.S.R., II, p. 418
117. A.S.K., X, p. 94
118. Roy, P.C. : Op. cit., p. 58; Interestingly, the earliest of Khajuraho records is related to this theriomorphic deily and is dated in V.S. 940. The pedestal inscription is non-official being a dedication by Golla, son and grand-son respectively of Gahila and Pahila. (B.P., p. 23)

119. A.S.R., XXI, p. 64
120. A.S.R., II, pp. 428 and 435
121. Bruhn, Klaus : Op. cit., p. 52
122. P.C., V, p. 177
123. S.E., pp. 404 and 415
124. P.C., III, p. 105
125. Ibid., p. 106
126. Ibid., p. 109
127. E.I., XX, No, 14
128. M.A.S.I., No. 8
129. I was shown a photograph of the icon by Secretary of the Gajarath Mahotsava Samiti, Damoh and my guide Shri S.D. Misra, Deptt. of AIHC and Archaeology, University of Saugar setteled the reading and palaeography of the record.
130. Bruhn, Klaus : Op. cit., p. 52 ff.
131. E.I., IV, No. 44
132. Bruhn, Klaus : Op. cit., p. 70
133. Jain, B.C. : Op. cit., p. 127
134. A.R., 1925-26, p. 15
135. Ibid.
136. Shah, U.P : *Studies in Jaina Art*, Banaras 1955. p. 19
137. E.I., I, p. 136
138. *Aspects of Indian History and Archaeology*, p. 119
139. Bruhn, Klaus : Op. cit., p. 53
140. A.S.R., X, p. 93
141. A.S.R., XXI, pt. II, p. 171
142. Mitra, S.K. : *Early Rulers of Khajuraho*, p. 207
143. A.P.R., 1915-18, p. 10
144. *Aspects of Indian History and Archaeology*, p. 122
145. Barth, A. : Op. cit., p. 143
146. P.C., III, pp. 99-100
147. Ibid., p. 122 : अस्माकमर्हतान् शासने सुरापान नास्ति ।
148. Ibid., p. 101-v. 6 : दूरे चरणप्रणाम: कृतसत्कारं च भोजनं निष्टम् इत्थमिले न कार्या ऋषीणा दारान रममाणावाम् ।।
149. Ibid., p. 126
150. P.C., V: pp, 177-78
151. Bruhn, Klaus : OP. cit., p. 57
152. Ibid., p. 59
153. *Aspects of Indian History and Archaeology*, p. 123 ; As a matter of fact *Sasanadevis* execute the commands of the *Tirthonkaras* and rank much lower in Jaina Pantheon. See Barth A. *Religions of India*, p. 143.
154. E.I., I, p. 136.
155. I.H.Q., XXX, pp. 183-85
156. E.I., I, p. 153
157. Ibid.
158. P.C. III, pp. 114-15
159. P.C., V, p. 175
160. P.C., IV, p. 164
161. P.C., I, p. 3
162. Puri, B.N. Op. cit, p. 48
163. Yadava, B.N.S, Op. cit. p, 375

7

Conclusions and Contributions

(No book having the bulk and dimensions as the one in hand is worth its price and time unless it also helps in reaping the rewards of effort made in its making. In terms of absolute certainty and concrete conclusion, a student of Ancient India can offer very little. Even otherwise, historical investigation is an ongoing process, and must always be so, since with each new dawn new evidence dawns displacing the clearest of conclusions. To this extent, conclusions contained in this chapter are bound to be partially modified or outrightly invalidated sooner or later. But they are worth-drawing, nonetheless, being based on an honest reading of the sources and, within their scope, represent the reality of religious life of a long epoch in bygone Bundelkhand.)

Bundelkhand at present is merely a 'geographical expression' but was not always so. It had political personality and administrative unity at one time or the other based largely on its geographic compactness. This independent identity of the region is reflected very well in historical records of ancient and early medieval period. The current lack of unanimity among the scholars on its physical frontiers stems largely from considerations other than historical. Linguistic basis is of much later origin and can made out a far larger area for the concept but at the cost of compactness which alone weighed with people in the past.

The idea of Bundelkhand has long been in the air and plenty of books on its history and culture have found place in library shelves but as regards the origin and antiquity of its name none has attempted an analysis, resting content with its British derivation from Bundela Thakurs who constituted the prominent warrior clan at their advent. The origin of the Bundelas is shrouded in mystery and lapped in a legend. They appear suddenly on the stage of history in the fourteenth century A.D. from nowhere In all probability, they emerged from the pulindas who inhabited the area all through and were warlike people of non-Aryan stock. With the passing out of Candellas at the close of thirteenth century goes also out of use Jejākabhuktī—a name they are believed to have given to the region. Jejā was an early Candella prince who is claimed to have christened the region and every author down to R K. Dikshit accepted it as such. But there are reasons to suspect that he merely seized upon an already existing fact officialising an informally current name. The name Jejā figures in Indian documents as early as sixth century A.D. and similarly Jujhotiā, an adjective applicable to the Brāhmaṇas and Banias of Bundelkhand, has origins in pre-Candella period.

Geography of any region is always a key to the understanding of its polity, society, economy and culture. The body of Bundelkhand is made of hard and black soil, Vindhyan fastnesses and dense forests. Together with low spring-level and deficient rainfall they militated against the emergence of a local centre of power, till the advent of the Candellas who put in extra efforts to generate a surplus by tackling water problem, promoting trade, encouraging industry and taping forest wealth. Prior to them political unity is difficult to establish though Cedi Janapada of Buddha's time might have approximated to the idea in some respects. In between, the region was either a part of an empire or fragmented into several pockets of power—Aryan side by side with non-Aryan. Under the Guptas Bundelkhand was a district administrative unit and the arrangement was based on its geographic compactness. Identical may have been its position under the Mauryas, though we have no means to ascertain.

The hand of geography may, again be seen in the coexistence of history and prehistory in the region. The Bundelkhand man switched over from food-gathering to food-producing early in the second millennium B.C. but his cave-dwelling and animal-hunting concomitant also continued well into history and sandwiched between these two extremes were aboriginal masses slowly coming under the shadow of Brāhmaṇisation. Eran Chalcolithic civilisation represents the first; painted rock-shelters prove the second and references to Śabāras, Pulindas and Kirātas in records authenticate the third section of this multi-faceted society. The exact identity of the authors of Eran culture is not settled and that of cave-painters remains a matter of guessing but the non-Aryan tribes of Sanskrit records can very well be taken to be Gonds, Bhils, Baigas, and Bharias of Bundelkhand. They remained a constant factor in regional polity down the ages. If Rāvaṇa's Laṅkā has to be located somewhere in Central India as a section of scholars feels, then the war of Rāma definitely constitutes an aspect of interaction between the Aryans and non-Aryans of the area. Historic parallels of this violent subjugation may also be found in epigraphic records. But political conquest did not prove to be as permanent as the cultural one which, in course of time, was completed by Brāhmaṇic support to non-Vedic cults of Viṣṇu, Śiva and Śakti.

The process of acculturation also progressed along lines laid down by geography. Bundelkhand was the heart-region on the Indian sub-continent. Any idea of political consolidation, commercial expansion and religious propagation was not to materialise without passing through it whether travelling from the North to the South or *vice versa.* Routes were bound to be built through it even if deeper penetration and absolute absorption was prevented by Geography. This is what happened. Acculturation was easy and early along the routes whereas vast areas waited till the comming of the Candellas under whom the pace accelerated to the maximum. Their aboriginal past is fairly evident and their support to Brāhmaṇical values and worship was assured once they get legitimation and lofty origin. Their adoption by the Brāhmaṇical ideologues is reflected curiously, but clearly, in a popular tradition referring to the imposition of four conditions on their ancestor—not to drink wine, not to put Brāhmaṇas to death, not to form improper marriage connection and adopt 'Varman' suffix in his as well as descendant's names. This recognition of as well as admission to Brāhmaṇa Varṇa was not easy to obtain since a true Brāhmaṇa would never subscribe to such a spurious proposition. But by early medieval period Brāhmaṇa Varṇa had also undergone proliferation of castes and subcastes pursuing a variety of professsons. Even now we have Brāhmaṇas suffering social degradation for rendering service to castes lower than theirs. Contemporary texts refer to ten categories of Brāhmaṇas, of whom six were decidedly degraded. Hence a willing priesthood to invent an epic or mythic origin for the Candellas was not altogether wanting. To clinch the issue, deliberate and frequent falsification of princely pedigrees commencing about the same time in South India stands already proved beyond the shadow of a doubt. [E.I, III, p. 171]

Since a local centre of power failed to emerge, a connected account of political history for the pre-Candella period is out of question. Even the structure of politics that shaped up is not fully reflected in our meagre and irregular sources. We can however, be reasonably sure of some of its features. Urban settlements were usually dominated by the commercial class and the royal officers were charged to run the administration in consultation with a board on which it was fairly and invariably represented. In rural areas royal representatives wielded all power and we have no reference to village assemblies. The situation was naturally different in case of villages wherefrom the royal income was made over to Brāhmaṇa beneficiaries or secular functionaries, who might have exercised civil and judicial authority though our records are far from conclusive on the point. Eminent officials—whether provincial governors, ministers or judges—were normally Brāhmaṇs who held their positions on hereditory principle. A new class that made spectacular entry into the structure of politics towards the close of our period was that of the Kāyasthas. It successfully rivalled with the Brāhmaṇas claiming a mythic origin and Ṛṣi ancestor. The scholar, soldier and trading classes owed their importance in political structure to the possession of knowledge, arms and wealth, respectively. The Kāyasthas acquired their share of authority from skill in drafting land records which had become central to the maintenance of state apparatus as never before. Of warrios class we hear very little but mobility of mercantile class into it is attested by at least one document. The eminent officials prided as much on their Brāhmaṇic back ground as on military qualities and achievement. The lower sections of the society enjoyed hardly any power but the fact that they found separate mention in epigraphic records of late Candella period shows that they had a sort of professional status in rural society which could not be ignored even by the King.

The picture of politics, presented above, is true only of the Brāhmaṇised parts. Vast tracts of forested territory were held by non-Aryan chief who stood in feudatory relationship with neighbouring potentate of the superior civilization. But feudal colour of this relationship was confined only to political sphere obliging the tribal chief to fight the battles of his superior. Economic content of feudalism based largely on administration of land is altogether lacking. In origin, the arrangement seems to have been based on realisation that neither civilization could absolutely annihilate the other. The tribals resented the Aryan advance but were powerless against superior technology and systematic warfare. The only way out was to offer submission and be secure against interference in tribal society. That the arrangement worked only in few cases is clear from constant headach of tribal revolts which the rulers had to suffer down to Bhojavarman Candella.

An Indian version of feudalism has been read into the records of early-medieval period, obviously including those of the Candellas as well. Feudalism is a phenomenon for which finality of definition is still far from settled. With its multi-level manifestation, this is naturally so. Viewing in terms of polity the essential feudal element lies in the emphasized form of lord-vassal complex with personal loyalty, leading to fragmentation of political authority and informing an administrative structure based on the possession of land.[1] Our study and analysis of the Candella records does not bear out this structure of politics. Barring a couple of copper-plates, all others were issued in favour of Vadic scholarship who were all-suited to articulate the Lord-vassal complex. Nowhere we come across delegation of civil and judicial authority. Some plates pertain only to permission granted for consolidation of land-pieces located in various villages. In one case there is mass assignment benefitting 309 scholars, jointly holding a dozen of villages. No phraseology in this case could turn them into feudal lord, particularly when the assignment was clearly qualified by a number of exceptions. Brāhmaṇas stood at the head of the society and the assignment of village income further added to their importance in local affairs. Reading feudalism in these records is possible only when we import meaning into them which could not only be questionable, but contrary to our commitment to history as well.

The few secular grants which are available come from the fag end of our period. Mostly made in favour of warriors, dead or alive, they might have contributed to feudal nexus, but even here the specific object of the king was to reap religious merit rather than reward bravery. References to the allotment of villages either as emoluments or as reward to high functionaries we do get but they are too few to form into a feudal pattern. Land-grants by the Candellas in no way contributed to feudalisation of political structure.

Of Ratnins we do not hear after the Vedic period anywhere in India. A refreshing memory of their constitutional status and importance is preserved in two of our records when we find the king assigning land only when assented to by the minister and the priest in one case and by the *Mahādevī*, the *jyeṣṭhakumära*, the *Pratihāra* and the *Akṣapaṭalika* in the other. A case of survival it is certainly not but a curious comment on the picture of oriental despotism presented by western imagination.

In addition to land-grants, building of forts has also been taken as factor in feudalisation. It is believed that a fortified place besides being used for storing collected taxes in kind, maintaining garrisons of soldier and offering shelter in times of emergency was final instrument through which a prince or chief could perpetuate his power over peasantry. Bundelkhand being dotted with numerous forts, the idea is applied to it. But we are far from sure how many of them are of Candella making. Again, it is curious that Mahoba, the very seat of government, should not be fortified at all. Khajuraho, the religious capital, was likewise unfortified. Further, the officer-in-charge of fort was to carry on the administration in consultation with a board of officials and non-officials. We find a feudal lord also acting in like manner. In fact, military nature as well as connection with Candellas seems to be fairly established in case of Kālañjara and Ajaygadh only. Contribution of forts in creating feudal nexus, therefore, is not conclusively proved.

The fact of Stone-Age man having inhabited the area being firmly established religious history of the region has to begin with the pre-Aryans. One of the earliest cults to emerge was that of the Mother. Anthropology has demonstrated beyond doubt that physical fact of paternity was unknown to the early man for considerable span of time who naturally wondered at the Creation and Transmission of life by woman. It is significant that Durgā, a deity of non-Aryan origin, has the name Vindhyavāsin with eternal abode among the Vindhyas and Bāṇa found her specially popular among the forest tribes.[2] Magic was another predecessor of religion which originated in material needs of primitive man—particularly animals, which were his staff of life as well as adversary. Mimesis was one of the means to acquire power over them and in rock-art we have human being wearing animal masks. Another and more probable explanations of the practice could be its connection with totemism which also turned out to be one of earliest reflections of religious consciousness in man. At agricultural stage, totem animals, were transformed into ancestors by slow process of rationalisation. This nature and content of totemism find clear reflection in the sept-names and folk-songs of Bundelkhand aborigines. From hoary antiquity trees were also held in high regard and even now constitute a substantial segment or the totemistic pantheon of primitive society. The greatest of their gods has his abode in a Sāj tree. Such was the simplicity of primitive mind that implements and weapons of chase also came to be deified in course of time. On change-over to food-producing stage new deities were bound to figure in their super-natural world and they did figure in variety of forms.

Aryan penetration of the region was not sudden or systematic but slow and sporadic, confined largely around the routes passing through the province. Even till the close of the Classical Age the process of Brāhmaṇisation had not made much headway and primitive communities went on with their ways behind the cover of woods. The absence of P.G. ware and the presence of microliths associated with red-painted sherds and followed by iron and N. B. P. ware at Eran and Tripuri indicate that these parts were Ayanised at a fairly later date. Epigraphic records leave us in no doubt that largest influx of immigrant Brāhmaṇas and their most widespread diffusion did not take place till the coming of the Candellas on the stage of history — somewhere around the close of the first millennium A .D. The interaction on religious plane took on a shape quite different from what we come across elsewhere. Offering accomodation to and absorbing aboriginal masses resulted in birth of new sects. Indications are fair that left-hand Śaivism—particularly Kāpālika sect—was born in Bundelkhand.

Symbols bearing religious sense appear very early in rock-art[3] and travel far into history, on pottery as well as numismatics. Significance of the former cannot be attributed to the latter since imaginative visualisation of the cave-dweller can hardly be equated with that of the people leading organised life in the plains below. An explanation could be that man on road to civilization retained and carried many beliefs and symbols born at earlier stage of existence. Resemblance resulting from contact also cannot be altogether ruled out but most probably symbols of rock-art had sense and significance not corresponding to what we know from Brāhmanic records.

The government of Aśoka was the first in the history of Bundelkhand to shape the religious life of the people by active and untiring efforts and helping indirectly thereby the process of Brāhmaṇisation. He created a special cadre of officials charged with religious responsibility. They were to see that all the sects—great or small—got equal opportunity to flourish and to propogate the imperial ideals envisaged in Dhamma, bearing a special Aśokan sense. It was noble attempt on the part of the emperor to suggest a way of life which was both practical and convenient, being moral at the same time. Apart from appointing *Dhamma-mahāmātās*, he also undertook *Dhamma-yātrās* to translate his ideals into life. He visited Bundelkhand in course of his tours in witness whereof put up the Minor Rock-Edict at Gujarra. The claim that he makes therein of having succeeded in effectine association of men with gods could be taken to stand for his success with non-Aryan masses. His 'theocracy without god' must have had far-reaching effect on an area like the one under study.

The art of Bundelkhand offers perhaps the earliest aniconic representation of Sun getting consecrated for worship in a temple. The Sun-dial of Unao (Distt. Datia) is circular in shape embedded in a high plateform and save for the unsculptured raised points at the periphery, it has no contours.[4] Partly aniconic and partly iconic figure of the same deity we have among the terracottas of Dhubela Museum collection (Distt. Chhatarpur).

Even before the dawn of the Classical Age, sacrificial religion of the *Vedas* had come to terms with folk cults and beliefs, evolving a new structure in which on mundane level the Brāhamaṇas wedded to the *Vedas* maintained supremacy over temple priests but on supramundane level Vedic deities accepted inferiority to non-Vedic gods Nārāyaṇa and Śambhu. Theories were pressed into service to rationalise the alliance and the structure based on it; cattle wealth was no longer sacrificed as religious requirement and *Ahiṃsā* was an important doctrine of the Vaiṣṇavas. The cow naturally came into her own obtaining apotheosis and equality with the Brāhmaṇas in heading the human society. Bundelkhand has preserved the earliest record making mention of this fact. A distinguishing feature of later day Hinduism was thus born.

Gift of land had acquired sacred character much earlier but it became an article of faith from classical period downward. Central Indian charters are among the earliest to quote relevant verses from Epic and Smṛti literature. Land-grants are usually in favour of Vedic scholarship and multiply in number as we travel down in time. A landless labourer could hardly hope for the favour since that was not supposed to earn any religious merit for the Sovereign. Lords Spiritual had successfully brainwashed the Lords Temporal on the subject through literature and education which was their monopoly.

Vedic gods numbered much less in comparison with non-Vedic ones, who were simply beyond calculation. In course of long interaction, attempts were made at evolving order out of chaos. Two unifying principles were at work in this world of bewildering diversity. One of them was oneness of the Ultimate Spirit and the other was Doctrine of Incarnation, and together, they made possible for Monoism and Pluralism to stay in complete harmony of neo-Brāhmaṇism or what we call Hinduism. Bundelkhand contributed a third principle enlisting geography in the service of religion. The earliest of Deogarh records mentions Viṣṇu as Keśavapursvāmin—the Lord of Keśavāpura, obviously the oldest name of Deogarh. In another record of the same time Viṣṇu is mentioned as Citrakutasvāmin. This tendency had far-reaching consequences. By being associated with hundreds of places and held as the presiding Lord there, Viṣṇu became an integrating factor enabling people with diverse backgrounds and different ethos to join a single cultural mainstream. With place-name becoming component part of his local name, the god could establish countries relationships remaining one in reality at the same time. Conversely it was also possible to identify a local deity with a super-god and obtain its affiliation to Hiudu hierarchy.

The theory of incarnation was bound to rest on bed-rock of mythology. The art of Bundelkhand has contributed the earliest lithic illustrations of Vaiṣṇava myths. The life-like representations of Karivarad and Nara-Nārāyaṇa themes are priceless contributions to Indian art. So also the sculptural transcriptions of *Kṛṣṇalīlā* and the *Rāmāyaṇa*.

Varāhāvatāra seems to be another contribution of the region to the cult of Viṣṇu. Boar may have been a totem originally, it maintained special hold on Bundelkhand all along. In cave as well as sculptural art the proliferation of Varāha representations speaks volumes for his popularity among the masses.

In realms of architecture, Gupta Temple of Deogarh is the earliest *pañcāyatana* shrine of India. Though we are far from sure of deities to whom the subsidiary shrines were dedicated, the temple is a rare contribution of Bundelkhand to the religious art and architecture of India.

By far the most remarkable landmark in religious history of the region and that of Classical India was the hermitage of sage Divākaramitra. Himself a Vedic scholar of no mean merit, he switched over to Buddhism and yet attracted students from the orthodox fold. Among the inmates of his Āśram Emperor Harṣa Vardhan saw the Buddhists, the Digambara Jainas, the Śvetāmbara Jainas, the Bhāgavatas, the Lokāyatikas, the pañcarātras, and the followers of Upaniṣadik, Paurāṇik and Dharmaśāstra teaching. The freedom of conscience and creed which he and his hermitage displayed is in sharp contrast to the persecution and intolerance practised elsewhere in the world at the time. It's a golden page in the annals of any country that describes the life and times of such a teacher and his institution.

A curious religious practice of Classical Age was that of putting up *gotra-śailikā*, a pillar in memory of dead ancestors or relatives. Though very few such *balayaṣṭis* have come to knowledge, the record incised on them clearly refers to the religious merit associated with the act. Since scriptural injunctions to the making of such a *balayaṣṭi* have not yet been located, the practice may have been special product of Central India.

The latter half of early-medieval period witnessed unprecedented dynamism in the life of Bundelkhand that nearly shook the people off from centuries of slumber. Attaining political unity under the sovereignty of a Brāhmaṇised native dynasty, the region produced one of the strongest armies of the time, one of the most renowned groups of temples and one of the most prosperous societies of the time. Trade and industry touched a peak scaled never before. Raising of majestic temples was no longer within the means of royalty only; a single merchant had enough surplus to finance and endow a shirne Influx of immigrant Brāhmaṇas surpassed all earlier figures. Kṛta Age was verily called back since the country was rendered fit enough for Aryan sacrificial religion, Manu's ideals having been materialised. Vedic Brāhmaṇism retained supremacy in religious structure but folk cults also had full growth and final shape. Apart from five Super-gods, some lesser ones also grew big enough to enjoy independent sects. Among these Cāmuṇḍa, Hanumāna and Brahmā merit particular mention. Temples sprang up as though from earth since very few epigraphic references we get to their making or maintenance. Gift of land, gold and cow went normally in favour of Vedic scholarship, though temple priesthood was not altogether neglected.[5] It is refreshing and interesting to see, at least, in one case that endowment was aimed at maintenance of sacred fire in the context of a Viṣṇu temple.

In urban economy temples had a vital role. They owned vast wealth of immovable property and industrial classes were bound by cash investments to supply materials of worship and money for maintenance. Merchants as makers of these temples mattered most in the management of their shrines. Richest among them were those dealing in salt, a dear, but indispensable commodity for all.

Early-medieval records of Bundelkhand reveal thirty different names of Śiva and nineteen of Viṣṇu. Place-names no longer constitute component parts of their names since there was no need now with process of absorption having reached optimum level. Names figuring in inscriptions therefore are based on iconography and mythology which found limitless lithic translations. Vaiṣṇavism had made full use of incarnation theory to exert an appeal over the masses but in Śaivism multi-dimensional personality of Śiva alone secured the popularity of his cult. In addition, a number of non-Vedic godlings found admission in Śaiva hierarchy enhancing its sweep and strength. Pāśupata Śaivas are known to have adopted anti-varṇa and anti-caste stance in admitting people to their fold. Their open-door policy had special effect in Bundelkhand in extending warm welcome to tribal masses. Besides, the Kaula and Kāpālika sects, which rose under the impact of Tantrism and openly violated the tenets of puratanic Brāhmaṇism, had special appeal to primitive communities through esoteric rituals and occult practices. Their aowed sensualism got unreserved support from aboriginal people who were free from puratanic rules and regulations. The Mātaṅgas were lowest of contemporary social orders equivalent to the Cāṇḍāllas. At Khajuraho one of the temples is dedicated to Mātaṅ geśvara Śiva. The 'puzzle of passion' writ large on the *jaṇghā* of Khajuraho temples has to be viewed in this context. The hold of Kāpālikas on Bundelkhand Śaivism of the time cannot be denied since even in contemporary drama the cult is represented by a Kāpālika and a Kāpālikī. The physical dimensions of the temples as well as their location demonstrate that they were made primarily for the king, his nearest courtiers and certain sects which indulged in esoteric rites now regarded as questionable. General causes responsible for the accommodation of erotic art on temple walls elsewhere in India might be applicable to Khajuraho as well but in our study of Bundelkhand archaeology we found the phenomenon confined to forest covered Khajuraho only.

The number of epigraphic records of the early-medieval period runs into hundreds but hardly any idea they offer us about the doctrinal changes and structural variations within various sects and systems. No cult was a royal cult in early-medieval period. Even father and son in kingly families happened to be devotees of two different super-gods. Hence, no cult got consistent royal support. Every system was to survive and flourish on its own. Its strength and spread depended mostly on mass appeal and innate ability to enlist affiliation of primitive deities to its pantheon. What is further interesting, polity seems to have prompted the princes to adopt plurality of cult affiliation. Bhoja Pratihāra was *Śrīmadādivarāha*, *Mihira and Paramabhagavatībhakta* all rolled into one. The Pratihāra *Koṭṭapāla* of Gopadri fort financed the making of a Viṣṇu shrine as well as that of Navadurgā. If it reflects eclecticism of the ruling class on the one hand, considerations of polity also seem to condition it on the other.

Comparison of kings with cult gods commenced very early in India. In the beginning only Vedic deities figured in the eulogies, Supergods like Śiva and Viṣṇu being left out of comparison. But in early-medieval period we frequently come across this equation as well. The early Candellas were content with comparison to minor deities but their successors verily proclaim self-apotheosization. To cite just one example, we are told that sublime appearance of Vīravarman made people wonder whether he was Viṣṇu riding his Garuḍa or Śiva roaming on his bull [EI. I No. 38(1)]. It is pure panegyric since it is beyond our belief that he might have actually mounted either of the vehicles. Equation with the twin super-gods seems to be the plain motive of the poet.

Another recurring theme of the courtly eulogies was the end of Sinful Kali Age and return of the Kṛtayuga in which Brāhmaṇical values stood translated into life. Such was the virtuous conduct of the kings and their officers that Kali Age ended out of season. A remarkable feature of life in Golden Age was physical manifestation of Gods on earth offering *'darśana'* to their devotees. Probably for *Praśastikāras* of early-medieval period their princely patrons were truly the divine phenomenon in flesh and blood on earth.

Bundelkhand records being mostly land-grants or lithic dedications of temples, only one kind of sinner looms large in their text—the person interfering with the grant or donation. Interesting are the contemplated courses and consequences prescribed for him. Saddling such a sinner with five Great and Minor sins is normal in early documents. In post-classical period he is cursed with consignment to Great Hell ; life of a worm in excrement for 66000 years ; earning Hell for his near and dear ones as well ; hundred births as dog followed by one among Cāṇḍālas ; habitation in a waterless hollow of a Vindhyan tree and birth as snake in a desert.

Variety of aims prompted people to raise temples. Religious merit for oneself or one's dears was natural and normal enough among them. But love of fame, honour to ancestors, attainment of wealth, boon of sons and grandsons, salvation of twenty-one generations and perpetuation of memory also figure as motives behind the building of temples in our inscriptions.

Religious tensions and dissensions cannot be ruled out as would be apparent from the play *Prabodhacandrodaya* of Srīkṛṣṇa Miśra, but eclecticism of the royalty and the nobility worked as much for harmony and unity as syncretism of the *Purāṇa-kāras* and mythmakers. About *Pañcāyatana* character of Deogarh Gupta temple we may not be sure, but of early-medieval period we can point out some temples of this variety. Sahasraliṅgeśvara temple of Chandpur (Distt. Lalitpur) was one of them. In fact, hand in hand with cults of the Super-gods flourished Smārta-worship and syncretic iconography, emphasising the unity and indivisibility of the godhead. The dichotomy of monism permeating pluralism was thus resolved.

The earliest among the cults manifesting in central India was that of the Mother. It maintained its popularity among the masses in one form or the other. Developing later into Śaktism one of its important offshoots was yogini kaul cult. It is noteworthy that though the cult was born in distant kāmarūpa, it found fertile soil in Central India. Out of nine known Yoginī centres spread all over India, five sprang up in this part of the country with beautiful circular shrines[6].

Jainism registered a distinct advance in the early-medieval period. At Deogarh in Classical Age, it was absolutely non-existent. Humbly manifesting thereafter, it swiftly acquired virtual monopoly of the place making it the holiest of holy Jaina enters in Central India. The records found there reveal proliferation *saṅghas* and *gacchas* among the Jaina laity and monk-orders. Under *Bhaṭṭāraka* influence Jainism also absorbed Tantric principles elevating the status of Yakṣīs who got life-size and multi-armed representations accommodating tiny figures of the presiding Jina. The *Jñāna-śilā* of Deogarh is a record of its own kind, verily an epigraphic curiosity containing several scripts. By any standards the production of Jaina art and iconography was prolific but hardly any panel has been handed down depicting Jaina mythology. A miniature Jina above the main one we normally do not get, such rare representation is offered by the Deogarh artist. Among other panels those depicting *Tīrthaṅkara's* mother, *ācāryas* and *upādhyāyas* are noteworthy. Mathematical principles also weighed with the devotees for increasing the religious merit of their donation in proportion to the number of figures carved. We have *dvi-mūrtikās*, *tri-mūrtikās*, *sapta-mūrtikas*. A solitary lithic translation of the concept of tri-caubīṣī from Banpur (Distt. Tikamgarh) is also noteworthy. The appeal of Jainism was ordinarily confined to urban trading class, part of which was enlisted by Vaiṣṇavism also, probably because extreme austerity of Jainism did not allow them the kind of freedom they desired in their dealings with other professional classes.

Buddhism did not die out till the close of our period. All through it maintained a sort of status quo neither rivalling with other sects nor suffering at their advance. Solitary Buddha icons from far-flung districts show that it retained some pockets of influence, never making active efforts to enlist new adherents to the Law of Buddha. The Buddhist iconography of Bundelkhand is also barren in representation of mythology. Towards the end we get Bodhisattva icons of whom meriting mention are Siṃhanāda Avalokiteśvara and Padmapāṇi—two rare gifts to Indian art.

On orthodox side also we have numerous iconographic contributions of Bundelkhand. Those from Khajuraho being too well-known hardly require mention. Elsewhere needing note are a hill-size *Gajāri*, Śiva, and a sixty-four armed Cāmuṇḍā, from Mahoba (Distt. Hamirpur), a *Padmāsana* Lakulīśa from Bharchā and a *Govardhanadhāri* Kṛṣṇa from Bhenswāhā (Distt. Sagar), a Nandi with Skanda climbing over from Chandpur and Gaṇeśa with Ardhanārīśvara in *Prabhāvali* from Dudhahi (Distt. Lalitpur), and Viṣṇu with Gaṅgā as his consort (Jhansi). Together with lithic rendering of epic and Paurāṇic mythology from Deogarh and khajuraho, this list of Bundelkhand contributions to religious art and iconography of India becomes frankly formidable.

REFERENCES

1. Yadava, B.N.S. : Op. cit., p. 179
2. Cowell, E.B. & Thomas, F.W. : Op. cit., p. 226; Also see—Kale, M.R., Op. cit., p.39
3. Srivastava, V.C. : *Sun-Worship in Ancient India.* Indological Publications, First Edition, 1972, p. 19. He is of the view that the testimony of beliefs and practices of primitive tribes may be taken into account to corroborate the tentative conclusions drawn on the basis of 'speechless' material evidences of the prehistoric and the protohistoric archaeology of India. Swastika Cross, and wheel of rock-art have been taken by him to represent the Sun. Further, Religion according to him had been the motive force behind the evolution of art all over the world (p. 272)
4. We should like to point out here that given in research monographs of Srivastava, V.C. *op. cit.*, and Pandey, L.P. *Sun Worship in Ancient India*, Motilal Banarasidass, (First Edition) New Delhi 1971 and Singh, S.B., *Brāhmanical Icons of Northern India*, Sagar Publications (First Edition) New Delhi, 1977, we have not found any reference to a Sun-dial representing the god and getting consecrated in a temple.
5. It seems down the ages a sort of social stigma continued to be attached to the profession of a temple priest.: D.H.I., 87-88.
6. Sharma, R.K.: *The temple of causatha-Yogini at Bheraghat* p. 32.

Bibliography

I. ORIGINAL SOURCES

(A) LITERARY

Aitareya Brāhmaṇa : (Edited, Translated and explained by—Martin Haug), Bharatiya Publishing House, Varanasi, 1976.

Bāṇa's Kādambari : A Literal English Translation of (tr. Kale, M.R.), Vaman Yashvant & Co., Bombay, 1924.

Manu Smṛti : Ed. Dave, J.H.) Bharatiya Vidya Series Vol. No. 33, Bombay, 1975.

Meghasandeśa of Kālidāsa: (tr. Shastri, S.R.) Sri Balmanoram Series No. 38, Mylapore, Madras, 1947.

The Harṣacarita o' Bāṇa : (tr. Cowell, E.B. and Thomas, F.W.) Royal Asiolic Society, London, 1897.

The Bhagvad Gitā : (tr. Swami Chidbhavanand) Tapovnam Series 94, Sri Ramakrishna Tapovanam Tirupparaitturai, 1976.

कूर्मपुराण : (सम्पादक—प. श्रीराम शर्मा आचार्य) संस्कृति संस्थान, प्रथम संस्करण, बरेली, 1970

परमाल रासो : (सम्पादक—श्यामसुन्दरदास) नागरी प्रचारिणीग्रन्थ माला 23, काशी, संवत 1976

प्रबोधचन्द्रोदय : चौखम्बा संस्कृत सिरीज, बनारस, 1955

ब्रह्माण्ड पुराण : शास्त्री, आचार्य जगदीश (संस्कृत), मोतीलाल बनारसीदास (   ) दिल्ली, 1983

बृहत्संहिता : (अनु. पण्डित अच्युतानन्द झाशर्मणा) विद्याभवन ग्रन्थमाला 41, चौखम्बा, वाराणसी, 1959

मत्स्य महापुराण : (अनु. शास्त्री, श्री रामप्रताप त्रिपाठी) हिन्दी साहित्य सम्मेलन, प्रयाग, संबत 2003

श्रीमद्वाल्मीकीय रामायणम्	: पण्डित पुस्तकालय, काशी, प्रथमावृत्ति, 1951
रघुवंशम्	: मिश्र, पण्डित श्री रामचन्द्रः, सुलभ संस्कृत ग्रन्थमाला श्री कामेश्वर सिंह दरभंगा संस्कृत विश्वविद्यालय, दरभङ्गा, 1979
विष्णुधर्मोत्तर पुराण	: वेंकटेश्वर प्रेस, बम्बई,
रूपक-षटम्	: सम्पादक-दलाल, चिमनलाल : सेन्ट्रल लाइब्रेरी, बडोदा, 1918

(*B*) *NUMISMATIC*

1. Altekar, A.S. : *The Coinage of the Gupta Empire* (corpus of Indian coins, Vol. IV) Numismatic Society of India, Banaras Hindu University, 1957.
2. Bajpai, K.D. : *Indian Numismatic Studies*, Abhinav Publication, New Delhi, 1976.
3. Roy, P.C. : *The Coinage of Northern India*. Abhinav Publication (First Edition), 1980.

(*C*) *EPIGRAPHIC*

1. Pande, R.B. : *Historical ond Literary Inscriptions*. Chowkhamba Sanskrit Studies, First Edition, Varanasi, 1962.
2. Sircar, D.C. : *Select Inscriptions bearing on Indian History and Civilization*. Vol. I, University of Calcutta (Second Edition), 1965.
3. Hultzsch, E. *Inscriptions of Asoka*. New Edition Indological Book House, Varanasi, 1969.
4. Fleet, J.F. : *Inscriptions of the Early Gupta Kings*, Indological Book House, Varanasi, 1963.
5. Mirashi, V.V. (*a*) : *Inscriptions of the Cedi Kalacuri Era* (2 Parts) Ootacalnand, 1955.

   (*b*) : *Inscriptions of the Vākāṭakas*, 1963.
6. Chhabra, B.Ch. Ed. : *Inscriptions of the Early Gupta Kings*, Published by A.S.I., New Delhi, 1981.
   Gai, G.S.
   Epigraphia Indica Volumes (Relevant)
   Calcutta and Delhi, 1892 onwards
7. Cunningham, A. : Archaeological Survey Reports—Vol. II, X, XXI.

(*D*) *ARCHAEOLOGICAL*

1. Cunningham, A. : Archaeological Survey Reports.
2. Annual Progress Reports of Archaeological Survey of India.

3. Indian Archaeology : A Review.
4. Memoirs of the Archaeological Survey of India.
5. Trivedi S.D. : *Bundela Khaṇḍa Kā Purātatva*, State Museum, Jhansi, 1984.

(E) *GAZETTEERS*

1. Imperial Gazetteer of India, New Edition, Today and Tomorrow's Printers and Publishers, New Delhi.
2. Madhya Pradesh District Gazetteers—Sagar (ed. Krishnan V.S.) 1967.
3. Central Provinces District Gazetteers—Damoh District (Ed...Russell R.V.) 1906.
4. Chhatarpur State Gazetteer (Compiled by Captain Luard C.E., and Lala Sohan Lal).
5. Datia State Gazetteer (Compiled by Luard C.E. and Lala Chhote Lal). 1907.
6. District Gazetteers of the United Provinces of Agra and Audh.

(A) Vol. XXIV, Jhansi District Gazetteer (Ed. Drake Brockman, D.L.) 1909.

(B) Vol.XXIV, Jalaun District Gazetteer (Ed. Drake Brockman, D.L.) 1921.

II MODERN WORKS

Agrawala, P.K. : *Gupta Temple Architecture*. Prithvi Prakashan, Varanasi, 1968.

Agrawala, U. : *Khajuraho Sculptures and their Significance, Delhi*, 1964.

Agrawala, V.S. : *Śiva-Mahādeva : the Great God* (on exposition of the Symbolism of Siva) Veda Academy, Varanasi, 1966.

: *Indian Art: A History of Indian Art from the Earliest Times up to the Third Century A.D.* Prithvi Prakashan, Varanasi, 1965.

: *India as known to Pānini—A Study of the cultural material in the Aṣṭādhyāyi*. Lucknow University (Second Edition), 1963.

: *Ancient Indian Folk Cults*. Prithvi Prakashan, Varanasi, 1970.

Asopa, J,N. : *Origin of the Rajputs*. Bharatiya Publishing House (First Edition) Delhi, 1976.

Bajpai, K.D. : *Sagar Through the Ages*, Sagar, 1967.

: *Development of Buddhism in U.P.* Lucknow, 1956.

: *Geographical Encyclopaedia of Ancient and Medieval India:- based on Vedic, Puranic, Tantric, Jain, Buddhist, literature and historical records*, pt. I, Indic Academy, Varanasi, 1967.

Banerjea, J.N. : *Development of Hindu Iconography*. University of Calcutta (Second Edition) 1956.

Barth, A. : *The Religions of India*. S. Chand & Co. (Sixth Edition) New Delhi, 1980.

Basham, A.L. : *The Wonder that was India*. Roopa & Co.(Second Impression), Delhi, 1974.

Bhandarkar, D.R. : *Asoka*
Calcutta University (Third Edition). Calcutta, 1932.

Bhandarkar, R.G. : *Vaisnavism, Śaivism and Minor Religious Systems*. Indological Book House, Varanasi, 1965.

Bose, N.S. : *History of the Candellas*. K.L. Mukhopadhyaya, Calcutta, 1956.

Brown, Percy : *Indian Architecture* (Buddhist and Hindu), D.B. Taraporevala Sons & Co. (Seventh Reprint) Bombay, 1976.

Bruhn, Klaus : *The Jina Images of Deogarh*. Leiden, 1969

Cunningham, A. : *The Stupa of Bharhut—A Buddhist Monument*. Indolagical Book House, Varanasi, 1962.

Desai, Devangana : *Erotic Sculpture of India—A Socio-Cultural Study*. Tata Mcgraw Hill, New Delhi, 1975.

Devahuti, D. : *Harṣa—A Political Study*, Oxford, 1970.

Dikshit, R.K, : *The Candellas of Jejakabhukti*. Abbhinav Publication, New Delhi, 1977

Dikshit, S.K. : *Mother Goddess: A Study regarding Origin of Hinduism*, Dikshit, New Delhi, n.d.

Dutt, Nalinaksha ; *Buddhist Sects in India*. Indological Book House, Varanasi, 1977.

: *Mahāyānā Buddhism*. Motilal Banarasidass (New Edition) Delhi, 1977.

Ganguly. O.C. : *The Art of the Candellas*. Indian Sculpture Series No. 1, Calcutta, 1957.

Goyal, S.R. : *A History of Imperial Guptas*. Central Book Depot (First Edition) Allahabad, 1967.

Gupta, Shakti M, : *Plant Myths and Traditions in India*. Brill, E.J., Leiden, 1971.

Gupta, S.P. & Ramchandran, K.S. : *Aspects of Indian History and Archaeology*. B.R, Publishing House, Delhi, 1977.

Ghurye, G.S. : *Two Brahmanical Institutions—Gotra and Charana*. Popular Prakashan, Bombay, n.d.

Hasan, Amir : *Meet the U.P. Tribes*. The Academic Press, Gurgaon, 1982.

Ions, Veronica : *Indian Mythology*. London, Paul Hamlyn, 1968.

Jaiswal, Suvira : *The Origin and Development of Vaiṣṇavism*. Munshiram Manoharlal, Delhi, 1967.

Jash, Pranabnanda, : *History of Śavisim*. Roy and Choudhuri, Calcutta, 1974.

Kane, P.V. : *History of Dharmaśāstra*. Bhandarkar Oriental Research Institute, Poona, 1941.

Kanwarlal, : *Immortal Khajuraho*. Asia Press, Delhi, 1965.

Kramrisch, Stella : *The Hindu Temple*. Calcutta, 1946.

: *Indian Sculpture*. *Calcutta*, 1933.

Law, B.C. : *Tribes in Ancient India*. Bhandarkar Oriental Series No. 4 (First Edition), Poona,1943.

: *Historical Geography of Ancient India*. Ess Ess Publications, Delhi, 1976.

; *India as Described in the Early Works of Buddhism and Jainism*.

Leeson, Francis : *Kama-Shilpa—A Study of Indian Sculptures Depicting Love in Action*. D.B. Taraporevala & Co., Bombay, 1962.

Mehta, R.J. : *Konarak* D.B. Taraporevala Sons & Co., Bombay.

Majumdar, R.C.(Ed). : *The Vedic Age*. London, 1952,

: *The Age of Imperial Unity*. Bombay, 1960.

: *The Classical Age*. Bombay, 1962.

; *The Age of Imperial Kanauj*. Bombay, 1955.

: *The Struggle for Empire*. Bombay, 1957.

Marshall, Sir John : *Mohenjodaro and the Indus Civilization* : (being on official account of archaeological excavation at Mohenjodaro carried out by the Govt. of India between the years 1911-27). Probsthain, London, 1931.

Mitra, S.K. : *The Early Rulers of Khajuraho*. Firma K.L. Mukhopadhyaya, Calcutta, 1958.

Mookerji, R.K. : *Chandra Gupta Mourya and His Times* (Madras University, Sir William Meyer Lectures) Third Edition, Motilal Banarsidass, Delhi, 1960.

Murray, Margaret : *The Genesis of Religion*

Nigam, M.L. : *Cultural History of Bundelkhand*. Sundeep Prakashan, Delhi, 1683.

Pande, G.C. : *Studies in The Origins of Buddhism*. Allahabad, 1957.

Pande, L.P. : *Sun-worship in Ancient India*. Motilal Banarasidass, First Edition) Delhi, 1971.

Pathak, V.S. : *Saiva Cults in Northern India*. Sagar, 1960.

Pagson. : *A History of the Boondelas*. B.R. Publishing Corporation (Reprint) Delhi, 1974.

Puri, B.N. : *India in the Time of Patañjali*. Bombay, 1968.

: *The History of the Gurjara-Pratiharas*. Hind Kitabs Ltd. Bombay, 1957.

Rao, T.A.G. : *Elements of Hindu Iconography*, Vols, I-II. Motilal Banarasidass, Second Edition, Delhi, 1968.

Ray, H.C. : *Dynastic History of Northern India*, Vols. I-II. Calcutta, 1931-36.

Raychoudhuri, H.C. : *Studies In Indian Antiquities*. University of Calcutta, 1958.

: *Materials for the Study of the Early History of the Vaiṣṇava Sect*. Orient, Reprint, New Delhi, 1975.

Rowland, B. : *The Art and Architecture of India*. Penguin, Middlesex, 1967.

Russell, R.V. & Hiralal : *Tribes and Castes of the Central Provinces of India*, Vols. I, II and III. Cosmo Publications. Delhi, 1975.

Sankalia, H.D. : *Prehistory and Proto-history of India and Pakistan*. Deccan College, (New Edition) Ponna, 1975.

Shah, U.P. : *Studies in Jaina Art*. Banaras, 1955.

Sharma, B.N. : *Harsha and His Times*. Sushma Prakashan, Varanasi, 1970.

Sharma, B.N. : *Socio-Cultural History of Northern India*. New Delhi, 1972.

Sharma. G.R. : *Excavations At Kausambi* (1957-59). Allahabad University, 1960.

Sharma, R.K. : *Indian Archaeology : New Perspectives*. Agam Kala Prakashan, Delhi, 1982.

: *Temple of Chaunsath ayogini at Bheraghat*. Agam Kala Prakashan, Delhi, 1978.

: *Kalacuris and their Times* Sundeep Prakashan, Delhi, 1980.

Sharma, R.S. : *Indian Society—Historical Probings*. People's Publishing House, New Delhi, 1974.

: *Indian Feudalism*. Macmillan (Second Edition). Delhi, 1980.

Shastri, A.M. : *India as Seen in the Bṛhatsaṃhitā of Varāhamihira*. Motilal Banarasidass, Delhi, 1969.

Srivastava, V.C. : *Sun-Worship in Ancient India*. Indological Publications (First Edition), Allahabad, 1972.

Singh, S.B. : *Brahmanical Icons In Northern India*. Sagar Publications (First Edition), New Delhi, 1977.

Sircar, D.C. : *Studies in the Religious Life of Ancient and Medieval India*, Motilal Banarasidass (First Edition), Delhi, 1971.

: *Studies in the Society and Administration oj Ancient and Medieval India*, Firma K.L.M., Calcutta. 1967.

Shukla, D.N. : *A Study of Vāstu Vidya*. Chandigarh, 1960.

Thapar, R. : *Asoka and the Decline of the Mauryas*. O.U.P. (Second Impression), Bombay, 1977.

Toynbee, A. : *A Study of History* (Abridgement of Vols I-VI by D.C. Somervell), London, 1946.

Tripathi, R.K. : *Spinoza in the Light of Vedanta*. Banaras, 1957.

Upadhyaya, V. : *Socio-Religious History of Northern India*. Chowkhamba, Varanasi, 1964.

Vaidya, C.V. : *History of Medieval Hindu India*. The Oriental Book Supplying Agency, Poona, 1924.

Vidya Prakash : *Khajuraho : A Study in the Cultural Condltions of Candella Dynasty*. Taraporevala Sons & Co., Bombay 1967.

Weber, Max : *The Religion of India*. The Free Press, Glencoe, Illinois, 1960.

Yadava, B.N.S. : *Society and Culture in Northern India*. Central Book Depot (First Edition) Allahabad, 1973.

Zannas, E. : *Khajuraho*. Mouton & Co., S. Gravenhage, 1960.

Zimmer, H. : *Myths and Symbols in Indian Art and Civilization*. (Fd. Joseph Campbell) Pantheon Books, Washington, 1946.

: *Philosophies of India*. Newyork, 1951.

अवस्थी रामाश्रय : खजुराहो की देवप्रतिमाएं. आगरा, 1967

बाजपेयी, कृष्णदत्त : **उत्तरप्रदेश की ऐतिहासिक विभूति**, लखनऊ, 1957

: **उत्तर प्रदेश का सांस्कृतिक इतिहास**, आगरा 1962

: **मध्यप्रदेश का पुरातत्व**, भोपाल, 1970

: **भारतीय वास्तुकला का इतिहास**, लखनऊ 1972

तिवारी, गोरेलाल : **बुन्देलखण्ड का संक्षिप्त इतिहास**, देवीप्रसाद ऐतिहासिक पुस्तकमाला, 10, काशी नागरी प्रचारिणी सभा, प्रथम संस्करण, संवत् 1990.

मिश्र, इन्दुमती : **प्रतिमा विज्ञान**, भोपाल, 1972

मिश्र, जनार्दन : **भारतीय प्रतीक विद्या**, पटना, 1959

त्रिपाठी भा. प्र. : **बुन्देलखण्ड की प्राचीनता**, वाराणसी, 1955

क्षुल्लक चिदानन्द स्मृतिग्रन्थ : उदासीनाश्रम प्रकाशन समिति, द्रोणगिरि, 1973

III. THESES

Gokhale, S. : *Studies in the Historical and Cultural Geography and Ethonography of Madhya Pradesh*. Poona University, 1960.

Mathur, M.M. : *Studies in the Historical and Cultural Geography and Ethnography of Uttar Pradesh*. Poona University, 1963.

Mishra, R.N. : *Development of Yeksha Cult with Special Reference to Yaksha iconography*. Saugar University, 1967.

Misṛa, S.D. : *'Prabodhacandrodaya'—A Cultural Study*. Lucknow University, 1969.

Pande, S.K. : *Painted Rock-Shelters in Madhya Pradesh with Special Reference to Mahakoshal*. Saugar University, 1970.

Saini, S.P. ; *Study of the Temple Architecture of the Vindhya Region*, Saugar University, 1965.

अग्रवाल क. ला. : **विन्ध्यक्षेत्र का ऐतिहासिक भूगोल**

: सागर विश्वविद्यालय, 1973

जैन, भागचंद : **देवगढ़ की जैन कला का सांस्कृतिक अध्ययन**, सागर विश्वविद्यालय, 1970

वर्मा, महेन्द्र : **चांदपुर और दुधई की चंदेली कला और संस्कृति**, कानपुर विश्वविद्यालय

वर्मा, शारदा प्रसाद : **मध्यप्रदेश में नागमत का विकास**, सागर विश्वविद्यालय, 1962

Singh, U.V. : *Proto-historic Pottery of Eastern Malwa*, Saugar University, 1966.

Singh, R. : *Palaeolithic Industries of Northern Bundelkhand*. Poona University, 1965.

IV. JOURNALS

Journal of Indian History, Trivendrum.
Proceedings and Transactions of All India Oriental Society, Poona.
Journal of the Madhya Pradesh Itihasa Parishad, Bhopal.
Jain Antiquary, Arrah,
Ancient India, Delhi.
Journal of the Asiatic Society of Bengal, Calcutta.
MARG, Bombay.
Prāchya Pratibhā, Bhopal
Indian Antiquary, Calcutta.
Annals of the Bhandarkar Oriental Research Institute, Poona.
Indian Historical Quarterly, Trivendrum.
Research Journal, Devi Ahilya University, Indore.
Journal of the Uttar Pradesh Historical Society, Lucknow.
Bulletin of Ancient Indian History and Archaeology, Sagar.
Journal of the Royal Asiatic Society, London.

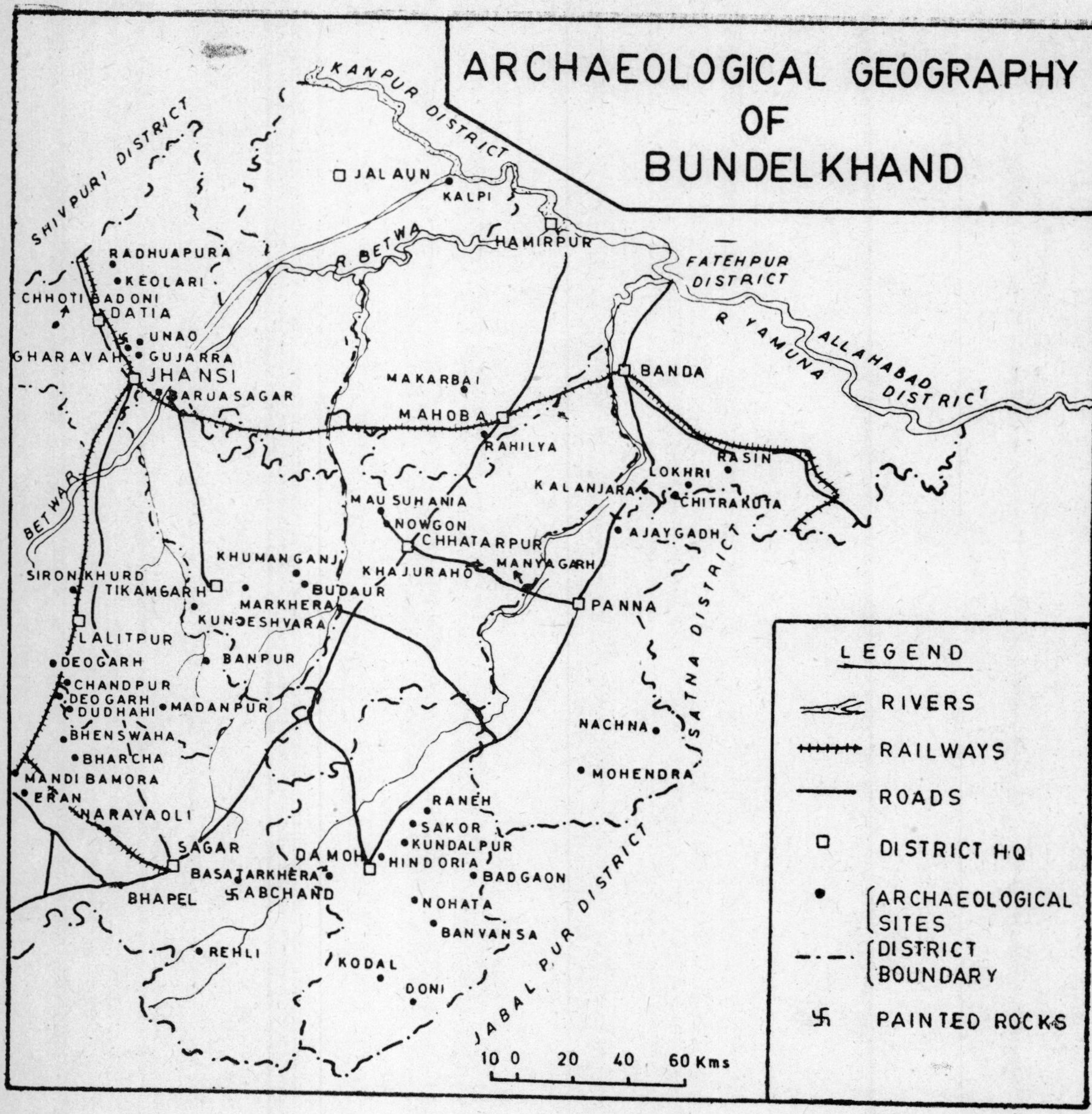
ARCHAEOLOGICAL GEOGRAPHY OF BUNDELKHAND
KANPUR DISTRICT
SHIVPURI DISTRICT
JALAUN
KALPI
HAMIRPUR
R. BETWA
FATEHPUR DISTRICT
R. YAMUNA
ALLAHABAD DISTRICT
RADHUAPURA
KEOLARI
CHHOTI BADONI
DATIA
UNAO
GUJARRA
GHARAVAH
JHANSI
BARUASAGAR
MAKARBAI
BANDA
MAHOBA
RAHILYA
RASIN
LOKHRI
KALANJARA
CHITRAKUTA
MAU SUHANIA
NOWGON
CHHATARPUR
AJAYGADH
BETWA
KHUMANGANJ
KHAJURAHO
MANYAGARH
SIRON KHURD
TIKAMGARH
BUDAUR
MARKHERA
PANNA
KUNDESHVARA
SATNA DISTRICT
LALITPUR
DEOGARH
BANPUR
CHANDPUR
DEOGARH
DUDHAHI
MADANPUR
BHENSWAHA
NACHNA
BHARCHA
MANDI BAMORA
MOHENDRA
ERAN
NARAYAOLI
RANEH
SAKOR
KUNDALPUR
SAGAR
DAMOH
HINDORIA
BASATARKHERA
BADGAON
BHAPEL
ABCHAND
NOHATA
BANVANSA
REHLI
KODAL
DONI
JABALPUR DISTRICT
10 0 20 40 60 Kms
LEGEND
RIVERS
RAILWAYS
ROADS
DISTRICT HQ
ARCHAEOLOGICAL SITES
DISTRICT BOUNDARY
PAINTED ROCKS

Index

Fig. 1
Yami, Lokhri (Dist. Banda)

Fig. 2
Kankālī, Lokhri (Dist. Banda).

Fig. 3
Nāgī, Lokhri (Dist. Banda).

Fig. 4
Mesamukhī, Lokhri (Dist. Banda).

Fig. 5
Kaumārī, Lokhri (Dist. Banda).

Fig. 7 : Ghaṇṭai Temple, Khajuraho
(Dist. Chhatarpur).

Fig. 6
Laksamana Temple, Khajuraho
(Dist. Chhatarpur).

Fig. 8
Temple Group, Mau Suhania
(Dist. Chhatarpur).

Fig. 9 : Brāhmaṇical Temple, Kundalpur (Dist. Damoh).

Fig. 10 : Siva Temple Nohatā (Dist. Damoh).

Fig. 11 : Siṃhanāda Lokeśvara, Mahoba (Dist. Hamirpur).

Fig. 12 : Padmapāṇi Avalokitesvara, Mahoba (Dist. Hamirpur).

Fig. 13 : Sixty-Four-Armed Cāmuṇḍā, Mahoba (Dist. Hamirpur).

Fig. 14 : Viṣṇu, Rahilya, (Dist. Hamirpur).

Fig. 16 : Viṣṇu Temple, Baruasagar (Dist. Jhansi).

Fig. 15 : Double storeyed Śiva Temple, Urwara (Dist. Hamirpur).

Fig. 17 : Tricaubīsī, Banpur (Dist. Lalitpur).

Fig. 18 : Smārta Liṅga, Chandpur (Dist. Lalitpur).

Fig. 19 : Nandī with climbing Skanda, Chandpur (Dist. Lalitpur).

Fig. 20 : Viṣṇu Temple, Chandpur (Dist. Lalitpur).

Fig. 21 : Jaina Remains, Chandpur (Dist. Lalitpur).

Fig. 22 : Temple group, Dudhahi (Dist. Lalitpur).

Fig. 23 : Headless Hanumāna, Dudhahi (Dist. Lalitpur).

Fig. 24 : Ganeśa, Dudhahi (Dist. Lalitpur).

Fig. 25: Gupta Temple, Deogarh (Dist. Lalitpur).

Fig. 26 : Gajendramoksa, Deogarh (Dist. Lalitpur).

Fig. 27 : Nara-nārāyana, Deogarh (Dist. Lalitpur).

Fig. 28 : Seṣaśayī Viṣṇu, Deogarh (Dist. Lalitpur).

Fig. 29 : Jaina Temple (No. 12) Deogarh (Dist. Lalitpur).

Fig. 30 : Jaina Temple (No. 15) Deogarh (Dist. Lalitpur).

Fig. 31 : Ācāryas, Upādhyāyas and Sādhus, Deogari (Dist. Lalitpur).

Fig. 32 : Mānastambha, Deogarh (Dist. Lalitpur).

Fig. 33 : Caturmukhanātha Temple, Nachna (Dist. Panna).

Fig. 34 : Caturmukha Siva-Liṅga, Nachna (Dist. Panna).

Fig. 35 : Visṇu Temple, Bhenswaha, (Dist. Sagar).

Fig. 36 : Govardhanadhari Krsna, Bhenswaha (Dist. Sagar).

Fig. 37 : Lakulīśa, Bharcha, (Dist. Sagar).

Fig. 38 : Sun Temple, Markhera (Dist. Tikamgarh).

Fig. 39 : Door-lintel of a Śiva temple (Khajuraho) (Dist. Chhatarpur).

Fig. 40 : Sadāśiva, Khajuraho (Dist. Chhatarpur).

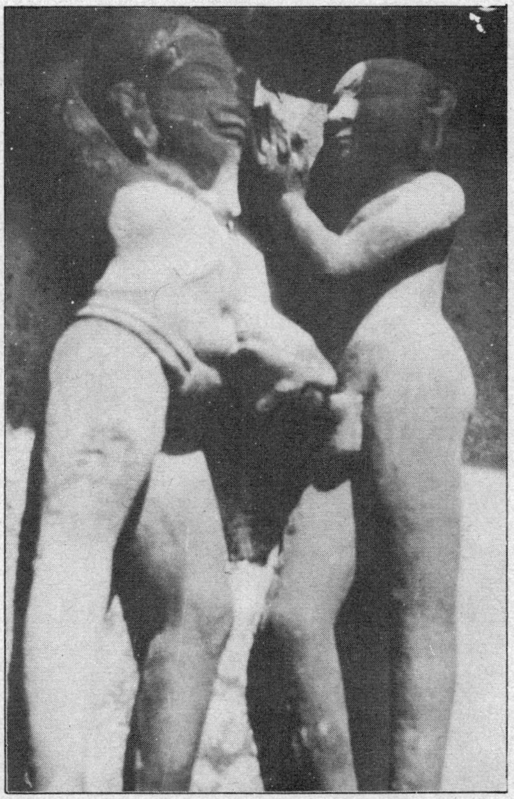

Fig. 41 : Kāpālika Teacher, Khajuraho (Dist. Chhatarpur).

Fig. 43 :
Viṣṇu-Gaṅgā Palace Museum,
Jhansi

Fig. 42 : Doorway Details,
Visnu Temple, Baruasagar
(Dist. Jhansi).

Fig. 44 : Chief Image of
Caturbhuja Temple, Khajuraho
(Dist. Chhatarpur).

Fig. 45 : Cāmuṇḍā, Nohatā (Dist. Damoh).

Fig. 46 : Acaryas flanlked by Upādhyāyas and Tīrthaṅkaras, Deogarh (Dist. Lalitpur).

Fig. 47 : Pañcopāsanā Panel, Palace Museum, Jhansi.

Fig. 48 : Siva Temple, Sakor (Dist. Damoh).

Fig. 49 : Remains of a Stūpa, Chhoti Badoni (Dist. Datia).

Fig. 50 : Siva Temple, Ajaygarh (Dist. Panna).

Fig. 51 : Siva Temple, Ajaygarh (Dist. Panna).

Fig. 52 : Pārvatī Temple, Nachna (Dist. Panna).

Fig. 53 : Pillar-base with representation of four incarnations of Viṣṇu, Nachna (Dist. Panna).

Fig. 54
Nrsimhāvatāra, State Museum, Dhubels (Dist. Chhatarpur).

Fig. 55
Sūrya, Rehli (Dist. Sagar).

Fig. 57
Hanumāna, State Museum, Dhubela
(Dist. Chhatarpur).

Fig. 56
Hanumāna, State Museum, Dhubela
(Dist. Chhatarpur).

Fig. 58 : Harihara, Rehli, (Dist. Sagar).